Redeemer Nation

*America had the infinite privilege
of fulfilling her destiny and saving the world.*

WOODROW WILSON

Redeemer Nation

The Idea of America's Millennial Role

Ernest Lee Tuveson

The University of Chicago Press

Chicago and London

The University of Chicago Press, Chicago 60637

The University of Chicago Press, Ltd., London

© 1968 by The University of Chicago
All rights reserved
Published 1968
Second Impression 1974
Printed in the United States of America

International Standard Book Number: 0–226–81919–1
  (clothbound)

Library of Congress Catalog Card Number: 68-14009

To Marjorie Hope Nicolson

Preface

Just at the turn of the century the statesman-historian Albert J. Beveridge, speaking in the United States Senate, stated the purpose and calling of the American nation as follows:

God has not been preparing the English-speaking and Teutonic peoples for a thousand years for nothing but vain and idle self-contemplation and self-admiration. No. He made us master organizers of the world to establish system where chaos reigned. He has given us the spirit of progress to overwhelm the forces of reaction throughout the earth. He has made us adept in government that we may administer government among savage and senile peoples. Were it not for such a force as this the world would relapse into barbarism and night. And of all our race He has marked the American people as His chosen nation to finally lead in the redemption of the world.

Here, in capsule form, are the elements of the idea I have called "the redeemer nation." Chosen race, chosen nation; millennial-utopian destiny for mankind; a continuing war between good (progress) and evil (reaction) in which the

United States is to play a starring role as world redeemer
—surely such an idea must be religious in origin; and so,
I shall try to show, it is.

This idea was by no means merely the reflex response to
a war. It has been present in some measure, as I shall try to
demonstrate, from the very beginnings of the republic; it is
present even yet. Only recently, Professor Henry Steele
Commager noted "a deep and persistent trait of the American mind: the belief in Old World corruption and New
World innocence. The men who won the independence
of America from the mother country were convinced that
the Old World was abandoned to tyranny, misery, ignorance, injustice and vice, and that the New World was
innocent of these sins" (Statement to Senate Foreign Relations Committee, February 20, 1967). Closely related to
this "shibboleth of Old World wickedness and New World
virtue" is, Professor Commager adds, a tendency to "transform our wars into crusades"—visible from the Mexican
War to the action in South Viet Nam. Closely associated,
too, with this idea of national innocence, Professor Commager says, is "the somewhat more activist notion of New
World mission." Providence, or history, has put a special
responsibility on the American people to spread the blessings of liberty, democracy, and equality to others throughout the earth, and to defeat, if necessary by force, the
sinister powers of darkness.

The relationship of "mantle of virtue" to "activist mission" is indeed close, but it is by no means inevitable that
the one would produce the other. Indeed, many of those
who like Jefferson were most convinced that the young
republic should be a haven of goodness in an evil world
were the most isolationist. Clearly, something has intervened
between the idea of "innocent nation, wicked world" and
the expectation that this country is to be "His chosen
nation to finally lead in the redemption of the world."
When and how did the conception of an American redemptive mission begin? The story has never yet been fully
told.

The crucial change came, I believe, with the reversal of
the Augustinian interpretation of history, which had pre-

vailed during the Middle Ages and the Renaissance. Augustine assumed that the City of God, the mystic body of the faithful, must live, usually subject to some degree of persecution, separate from the world of action—the City of God —until the Last Judgment would roll up history itself. Although the Book of Revelation predicts that there will be a time when the power of evil is to be "bound"—the millennium—that prophecy is to be interpreted only allegorically; the millennium, Augustine concluded, began with the Resurrection. If the power of Satan is "bound" even in this age, with all its woes for mankind, then the outlook for mankind in this world can never be hopeful.

Yet, even during the Middle Ages, isolated groups were never content with such an interpretation. The Bible, both Old and New Testaments, has many passages describing a glorious time when the kingdoms of this world shall become in literal fact the kingdom of God, when swords shall be beaten into plowshares, when "the kingdom and dominion, and the greatness of the kingdom under the whole heaven, shall be given to the people of the saints of the most High, whose kingdom is an everlasting kingdom, and all dominions shall serve and obey him." In the light of such promises, was it reasonable to believe, with Augustine, that God had condemned his people to suffer under the heel of the wicked, to allow the creation which he had made so fair, originally, to be marred by the dominance of evil until the very end of time? May the prophecies of the Revelation not be literally true after all—may not God's plan envisage the step-by-step triumph of good over evil?

Only isolated and radical minorities, however, asked such questions until, when the Reformation was established, a new examination of the whole Scripture occurred. Even in the late sixteenth century some biblical scholars began to conclude that perhaps, after all, there was to be a millennium, a period in which Christ would rule. In the next century, however, the conception took a new and momentous turn. It might be, as Augustine had thought, that the Revelation should be taken partly in an allegorical sense —but with a very different significance. Perhaps the millennium was to be an earthly *utopia*, an age at the end of all history, in which, not Christ in person, but Christians and Christian principles would really be triumphant. Human life would go on as before, but how much more happily! War would cease; poverty would be largely if not completely eliminated; knowledge would increase as never before; men would at last know true justice and mercy.

Read in the light of this expectation, the Revelation and the other prophecies took on a new and revolutionary meaning. The course of all history was seen as a great series of struggles, in which the Prince of Darkness is progressively defeated, according to a preconceived plan. The plan, moreover, was already far advanced; the interpreters generally felt that, with the Reformation, the turning point had been reached, and that the source of the evil had already received his death blow. How glorious the future would be! What a great part men living in the last days might play in bringing about the true utopia! Yet, it was frequently warned, great battles still lay ahead; the powers of evil were doomed to defeat, but their resources still were large, and the Revelation had predicted that Satan in his death pangs would rage more strongly than ever before.

In such a pattern of history it was inevitable that God would have to operate through certain nations. The old conception of a "chosen people," called to fight the battles of the Lord, was revived. Augustine had replaced the chosen people with the mystical conception of the hidden City of God; now it appeared that God must use peoples, armies, governments, to attain his ends; God had re-entered secular history as a participant.

Many factors contributed to point to one race and one nation as chosen to perform God's work in the last days. It seemed as if the finger of Providence had pointed to the young republic of the West. The image was a popular one with commentators, and, as I shall try to show, it was taken literally, not only by a minority, but by what seems to have been a majority of the Trinitarian Protestants of the United States. The mission of the nation, Wilson remarked, is to "the redemption of the world." This idea of American destiny, how it arose and something of how it has operated in our history, is my subject. I do not claim completeness for the story; but the ideology and its sources must be understood before its immense ramifications can be appreciated in their entirety.

I am grateful to my colleague Professor Henry Nash Smith, to Dr. Martin E. Marty, and to Professor Benjamin Nelson, who have made many valuable comments on this book in manuscript.

Berkeley, California

Contents

I

Apocalyptic and History

Christianity is a religion of expectation. The literal meaning of "Christian" is "Messianist." The Gospels are permeated by eager anticipation of the blessed day, shortly to arrive, when the "Kingdom of God and His Christ" will be all in all: the final triumph of good over evil, the end of all the sorrows and fears of this life. Yet no one is surprised to hear of "Christian pessimism about the possibility of happiness on this earth." [1] For in the succeeding centuries it came to be assumed that the Kingdom is to be transcendent, otherworldly, and unhistorical; lives and institutions in this world are to be cursed by the ubiquitous power of evil until the consummation of all things. To expect to make the world's City truly righteous is, indeed, an egregious manifestation of pride.

Yet, beginning over three centuries ago, a movement among a large segment of Protestants effected a reversal of this dark belief. There sprang up a hope, what might be called a "Christian optimism" about the future of humanity and human society. And, for reasons to be explained later, that hope came to center peculiarly on one nation—the young republic of the United States. How this change came about and some of its consequences in history have not yet been fully investigated. [2]

[1] From a BBC address by John Weightman, "Madame de Lafayette," reprinted in *The Listener*, March 3, 1966.
[2] See the Bibliographical Note, below, for reference to books and articles on American millennialism.

The hopes and expectations for the United States were not exclusively chauvinism. Their alpha and omega were the "prophetic" parts of the Scriptures, especially the book known as the Revelation of St. John. Christianity took over, revised, and transformed in its own image the ancient Jewish tradition of apocalyptic.[3] St. John's Revelation, fittingly placed at the end of the canon, by no means represents the whole of Christian thinking about the meaning and end of history, and throughout the centuries there has persisted skepticism about whether it is rightly to be accepted as inspired. Nevertheless, it did establish itself as canonical, and it surely ranks as one of the most influential books in the whole of western history. There has never been a time when it did not engross the imagination of the Christian world— usually as an ominous, fearful warning of judgment and other terrible things to come. Yet in recent centuries its fires became a beacon of hope for mankind, and this change has been one of the most momentous events in the intellectual history of the West since the Reformation.

Jewish apocalyptic envisioned a final battle between the armies of God and those of the enemies of the chosen people. The Book of Daniel predicts that after four beasts, symbolizing four world kingdoms, have been defeated or slain, the "Son of man" will lead the armies of God to the last victory, after which an eternal divine kingdom will be established over the entire world. This vision of future glory is the more remarkable in that it arose out of a perennially oppressed and seemingly insignificant people. In consequence, perhaps, it assumed peculiar forms. Weakness and suffering under despotism are themselves virtues and means of attaining strength; the Great Day of the Lord will come only after his enemies have, apparently, reached the pinnacle of power. Then, when the chosen people have been reduced by extreme misfortune to true penance and have been brought back to observance of the divine commandments, the supernatural power of the God of Battles will

---

[3] See my *Millennium and Utopia: A Study in the Background of the Idea of Progress* (Berkeley: University of California Press, 1949), chap. 1, for a fuller account of the Book of Revelation.

descend upon them; Jehovah, not a great, conquering nation like Rome, will win the victory.

In St. John's Revelation the Christos figures as the "Son of man." Superficially, it would appear that this apocalyptic rhapsody is simply an adaptation of the messianic expectations, in which the Christians, the redeemed people, take the place of the national Jews; consequently the power and faith associated with the ancient Hebraic traditions are transferred to the new religion, after the crushing defeat the Jewish kingdom had suffered in its rebellion against Rome. A closer look, however, shows that there are crucial changes. The author of the Revelation utilized all the prophetic tradition, including parts not in the scriptural canon as we have it, but his work was by no means only a pastiche; it was truly a new creation.

In the New Testament there are many apocalyptic passages. In general, all of them—except for the Revelation—follow the relatively simple plan of the Jewish prophecies. There will be omens, "signs of the end," as described, for example, in Matthew 24. They will include such items as wars and rumors of wars, famines, pestilences, earthquakes, incredibly great iniquity, and the emergence of many "false prophets." But first the "gospel of the Kingdom" must be preached, and a saving remnant, a new kind of chosen people, must be formed. This nucleus of the kingdom must suffer unparalleled tribulations, as the earlier prophets predicted that Israel must be humbled before the Son of man could appear. Just before the end, new and supernatural cosmic portents will be seen. The sun will be darkened

and the moon shall not give her light, and the stars shall fall from heaven, and the powers of the heaven shall be shaken: and then shall appear the sign of the Son of man in heaven: and then shall all the tribes of the earth mourn, and they shall see the Son of man coming in the clouds of heaven with power and great glory. And he shall send his angels with a great sound of a trumpet, and they shall gather together his elect from the four winds, from one end of heaven to the other.[4]

---

[4] Matt. 24:29 ff. I have quoted throughout from the King James Version, the only translation my authors used.

There are several other passages of similar import. Thus 2 Peter 3 foretells a "second deluge," of fire, which will destroy the "ungodly men" and make way for "new heavens and a new earth, wherein dwelleth righteousness." There is the further point (recalling Old Testament prophecy) that "one day is with the Lord as a thousand years, and a thousand years as one day"; it was to become essential for commentators who tried to establish prophetic time-tables. All these passages in the Gospels and Epistles warn that, despite the premonitory omens, the Son of man will come suddenly, "as a thief in the night."

Jesus, it would seem, realized that this Kingdom of God would require inhabitants of a very different kind from actually existing men, even those who faithfully observed the law. Flesh and blood cannot inherit the Kingdom; a transformation in human nature is urgently necessary. The duty of the believer is not to peer into the darkness of God's will, or to engage in futile uprisings against the rulers of this world, but to prepare himself spiritually to be fit to enter the Kingdom and to maintain the integrity of the faith against the "false prophets" who will be sent to undermine these indispensable preparations for the new order.[5] The two eschatologies—of the individual soul, and of the world—are interlocked, the first making possible the second. There is, however, a strong emphasis on the redemption of the world: unlike mystery religions, where the immortalization of individuals is the primary purpose, Christianity always has in view as the true and only solution to the world problem the inauguration of a new heaven and a new earth.

St. John's Revelation, from one point of view, is the extended and completed version of such prophecies. Yet the

[5] 2 Peter 1 and 2. I have not been concerned with the enormous body of scholarship of recent decades about the prophetic tradition and books. None of this was known to any of the authors whom I discuss; and it is obviously with their ideas of the prophecies, rather than with those prophecies as things in themselves, that I am concerned. It should be added that biblical commentators in the United States during the period in which I am interested were little affected by the "higher criticism." I have not found interest, even, in the seventeenth-century critical studies of authorship and integrity of the biblical texts.

form of the composition has been changed. Before it, apocalyptic might be said to be something like the epic; but, as readers have always recognized, the Revelation of St. John is a drama. The reader, like the prophet himself, seems to see the events occurring, in a setting unparalleled for sublimity and scope—on earth, in the heavens above, and in the abyss beneath. There is the sense of actions proceeding through scenes to a conclusion, and there is suspense. Above all, there are dramatic confrontations, with what might be called cosmic melodrama. Yet the Revelation in no sense invented Christian apocalyptic. The letters to the angels of the seven churches, dictated by the titanic figure of the Son of man, extensively repeat the generalized warnings of Peter about the dangers of heresy and lukewarmness of faith and of impurity; the vision of the tremendous final war is an imaginative realization in dramatic form of (possibly) earlier, more abstract, and briefer accounts; the great final judgment is presented in immensely powerful images, but essentially it is nothing new. If the author of the Revelation had never been in the spirit on the Sabbath, or if his work had been rejected as were other Christian apocalypses, the expectation of judgment would have remained, and the preeminent concern of Christians would still have been to make ready for it.

What then, apart from form, is new? First, there is the very fact that these sublime terminal events, only briefly described before, are expanded into a symbolic, detailed history. John combined and expanded the vague chronology of Daniel with the Christian predictions of the "Last Days" to form a *programmatic* sequence. Previously, the apocalyptic time had been sharply separated from the historical one. The disasters in the heavens which were to precede the arrival of the Messiah signified that the earth must be changed: the measure of time, the sun's revolutions, for example, must be interrupted or discontinued when the Day of the Lord shall arrive. In Revelation, by contrast, the apocalyptic events are seen as beginning to occur contemporaneously; reading it, we get the sense that the apocalyptic age is *in* time. The messages to existing churches, delivered from the hero who is to defeat Satan, indicate this fact.

There is to be a series of judgments—the pouring out of the "vials" of divine wrath on various parts of the earth—which constitute the engagements of the final apolcalyptic war. Presumably, the figures in the visions can or will be recognized as actual persons, institutions, or nations: the Four Horsemen, for instance. The second vial is poured out "upon the sea" (Rev. 16:3); the angel who interprets the vision for the author explains, "The waters which thou sawest, where the whore sitteth, are peoples, and multitudes, and nations, and tongues" (Rev. 17:15).

But the apocalyptic time does not begin only with the Redemption. The fact that the images are largely taken from the historical and prophetic books of the Old Testament makes us see that *all* history finally is apocalyptic. The events in which we ourselves participate are parts of the pattern; we find ourselves in the Apocalypse. Other gifted poets, like the second Isaiah, had depicted intensely moving confrontations between the people and God and the servants of the Enemy, and had seen in vision the new world of God. But John worked what had been detached dramatic moments into a cosmic unity. All that seemed mysterious and accidental, or isolated, is now revealed to have had its place in the great whole. Daniel related a number of dream-visions about the future, and they furnished materials to John; but the book of Daniel forms no clearly unified composition.

In the Revelation we see a great drama which joins angels, demons, monstrous villains, and the people of God in one great action. It involves the human race, which is inescapably divided into redeemed and condemned—there can be no neutrality, no "third force" here. Everything is dualistic, good or evil. It is possible, moreover to conclude from this prophecy that men are by no means mere spectators of the great final events; their part is not only to prepare spiritually for the kingdom, but to play a part in bringing about the defeat of evil. For this reason, the book has a strange, exhilarating effect that, logically, one might not expect. For, of all the compositions of all time, it is one of the most "awful" in the old, literal sense of the word. Consider, for one instance, this terrible passage:

And the angel thrust in his sickle into the earth, and gathered
the vine of the earth, and cast it into the great winepress of
the wrath of God. And the winepress was trodden without the
city, and blood came out of the winepress, even unto the horse
bridles, by the space of a thousand and six hundred furlongs.

The combination of the pastoral scene and the slaughter
gives the description the highest effect of horror. But what
redeems this frightful prediction is the confidence that ultimately good is, act by act, destroying evil. Mankind has
suffered and still suffers many woes, but they are being
eliminated. The author, unlike previous prophets, does not
depict a long and dreary sequence of unrelieved calamities,
increasing in intensity until, at the very end, the Messiah
appears and all is set right, as in the last scene of a harrowing
melodrama. The vivid descriptions of the sufferings and
bloody conflicts are arranged in series, each leading up to a
hymn of triumph and rejoicing. There is the sense of a
rising movement, each victory being on a higher level than
the one before.

Thus, strange as the idea may seem at first glance, the
movement of the Revelation is in its way *progressive*—
perhaps the first expression of the idea of history as progress. In other prophecies there is the pessimistic implication
that the sorrows must itensify simply because, in this hopeless world, evil breeds evil until God puts an end to the
whole sorry mess. John, too, implies that the violence will
intensify as the end approaches. But there is a very different
reason: history is something like the invasion of an enemy
nation, in which the conquering army progresses inexorably
from one stronghold to another, approaching the capital. As
the conquered territory increases in extent, the desperation
of the defender grows. Satan in this world, despite his
seeming invincibility, is now really the defender, and his
territory is shrinking.

After the war in heaven, and the casting-out of Satan
(chap. 12), a "loud voice" proclaims: "Therefore rejoice, ye
heavens, and ye that dwell in them. Woe to the inhabiters of
the earth and of the sea! for the devil is come down unto
you, having great wrath, because he knoweth that he hath
but a short time." We are so familiar with Milton's account

of the war in heaven as preceding the creation, and all that followed, that we do not realize this episode in the Revelation occurs *after* Satan has suffered decisive defeat in history, of this world as well as of heaven. In chapter 11 the seventh trumpet has been sounded, and the second "woe" has occurred; "great voices in heaven" have said, "The kingdoms of this world are become the kingdoms of our Lord, and of his Christ." The word "woes," like "judgments," has an ambivalent meaning. They are unspeakably terrible in themselves, but as each is completed a part of the power of darkness has been ended. So the "judgments" are not only punishments of evil but definitive victories. The situation may be compared with the last days of the Second World War. And that war, evil in itself, yet was curiously inspiring; for, obviously, nothing less than a great war could rid the world of the tyrant who so much resembled the Antichrist of the Revelation, and thus war was infinitely preferable to a fallacious "peace." So the warning of "Woe!" to the children of light is the signal for hope, not despair.

A great voice exultantly announces that "Babylon is fallen, is fallen, that great city . . ." (Rev. 14:8). Her "smoke" will rise up "for ever and ever." Satan has been conquered in heaven. Babylon, symbolizing the domain of the Enemy—in fact, the whole world—is "fallen," however, only in the sense that the turning point, not the full defeat, has occurred. Much remains to be done; a "mopping-up operation" of the large remaining territory, on earth, under Satan's control has to be completed. In a series of actions, represented by the "pouring out of the seven vials" of judgment, the final, desperate, and cunning resistance is overcome. The cohorts of the Enemy gather for a last stand, at a mysterious place called Armageddon. This final, greatest battle is won by the armies of God as the last angel pours out his "vial" into the air (in which recent commentators of course can see a forecast of air forces); and the triumph of God is accomplished. "And the great city was divided into three parts, and the cities of the nations fell." It is a realistic account of the siege of a huge metropolis, like the taking of Berlin. Now an angel binds the "Dragon" for a thousand years. The souls of those martyred saints who in this life have striven for the good cause are to be raised from the tomb to "live and reign" with Christ. This period is the "millennium." When the period of the occupation by the servants of God has ended, Satan will be "loosed" and will return, rather like Napoleon from Elba. His followers, like the Grand Army, have been "bound," not annihilated, and presumably have been brooding on revenge. Satan, escaped from his prison in the bottomless pit, will rally them for one more effort, again like Napoleon's Hundred Days. But this demonic army will have its Waterloo—the "beloved city" will be besieged, but "fire from heaven" will destroy the invaders. Then, and only then, will occur the transformation of the earth often attributed to the beginning of the millennium: there will be a "new heaven and a new earth," the holy city will descend out of heaven, and "second death" after the universal judgment will be allotted to those who have adhered to Babylon.

The account of the millennium in fact occupies only a few verses in the twentieth chapter; but surely no other passage of comparable length has ever had such great and long-lasting influence on human attitudes and beliefs. It is clear that this period is, quite literally, only an "occupation." Since the servants of God rule, it is also what we should call a utopian age. It is, in fact, the last stage of human history, and not something beyond and outside the historical process and time. The fact that a supernatural event—the resurrection of the martyred saints—is foretold seems to us to make the whole thing supernatural; but, I think, such a conclusion is exaggerated. People of earlier times thought of history as interpenetrated by the supernatural. Matthew relates that, after the Crucifixion, "the graves were opened; and many bodies of the saints which slept arose, and came out of the graves after his resurrection, and went into the holy city, and appeared unto many." Yet these supernatural happenings by no means ended the history of this world. The personal rule of the Son of man could also be an event within history. The interpreting angel explicitly warns the prophet against worshipping him, and adjures "worship God: for the testimony of Jesus is the spirit of prophecy" (Rev. 19:10). The text of the whole book, in fact, seems to give the impression that the "Dragon" and the "Son of man" are on a comparable level, the supreme commanders of eternally opposing armies. Furthermore, beings with supernatural attributes figure in the action throughout. Thus Nero is probably the "beast" who has been fatally wounded but restored to life. The Roman emperor received divine honors, and early Christians refused to honor the cult, since they considered him an evil power who usurped the worship due to the one God alone; but the Revelation gives the impression that he combined human and demonic attributes.

The Revelation of St. John has presented many, and very different, aspects to various ages of Christianity. One of those is "progressivism." Progress, the book seems to teach, is the law of history; but it is to be attained not through regular, linear advancement but by successive defeats of the sources of all evils. For, it is assumed, the ancient afflictions of mankind—ignorance, poverty, war, injustice—have been caused by a monstrous conspiracy. Spiritual, political, military, social means of defeating this conspiracy all must be employed. The program, furthermore, is as definitely set forth as any purely secular idea of progress. The "vials" give the outlines of that program. Thus, it seemed to Protestant commentators on the Bible, the Reformation was primarily a spiritual event, but it had to be defended and consolidated by the armies of the Commonwealth; and the American Revolution, too, was both a political and spiritual victory, since it was a further step in the purification of society which enabled the redeeming message of the Gospel to achieve its effect. The Christian is called upon not only to make ready for the Day of the Lord but, with divine assistance, to bring it about. "Onward, Christian soldiers" epitomizes this conception of the work of the believer. That hymn, we may safely speculate, would never have been written if the vision had never come to St. John.

The idea that there should be an age of righteousness and peace on this earth as we have known it has a logic of its own. God created the universe good, and man's life was intended to be led in harmony with the divine will; and so it should be happy and noble. But in fact, as the prophets constantly trumpeted, the reality has usually been the reverse; it appears that some malign power has almost always frustrated the plan of the one God. Should the Omnipotent be thus constantly mocked in his own creation? Should it be necessary to burn the earth, to create new heavens and a new earth, in order to fulfill God's original intention? If so, there is a sense in which he is not omnipotent after all. It is appropriate, then, that in the Sabbath of God's week—the historical duration of humanity—the "Kingdom of God and his Christ" should be established in this creation and among the human family he created. In this last millennium, logically, the present situation will be reversed. Hitherto, the servants of God have for the most part been a persecuted minority; in the divine utopia the righteous will be on top. This will be a revolution indeed, for, as a conservative clergyman of the Church of England takes for granted, in the eighteenth century, the figure of "Babylon the Great" in the Revelation is the same as the "reigning City, or prevailing State of the Governments of the World."[6] The changed state of the governments of the world is symbolized by the prediction that Christ and the saints will rule in the millennium. There is and has been a tendency to emphasize the theocratic form of government. This, I suspect, is to miss the real point, which is that things will be restored to the state in which God created them: that, for the first time since the Fall, the prevailing powers will permit the Children of Adam to live their really "natural" life.

This reading of the Scripture ultimately helped make possible a revolution in thinking about the possibilities of history and society. The word "utopia," we recall, means literally "no place." That there could ever come out of history a state of affairs in which human life generally should be lastingly happy, just, and prosperous has seemed impossible. It is hard to believe that Plato could ever seriously have expected to see his Republic in existence. Until modern times dreams of universal harmony and happiness have been no more than fantasies of far-away lands, or of a

---

[6] James Knight, *A Discourse on the Conflagration and Renovation of the World* (1736), p. 33.

golden age in the past. But the Apocalypse, interpreted in this way, seems to hold forth not only a vague hope but an unequivocal promise that these fantasies will become fact; the golden age is coming.

Such expectation reversed the attitude dominant in Christianity for many centuries. Christians, as I remarked, have assumed that nothing but darkness lies this side of the final judgment; as Michael predicts to Adam,

> . . . so shall the World goe on,
> To good malignant, to bad men benigne,
> Under her own waight groaning, till the day
> Appeer of respiration to the just,
> And vengeance to the wicked, . . .

The only consolation is that Christ will return

> . . . to dissolve
> *Satan* with his perverted World, then raise
> From the conflagrant mass, purg'd and refin'd,
> New Heav'ns, new Earth, Ages of endless date
> Founded in righteousness and peace and love,
> To bring forth fruits Joy and eternal Bliss.
>   [*Paradise Lost*, XII, 537 ff.]

But in the seventeenth century a revolution in thinking about eschatology had already begun: the idea that God predicted the defeat of evil before the conflagration, and is redeeming that promise, began to be taken seriously throughout English-speaking Protestantism. God, it began to be thought, is redeeming both individual souls and society in parallel course; and, in the next century, a new nation in a recently discovered part of the world seemed suddenly to be illuminated by a ray of heavenly light, to be at the western end of the rainbow that arched over the civilized world.

2

Such Fathers as Tertullian, Irenaeus, and Justin Martyr believed that a millennium was shortly to be inaugurated. Although the book actually describes no earthly paradise, there was a natural tendency to think of this time as some kind of ideal state, material as well as spiritual. Yet, so unimaginable was a perfect society that only wild fantasies of such a condition could be envisioned. The earth, said Papias (who was alleged to have been a disciple of John the Apostle), will be transformed by a fertility miracle: "The days will come in which vines shall appear, having each ten thousand shoots, and on every shoot ten thousand twigs, and on each true twig ten thousand stems, and on every stem ten thousand bunches, and in every bunch ten thousand grapes, and every grape will give five-and-twenty metres of wine." These wonders, it was considered, would be a fitting reward for those who have suffered for the faith. They would, for example, have the Christian satisfaction of seeing their old enemies bound in perpetual slavery to themselves.

Augustine confesses that at one time he leaned toward this opinion, but that on further reflection he was repelled by the "sensuality" of such notions of the reign of Christ. The chiliasts, who hold that the millennium is to be a spiritual Sabbath, actually "assert that those who then rise again shall enjoy the leisure of immoderate carnal banquets, furnished with an amount of meat and drink such as not only to shock the feeling of the temperate, but even to surpass the measure of credulity itself." [7] One suspects that Augustine found the book an embarrassment, and would have preferred to forget about it; but it was entrenched in the canon, and had to be reckoned with. Anything like a notion of a progressive conquest of evil in history was of course out of the question in his age. Instead, he fitted the Revelation into the pessimistic view of temporal history which the events of the fifth century made inevitable. There are and have been from the time of Cain and Abel two divisions of the human race: ". . . the one consisting of those who live according to man, the other of those who live according to God. And these we also mystically call the two cities, or the two communities of men, of which the one is predestined to reign eternally with God, and the other to suffer eternal punishment with the devil" (15.1). The fundamental premise of this theory is that the two cities, although they will exist together in one

---

[7] Augustine, *The City of God*, trans. Dods *et al.* (New York, 1950), 20.7.

community until the end of time, are separated by an invisible but very real barrier. To regard the goods of this world as the true goals of the human spirit is to pay allegiance to the City of Man:

But the earthly city, which shall not be everlasting . . . , has its good in this world, and rejoices in it with such joy as such things can afford. But as this is not a good which can discharge its devotees of all distresses, this city is often divided against itself by litigations, wars, quarrels, and such victories as are either life-destroying or short lived. [15.4]

It follows that

. . . the earthly one has made to herself of whom she would, either from any other quarter, or even from among men, false gods whom she might serve by sacrifice; but she which is heavenly, and is a pilgrim on the earth, does not make false gods, but is herself made by the true God, of whom she herself must be the true God, of whom she herself must be the true sacrifice. Yet both alike either enjoy temporal good things, or are afflicted with temporal evils, but with diverse faith, diverse hope, and diverse love, until they must be separated by the last judgment, and each must receive her own end, of which there is no end. [18.54]

Even the good the City of Man seeks—although absolutely a legitimate good—peace, for instance—is in the long run an evil, because it is sought for the wrong reasons.

The City of Man, however, is destined to retain supremacy in this world until the end. The Heavenly City lives, as it were, furtively, keeping out of the way and cultivating its spiritual life which is its one and only interest; it "lives like a captive and a stranger in the earthly city, though it has already received the promise of redemption, and the gift of the Spirit as the earnest of it" (19.17). Obviously, therefore, social reform may to some extent ameliorate but can never cure the ills men must suffer. Society can never be "redeemed" for the same reason that the fallen angels will never be saved. In theory, the latter may at any time repent and be reconciled with heaven; but their wills are so intent on their own egocentric ends that their own natures inhibit them. So, too, the City of Man desires peace but makes war in order to "enjoy earthly goods" and for no other reason; hence it is caught in a never-ending cycle of wars, "glorious victories," and temporary peace (15.9). Earthly and heavenly goals are irreconcilable.

Although Augustine could hardly deny that a millennial age when Satan was to be bound had been prophesied, he was compelled to dispose, by rather tortuous reasoning, of any thought that the City of Man could ever become the Kingdom of God and his Christ. His main objection, we may speculate, was that human nature as a whole would have to be miraculously transformed first. His theory of the millennium is in fact an implied compliment to the irresistible power of Satan over the generality of mankind. The "binding" of the Prince of the Air is only "his being prevented from the exercise of his whole power to seduce men, either by violently forcing or fraudulently deceiving them into taking part with him. If he were during so long a period permitted to assail the weakness of men, very many persons, such as God would not wish to expose to such temptation, would have their faith overthrown, or would be prevented from believing; and that this might not happen, is he bound" (20.8). God's predestination seems to work in environmental ways. And if the Devil is now "bound," in this desperately unhappy world, the idea of progress would seem the most foolish of dreams!

A great modern scholar has strikingly expounded this attitude toward history.

One of the things that surprised me when I first read the New Testament seriously was that it talked so much about a Dark Power in the universe—a mighty evil spirit who was held to be the Power behind death and disease, and sin. The difference is that Christianity thinks this Dark Power was created by God, and was good when he was created, and went wrong. Christianity agrees with Dualism that this universe is at war. But it does not think this is a war between independent powers. It thinks it is a civil war, a rebellion, and that we are living in a part of the universe occupied by the rebel.[8]

[8] C. S. Lewis, *Mere Christianity* (London, 1955), p. 47.

Our only hope is a sort of resistance movement.

Enemy-occupied territory—that is what this world is. Christianity is the story of how the rightful king has landed, you might say landed in disguise, and is calling us all to take part in a great campaign of sabotage. When you go to church you are really listening-in to the secret wireless from our friends: that is why the enemy is so anxious to prevent us from going.

God delays the rescuing invasion only because

He wants to give us the chance of joining His side freely. I do not suppose you and I would have thought much of a Frenchman who waited till the Allies were marching into Germany and then announced he was on our side. God will invade. . . . When that happens, it is the end of the world. When the author walks on to the stage the play is over.[9]

The premise behind such a belief is that the rescue, like that of occupied France, must be effected wholly by an outside power. But what if the loyal inhabitants of the occupied territory have begun to rescue themselves?

Augustine, moreover, made another innovation which was to prove of first importance. To make possible his interpretation of the Revelation, he had to assume something new: that the millennial predictions are in fact allegorical only. The saints "reign" with Christ because they enjoy an inward spiritual triumph, whatever may happen to their bodies. Following a suggestion of Tichonius he thought the "millennium" is a round figure indicating a long period of time, and not to be considered as precisely 1,000 years. And as to the "Beast," which seems to designate a person or institution, "it is not inconsistent with the true faith to understand it of the ungodly city itself, and the community of unbelievers set in opposition to the faithful people and the city of God. 'His image' seems to me to mean his simulation, to wit, in those men who profess to believe, but live as unbelievers" (20.9).

The doctrine of an allegorical millennium became official. Although the expectation of an earthly millennium never completely died out, and although it was the motivating

⁹ *Ibid.*, p. 63.

force in local uprisings during the Middle Ages, this chapter in the vicissitudes of John's book is not of much concern to us. For, as I have recounted elsewhere, with the Reformation there began a largely new apocalyptic tradition, and when, in the seventeenth century, the belief in a literal millennium was revived, it was in new terms and after a fresh study of the Bible.[10] No one more abominated the "bestialities" of the Anabaptists than did the biblical scholars who revived the millennialist theory of prophecy. And they sharply rejected the "carnal" notions of the millennium found in early writers. The Protestant eschatology was substantially new, and by the end of the seventeenth century the novel idea that history is moving toward a millennial regeneration of mankind became not only respectable but almost canonical.

The first step in the development of this idea came with the Reformation. The Johannine Revelation, the reformers soon recognized, provided the justification they sorely needed. The greatest logical objection to their work was: why had God allowed the whole Church to become "apostate," nothing less, the reformers maintained, than the "synagogue of Satan"? Could the ostensible Christian institution really have departed so far from the true Gospel message and organization? The question might have been unanswerable if scriptural prophecies could not have been made to yield a plausible explanation. Peter's warning against many "false prophets" to come was recalled. But more important, the Revelation could be taken literally and not allegorically, and therefore refer to the whole history of the Church, not merely to the very last days. There seemed to be a clear warning that "Babylon" would reign supreme for a period signified by the prophecy that "a woman clothed with the sun," who would give birth to a child, destined to rule the nations, would be driven by the dragon into the "wilderness," and would remain there for 1,260 days (Rev. 12). Since a "day" is a year in prophecy, it follows that the dark age of the Church and hence of Christendom as a whole was destined to endure for 1,260 calendar years.

[10] *Millennium and Utopia*, chaps. 2–4.

If, as the Protestants maintained, this time of travail began at the time the papacy gained full ascendancy, it could be concluded that the true Church was restored about the time the Reformation began. So the fall of Babylon has begun with the Reformation itself! "And the beast was taken, and with him the false prophet that wrought miracles before him, with which he deceived them that had received the mark of the beast, and them that worshipped his image" (Rev. 19:20).

There can be no doubt that such a propagandistic theory had immense effect. It is not too much to say that the prophetic plan which Protestant commentators discerned in the Bible and which innumerable preachers constantly expounded from their pulpits sustained the morale of their followers and gave them a philosophy of history that seemed to make them partners with God in the redemption of the world; for it was the armies of Protestant princes that preserved the Protestant faith.

After the religious wars had failed to re-establish the universal church, more consequences of the historical theory became apparent. At first, its importance was only that the prophecies guaranteed the righteousness of the Protestant cause, that they guaranteed the Protestant theology against the charge of heresy. In time, however, the very fact that the Reformation had occurred became a source of optimism about the future. The fall of Babylon, as I remarked earlier, is the pivot of the Johannine account of history; the Redemption had made possible the ultimate salvation of the City of God; the destruction of its enemy was the event which would consolidate this great potential and turn it into tangible victory. Yet, even though the "false Church," Babylon *redivivus*, had been dealt a great wound and its ultimate fate sealed, the more radical reformers feared that much of the old papal corruption remained even in the reformed churches, and that Reformation itself still needed reforming. In the Revelation, the proclamation of the fall of Babylon is by no means the terminal victory. Satan, then, far from being paralyzed by his great defeat, was working harder than ever. But the war against evil took on a new character, now that actual events had demonstrated that the prophecy was reliable. Christians need no longer lead the furtive existence of Augustine's City of God; militant action against the remaining wrongs had now a great promise of success. And in time, as we shall see, the conception of those evils expanded to include social and political ills generally. Mankind might be over the hump at last. Thus the Reformation became the assurance that the long era of superstition, injustice, and poverty was ending and that light was breaking over the world. A great age of achievement had begun. The young Milton expressed this exultant attitude:

> But to dwell no longer in characterizing the depravities of the
> church, and how they sprung, and how they took increase;
> when I recall to mind at last, after so many dark ages, wherein
> the huge overshadowing train of error had almost swept all the
> stars out of the firmament of the church, how the bright and
> blissful Reformation (by divine power) struck through the
> black and settled night of ignorance and antichristian tyranny,
> methinks a sovereign and reviving joy must needs rush into the
> bosom of him that reads or hears; and the sweet odor of the
> returning gospel imbathe his soul with the fragrancy of heaven.
> Then was the sacred Bible sought out of the dusty corners
> where profane falsehood and neglect had thrown it, the schools
> opened, divine and human learning raked out of the embers of
> forgotten tongues, the princes and cities trooping apace to the
> new erected banner of salvation; the martyrs, with the unresistible might of weakness, shaking the powers of darkness, and
> scorning the fiery rage of the old red dragon.
>
> [*Of Reformation in England*, Book I]

What a sense of power the Christian now has, since he knows he can scorn the worldly might of the dragon! That dragon comes out of the Revelation, and suggests that all these events have occurred in accordance with God's plan. What great things may we who live in the last age accomplish! The mood that gave rise to the "idea of progress" must certainly owe much to this feeling of release and confidence.

Although the "dragon" is behind all human sorrows from the time of Adam and Eve, we should think of the Antichrist as less a magician than a politician. The more responsible authorities held that the Enemy, by superb maneuvers, had arranged a compact between church and state. It was often said that the apparent triumph of Christianity when Constantine made it official was really the beginning of its "captivity." Satan appealed to the selfishness of both prelates and generals, gradually bringing them to see how, by repressing the Gospel and perverting its message, they could advance themselves. The prelates became the medieval popes, claiming absolute authority both spiritual and temporal, even over the next life. The technique of subversion involved the re-establishment of "idolatry"—for example, transubstantiation and "worship of images" in place of "pure religion." The ultimate purpose overtly was, of course, not to exalt the Antichrist, but to establish a system which he could control. It succeeded because rulers were all too eager to hold the majority of mankind in the bondage of ignorance, superstition, and brutishness, since the true "Gospel freedom" purchased by the Redemption would liberate mankind from every kind of tyranny. This unholy alliance of religion and politics, as commentators—especially American—came to emphasize, was the evil seed from which the evil tree of feudalism grew.

Defoe has given us a trenchant account of the orthodox Protestant view. The Devil,

having secretly managed both temporal and spiritual power apart, and by themselves . . . now united them, in point of management, and brought the church usurpation and the army's usurpation together. . . . A blessed compact! which at once set the Devil at the head of affairs in the Christian world, as well spiritual as temporal, ecclesiastic and civil. Since the conquest over Eve in Paradise, by which Death and the Devil, hand in hand, established their first empire upon earth, the Devil never gained a more important point than he gained at this time." [11]

To get a Pisgah sight of the theory and its application to the American people, we may turn not to a theologian but a statesman, a product of both Protestantism and Enlightenment. In August, 1765, John Adams' *A Dissertation on the Canon and Feudal Law* was printed in the *Boston Gazette.*

[11] Daniel Defoe, *The History of the Devil*, Bk. 2:2 and Bk. 2:1.

Thomas Hollis immediately reprinted it in the *London Chronicle;* a separate publication three years later was entitled *The True Sentiments of America.* It was, Hollis said, "one of the very finest productions ever seen from North America."

During the Middle Ages, Adams wrote, people "became more intelligent in general." Why, we do not know for sure, "but the fact is certain; and wherever a general knowledge and sensibility have prevailed among the people, arbitrary government and every kind of oppression have lessened and disappeared in proportion." [12] A common principle in human nature—"that aspiring, noble principle founded in benevolence, and cherished by knowledge; I mean the love of power, which has been so often the cause of slavery" —has been responsible both for the soaring ambitions of princes and for the efforts of "the common people to aspire at independency, and to endeavor at confirming the power of the great within the limits of equity and reason." For, he says in phrases anticipating the language of the Declaration of Independence, all human beings have *"Rights,* that cannot be repealed or restrained by human laws—*Rights,* derived from the great Legislator of the universe."

All this would seem to be derived from rationalistic theories of the Enlightenment rather than from traditional religious doctrine. Yet, in explaining what has actually happened and why, Adams clearly betrays a very different kind of background. For we find that the source of the usurpation of human rights is the perversion of true religion. Canon and feudal law, he says, have ever worked in close alliance. One could not have succeeded without the assistance of the other. But religious *corruption*—not the familiar deception of "priest-craft" in general—is the true villain. And the pattern, recognizably, is similar to Defoe's.

By the former of these [canon law], the most refined, sublime, extensive, and astonishing constitution of policy that ever was conceived by the mind of man was framed by the Romish clergy for the aggrandisement of their own order. All the epithets I have here given to the Romish policy are just, and

[12] *Works of John Adams* (Boston, 1865), 3:447.

will be allowed to be so when it is considered, that they even
persuaded mankind to believe, faithfully and undoubtedly, that
God Almighty had entrusted them with the keys of heaven,
. . . Thus was human nature chained fast for ages in a cruel,
shameful, and deplorable servitude to him, and his subordinate
tyrants, who, it was foretold, would exalt himself above all
that was called God, and that was worshipped.

This is not a diatribe, of the conventional Enlightenment
kind, against religious deceit in general; no disciple of Rousseau or of Voltaire would have said "it was foretold." And it
is far from Gibbon's explanation of the fall of the Roman
Empire. A deliberate, evil conspiracy is assumed, and
"human nature," not only men, has been "chained"; of this
idea we shall hear much more. There is something like
Defoe's "blessed compact":

Still more calamitous to human liberty, was a wicked confederacy
between the two systems of tyranny above described. It seems
to have been even stipulated between them, that the temporal
grandees should contribute everything in their power to maintain the ascendancy of the priesthood, and that the spiritual
grandees in their turn, should employ their ascendancy over the
consciences of the people, in impressing on their minds a blind,
implicit obedience to civil magistracy.

Surely a man as well informed as Adams would know that
the lords spiritual and temporal, far from being scheming
confederates, were usually at loggerheads. What of Thomas
a Kempis? But the idea Adams here sets forth was to be
dominant, especially in the United States, and to form a
cornerstone of the popular philosophy of history.

The belief in the evil confederation was necessary if one
were to attribute the evils of the past—centering in the
Middle Ages—solely to the machinations of Antichrist.
Since he has been the moving spirit of all oppression,
we can expect that the beginning of his downfall has begun
the restoration of human liberty. And, as we might expect,
all has been ordained.

Thus, as long as this confederacy lasted, and the people were
held in ignorance, liberty, and with her, knowledge and virtue
too, seem to have deserted the earth, and one age of darkness
succeeded another, till God in his benign providence raised up

the champions who began and conducted the Reformation. From the time of the Reformation to the first settlement of America, knowledge gradually spread in Europe, but especially in England; and in proportion as that increased and spread among the people, ecclesiastical and civil tyranny, which I use as synonymous expressions for the canon and feudal laws, seem to have lost their strength and weight.

The "execrable race of the Stuarts" were of the party of Antichrist; and only after their final downfall did men— most fully in the New England colonies—move out into the sunlight of liberty.

Thus all stems from the Reformation. We hear nothing of the "revival of learning," the printing press, or the new science as causes for the enlightenment of mankind. Again, increase in knowledge and intelligence is accompanied by increase in virtue. Not simple ignorance, historical disaster, or the expected folly and vice of imperfect men, but a diabolical scheme to prevent Christianity from having its effect, has caused all our woe.

It is important also to understand the ideological basis of the connection between religion and "liberty." The essential idea of the reformers was that the Gospel must be brought, in its integrity, into immediate contact with each soul, and that human doctrines cannot therefore be permitted to stand as barriers between the means of grace and the believer. When the Gospel, devotedly expounded by its ministers, can do its work, it almost miraculously affects the mind and spirit. When a whole community is impregnated with this redeeming grace, a new state of affairs arises, one in which justice, charity, and truth are the common motives of conduct. Jonathan Edwards thought such a condition prevailed for a time in Northampton, after the Awakening. To prevent the Gospel from changing the world, Satan has used both political and religious tyranny to repress the Word. Thus, in the final analysis, political oppression is intended to serve a religious end.

It follows that the plain duty of Christians is to forward the work of Reformation. Adams says that, although the "struggle between the people and the confederacy aforesaid of temporal and spiritual tyranny, became formidable, violent, and bloody," the people have the confidence that they are supported by God's "benign providence." The discovery of America, and later the American Revolution, were placed in a sequence of victories beginning with the Reformation. The apocalyptic struggle was eventually to be seen as assuming new forms in the fight against slavery, in the campaign to "make the world safe for democracy," as well as in the seizure of new territories, in the New World, from the grasp of Antichrist.

The apocalyptic background of Adams' thesis emerges plainly in his statement of the motives of the first colonists. Although no enthusiasts, "they saw clearly, that popular powers must be placed as a guard, a control, a balance, to the powers of the monarch and the priest, in every government, or else it would soon become the man of sin, the whore of Babylon, the mystery of iniquity, a great and detestable system of fraud, violence, and usurpation." Here is an interesting amalgam of ideas. The balance of powers, of course, is rooted in Renaissance political philosophy and is a feature of Whig thought in the century. It is surely secular enough. But the menaces are the whole collection from the Revelation; the man of sin is a diabolical figure quite alien to Lockean philosophy. The combination might be called apocalyptic Whiggism; it is the prototype of what was to be perhaps the central American attitude toward government.

Against this ever-present danger there were established such safeguards as the "fine institution of the late Chief Justice Dudley, of a lecture against popery, and on the validity of presbyterian ordination." The early settlers, Adams says, framed their institutions in direct opposition to canon and feudal law; but they were no Anabaptists, and carefully avoided anything like revolutionary destruction. They decided, for example, not to hold lands alodially, as constituting a government "too nearly like a commonwealth." But, most important of all, they transmitted to their descendants "a hereditary ardor for liberty and thirst for knowledge." Why "hereditary"? Here he touches on another theme which was to become of first importance. There is some quality—represented in part only by desire for knowledge—in the English makeup that has made Englishmen take the lead in the Reformation. It is not merely what we should call a "cultural" trait; it is something that can, literally, be inherited.

Throughout the published *Dissertation*, Adams describes the people of the New England colonies as establishing their own righteous state, eliminating the rags and tags of the Whore of Babylon, which, regrettably, remain in Britain itself. There is no overt concern about other nations, except a Christian desire to see them also liberated; there is no sense of a special mission to save them. The motivation of the Puritans in the New World seem to have been a kind of holy self-interest. But the original draft, as recorded in his diary for February, 1765, contains one sentence of very different import: "I always consider the settlement of America with reverence and wonder, as the opening of a grand scene and design in Providence for the illumination of the ignorant, and the emancipation of the slavish part of mankind all over the earth." Here is a very early suggestion that the American settlements may be destined to be the nucleus not only of a holy but of a *millennial* people. Is it possible that the Reformation was the beginning of a process, within history, which is to lead to the establishment of God's kingdom in all the world? If so, it seems almost as if the "finger of prophecy" must point to this, the last, the best child of the Reformation. Why, many were to wonder, did Providence hold back the discovery of this vast part of the earth until the very time when the mystical Babylon began to suffer her death pangs?

II

The Rationale of the Millennium

The Protestant Revolution set in motion a new study of the Scriptures. Over the centuries there had grown up a great body of interpretations which, the reformers asserted, had taken the place of the saving text itself. The Old Testament in particular had lost much of its historical meaning, having been resolved into many spiritual "types" and allegories referring forward to the supreme mysteries of the Incarnation and Redemption. Protestants, however, were obligated to reconsider everything, the spirit in which interpretation was made as well as detailed explanations; for the assumption that Rome was the great "usurpation" made all its works suspect per se. How much, preachers and congregations constantly had to ask themselves, did the subtle misrepresentations of the False Prophet still infect even the "reformed" churches?

Especially dubious were "scholastic subtlety" and "metaphysical system"—means by which, it was alleged, a vast superstructure had been erected in front of the true message. The books of the Bible must not be made to speak in elaborate riddles which could be understood only by the most sophisticated minds, and which must be taken on trust; the Book must plainly protest its own meaning.

As would be expected, in time this idea produced revolutionary results—often, as the responsible clergy were to find in the Great Rebellion, going to the most fantastic extremes. But one major consequence on which most could agree was that the historical sections of the Old Testament again became historical. The people of God have had a continuous history, throughout Jewish and Christian eras. Augustine's thesis, that the two cities have had each its unbroken continuity from the beginning, took on new force. As Milton remarked, Protestants think the various parts of the Bible all have meaning for all time, and were not written for occasions. The events of the Old Testament, it seemed, bear much the same relation to those of the sixteenth or seventeenth centuries A.D. as, say, events of early English history bear to those of later days. Jews in the time of Jeremiah faced the same kinds of problems and temptations as did the English in the seventeenth century. Even names could be interchanged, for the very patterns of action are repeated. History is the account of one great war, in which there have been many campaigns; but, unlike long wars between nations, the high commands have remained the same throughout. It is as if Louis XIV, Napoleon, Bismarck, and Hitler all were only agents under the direction of one guiding mind. Thus, in Jonathan Edwards' words, "The religion that the church of God has professed from the first, has always been the same. . . . The Church of God, from the beginning, has been one society. The Christian church is manifestly the same society continued, that was before Christ came; grafted on the same root, built on the same foundation." [1] It follows that "The church that was before the Israelitish church, was still the same society, and it was essentially the same religion that was professed and practised in it. . . . So that the opposition which has been made to the church of God in all ages, has always been made against the same religion, and the same revelation." To speak of the medieval church as "Babylon" goes beyond metaphor; the old and the new persecutions are more than just alike in purpose. "Heathenism and Popery" are parts of the same conspiracy.

[1] Edwards, *History of the Work of Redemption*, vol. 3 in *Works* (New York, 1830), p. 381.

Such a theory might appear pessimistic. If the story of mankind is one lamentable chronicle of unremitting struggle between the children of darkness and the children of light, in which the former usually seem to have the upper hand, what hope is there for the future? Might it not even be prudent to adhere, like the witches, to the seemingly victorious side? Satan "endeavoured to frustrate [God's] design in the creation of this lower world, to destroy his workmanship, to wrest the government of it out of his hands, to usurp the throne, and set up himself as the God of this world, instead of him who made it." [2] And how well Satan has succeeded in making "man God's enemy" is only too apparent. Is there to be no end to this dismal tale? There is, Edwards tells us, for God has partially, though sufficiently, let us in on his grand strategy. The aim of the scheme of redemption is to subdue all the enemies of God. And, unlike Augustine, Edwards looks for the victory to be won in this world as we know it; we now can see what Augustine could not—how such a thing could be possible. It is a curious fact that those who, like Edwards, restored the spirit of Augustine's doctrine of original sin were the ones who reversed his theory of history.

Those holding the Augustinian view that secular history is of no lasting importance could accept with equanimity the prospect that Satan's primacy will endure until the end. The wise man will concentrate on this lasting, this only truly valid fact. But if the story of redemption coincides with that of human secular life, if the revelation is composed in large part of history related for its own sake, the terms must be altered. If there is to be an optimistic solution to the mystery of evil, it must be revealed within the events in time and this world as well as in eternity. Why have we been given such a detailed account of the conflicts of good and evil in the story of God's people if the evil is destined to win, over and over again? There surely must be some kind of direction. There must be more than local judgments on peoples that occasion may call for. The intensely historical nature of the Old Testament, taken at its face value, strongly intimates that God works as much through history

[2] *Ibid.*, p. 172.

as through the lives of individual souls. But in terms of the traditionally accepted eschatology, it was hard to find any basis for such a conclusion; the two Cities have two paths and two ends, and never the twain shall meet. But can we ignore the many passages that prophesy, in language that seems to apply to this world, a wonderful age when the wilderness will flower and men will make war no more?

In the second quarter of the seventeenth century a study of the Biblical texts provided the revolutionary change of interpretation that was needed to solve the dilemma. Joseph Mede, one of the greatest biblical scholars the Church of England has produced, came to look again at the Revelation of St. John in the light of improved understanding of Hebraic literary practices. Read without the presuppositions inherited from Augustinian tradition, it had an unmistakable historical significance. Its imagery and its arrangement of actions, could and must be referred back to Isaiah, Jeremiah, Ezekiel, Daniel, Micah, and others. And these prophets dealt with events forming part of the history of the one church and its fate in this world. So it follows that the prediction of a millennial state in the future must be more than an allegory of the spiritual order: there is, God has promised, an actual historical kingdom of God to be expected, one inhabited by persons in this mortal flesh. It follows, too, as earlier Protestant commentators had begun to assume, that the stages described by St. John—the events forecast in the scroll the Lamb opens before the company of heaven—likewise must refer to historical happenings, past, present, or to come. The last of them, therefore, the "binding" of the Dragon, must not be supernatural, but rather some great defeat of evilly inclined men, by means familiar to us. The history, political as well as spiritual, of mankind is not a record of the City of Man alone; but rather a program in which God, step by step, is redeeming *both* separate souls and the whole community of men. The twain shall meet. As a later writer says, the millennium is the vision of "the Civitas Dei within whose sacred walls our race is at last to dwell"—"our race," not only the mystical body of the redeemed.[3]

---

[3] Edward D. Morris, "The Future of Humanity on Earth," *Presbyterian Review*, 1 (1880): 426.

Just as the redemption of the soul has its stages—the calling, the renovation, the regeneration, imperfect glorification, final perfection beyond this life—so the scheme of redemption of society has its appointed progression. In Edwards' account, the scheme of all redemption is a great "machine" with many harmoniously operating "wheels." The machine is mobile and it majestically, but not without great destruction, goes forward from one position to the next; these he identifies as the "preparation, purchase, application, success" of the redemption.[4] "Success" has its literal meaning: triumph in this world. The study of Daniel and Revelation shows us that we are in the last of the stages, or close to the beginning of "success." Just as no individual sinner is perfected wholly in this life, moreover, but is psychically regenerated, society too is not to become absolutely perfect, but is to be immensely improved as the forces of righteousness finally gain the upper hand. The great events of all history, rightly read, "are but so many steps and degrees of the accomplishment" of Daniel's vision of the Son of man possessing "dominion, and glory, and a kingdom, that all people, nations, and languages, should serve him."[5] But, to repeat, this will be no sudden, miraculous manifestation of overwhelming divine power; it has been occurring, in fact, from the very time of the Fall. God has struck down Satan's power again and again; and although the Adversary seems to come back strong every time, the prophets have assured us that God "by every step advances [Christ's kingdom] still higher and higher, till at length it is fully set up, and Satan perfectly and eternally vanquished."[6]

The Kingdom of God on earth, Edwards assures us, is to be no fantastic, preposterous dreamland in which the saints get their rewards and their revenge, but such a condition as we should expect if honest, rightly motivated men, filled with the grace of the Gospel, were to exercise supreme control. Thus it is a form of utopia. And one of the marks of any utopia is great "temporal prosperity." In this connec-

---

[4] Edwards, *Work of Redemption*, p. 168.
[5] *Ibid.*, p. 127.
[6] *Ibid.*, p. 329.

tion, we should look briefly at a most important but not well understood aspect of Protestant thought.

Any reader of the Old Testament can hardly fail to notice that the prophets consistently stress the point that worldly flourishing is the sign that the chosen people is keeping its covenant; defeat and poverty come upon the nation when it violates its obligation to do God's work, and so incurs his wrath. A preacher named Thomas Barnard, in a Thanksgiving sermon in 1795, asserted that "publick blessings are evidently granted upon condition of good behaviour, and are lessened, or entirely recalled whenever societies persist in wrong conduct." [7] Prosperity is a consideration in the contract of God with the nations and individuals whom he calls to carry out his program; Job is the only exception to this teaching. Thus prosperity is the outward sign of an inward grace, for it demonstrates that the covenant is being fulfilled. God does not simply hand out goodies as compensation for good behavior. Thus, Barnard concludes, the people of the United States "may . . . say to each other with cheerful countenances—'We are a people peculiarly favoured of Heaven.'" Thus a "cheerful countenance," optimism bubbling over, is a sign of one's recognition as a citizen of the chosen country. The extraordinary good fortune of this country is the visible testimony to all the world that "the UNITED STATES OF AMERICA are now his vineyard" (referring to the text of the sermon, Isa. 5:3). The medieval doctrine of "holy poverty" is finally wound up; for poverty, far from being the sign of one's separation from the City of Man, is the evidence of alienation from the City of God. Logically, therefore, the period of the binding of Satan, when the original covenant of God and humanity is in large measure restored, will be a time of unexampled material well-being.

The radical movements of the English Civil War period, often called the "Fifth Monarchy" agitations, were in fact only the lunatic fringe of the central ideology of millennialism. The Fifth Monarchy, technically, is the name of the kingdom of righteousness, however its advent and character

[7] Sermon at Salem Congregational Church.

are understood, since it succeeds the four regimes thought to be predicted in Daniel. Even the most conservative theologians soon regarded its coming as a distinct certainty. It will not, they thought, be a revolutionary destruction of all civil order but rather the perfection of that order, government realizing its true purpose. In 1654 the leading Independent preacher Thomas Goodwin preached a sermon setting forth the reasonableness, one might almost say the aesthetic as well as moral propriety, of the conception that God's kingdom will come as the end of the historical process. If the millennium is no more than an allegory of the age after Christ, if conditions are to continue in their old way up to the last judgment, the triumph of God lacks completeness, and history ends in an unsatisfactory way: the devil has a kind of victory after all, if he is able so to frustrate the will of God that a miraculous intervention is necessary to bring him down. We are not satisfied when the author of a play has to invoke a *deus ex machina* to set things right in the last act. We feel that the interplay of plot development and character should produce the desired result. Just so, the traditional theory of eschatology is unsatisfying. It is essential, therefore, "that after all the Kingdoms of the world have had their time and their date, by which the Saints have all along been opprest and injured, there is, even on earth, a Kingdom to be given unto them, when all Nations shall be converted unto God, and the Saints in them be the prevailing party in this World." [8] The whole plot of the Revelation (which he describes as a kind of "comedy," presumably because its conclusion is fortunate) "is but the story of Christ's conquering of his Kingdom with his bowe, and with his arrows, [i.e. the Word of God] and executing the decrees that were contained in the roll he took out of his Fathers hand." [9] Yet this great result, although accomplished essentially by the true preaching of the Gospel, is by no means wholly peaceful; the book of Revelation, for example, 19:11, makes it clear the sword also must be used. The

---

[8] Goodwin, *A Sermon of the Fifth Monarchy* . . . (London, 1654), p. 18.
[9] *Ibid.*, p. 12.

kingdom is not to be achieved by ministers alone, even aided by devout congregations. Each person, even the non-believer on occasion, has his part, which will include soldiering. For God, in redeeming history, works *within* history; his grace operates through inspiration of people and nations who actually make that history. Finally, the course of redemption is not linear and continually upward. The fact that God permitted the Antichrist to bring darkness over all Christendom, as well as the story of the chosen people, suggests, rather, a campaign in which success seems to alternate between the sides, and the outcome is uncertain until the last engagements; but we have what every general would give anything to have: the assurance of ultimate victory.

Goodwin specifically disclaims any knowledge of or interest in the touchy question whether this is all to be achieved before or after the visible return of Christ to earth. The sermon is of special interest because it concentrates on the essential question—anterior to any specific theories—why there is any reason to expect a millennial utopia at all. It asserts there are good arguments, a priori, for the proposition that utopia is not something only to be dreamed about and argued about theoretically, or merely wistfully hoped for.

If Goodwin does not overtly commit himself as to whether the millennium will occur before the personal advent of Christ, it is clear, nevertheless, that his heart is with what is called the "post-millennialist" school. This opinion represented an interesting amalgamation of elements from previous views of the millennium. The most ancient theory, as we have seen, expected a literal reign of Christ and the saints, to be inaugurated by a series of wonderful, at least preternatural occurrences. It would be sudden daybreak after a long and deepening night. The Augustinians, on the contrary, thought that all these predictions must be considered only allegorical. The "third force" interpretation of the Protestant millennialists held that a literal millennium would indeed occur, but that the description of it was in many respects allegorical, and that nothing preternatural would be required to bring it about. Thus the first advent of Christ, before the millennium, symbolizes the triumph of the true Christian spirit rather than a visible descent from heaven. The "first resurrection," likewise, refers to the regeneration of the spirit of the saints, the rise of their righteousness rather than their bodies. To the earlier opinion—which expects the physical return of Christ—I have given the name "millenarian." To the belief that history, under divine guidance, will bring about the triumph of Christian principles, and that a holy utopia will come into being, I have assigned the name "millennialist." ("Progressive-millennialist" would be more accurate, but it is too cumbersome.) It has not been generally realized that some version of the "millennialist" doctrine has probably been predominant among English-speaking Protestants since the later seventeenth century. Minority groups, however, have continued to maintain that Christ will visibly appear in the air, graves will be opened, the saints then living will be caught up in the air, etc. Such a view, it is important to note, is *anti*-progressivist in attitude. This school believes that "It is not the intention of God to convert the world before that advent. . . . No radical spiritual change in the condition of the world will take place, on the contrary, it will grow worse and worse, under the present dispensation. Its subjection to Jesus is only to be brought about by unprecedented displays of his wrath, and most notably by the revelation of him, in flaming fire, taking vengeance on his adversaries." [10] The Millerites of the 1840's and the Jehovah's Witnesses of a century later belong to this "millenarian" category.[11] It is important to remember that, although both millennialists and millenarians expect an ac-

---

[10] R. M. Patterson, "Pre-Millennialism," *Princeton Review*, 55 (1879), p. 415.
[11] Joshua Spaulding, for example, in *The Coming and Kingdom of Christ* (Salem, 1796), distinguishes between "millenists" and "millenarians." I find the traditional terms "pre-" and "post-millennialists" unsatisfactory because, I believe, the attitudes toward the question of the millennium divide into three, not two categories; there are Augustinians as well as millennialists and millenarians. The term "post-millennialist" technically would include both Augustinians and millennialists, for both believe the millennium precedes the Parousia; but their conceptions of the millennium are diametrically opposite.

tual millennium, their ideas of it and how it is to come about are totally different. It is, however, a common mistake to confuse them. To do so is as misleading as to put Calvinists and Christian Scientists into one category because both identify themselves as Christian churches. The Chorus in T. S. Eliot's *The Rock* asks:

> And what shall we say of the future? Is one church all
> we can build?
> Or shall the Visible Church go on to conquer the World?

The millennialists resoundingly answer, Yes! On the other hand, both Augustinians and millenarians would hold that the believer must separate from an incurably evil world. In the words of the same Chorus:

> The great snake lies ever half awake, at the bottom of
> the pit of the world, curled
> In folds of himself until he awakens in hunger and mov-
> ing his head to right and to left prepares for his hour
> to devour.
> But the Mystery of Iniquity is a pit too deep for mortal
> eyes to plumb. Come
> Ye out from among those who prize the serpent's golden
> eyes,
> The worshippers, self-given sacrifice of the snake. Take
> your way and be ye separate.

The dramatic change of attitude in the seventeenth century can be seen if we compare two works by the celebrated non-conformist (and certainly conservative) divine, Richard Baxter. In his tract *A Holy Commonwealth*, one of the publications in the crisis after Cromwell's death, he states that "I live in hope of the coming and appearance of our Lord Jesus Christ, and pray that he may come quickly: But that he will after his coming reign visibly on earth, and if so, in what manner, are things that I have read much of, but am uncertain after all, . . ."[12] The conclusion of the book is that we can expect to have anything like a really good state only through the ordinary, accepted means of improving government—by selecting good men for office, by faithfully obeying the laws, by observing our assigned

[12] Baxter, *A Holy Commonwealth* (London, 1659), p. 222.

position in the constitution. "The discovery of an *Utopia*, or *City of the Sun*" is only a dream. There is no other means by which the kingdoms of this world can "become the Kingdoms of the Lord, and of his Christ." That is so much as to say never; for Baxter emphasizes the great inherent sinfulness of human nature, and the little and slow improvement we can expect in this life. The author of *The Saints' Everlasting Rest* at this time fundamentally agrees with Augustine, Thomas More, Erasmus, and the rest of the Christians in the old tradition.

It comes, therefore, as a great surprise to find the same man, over thirty years later and after a life of troubles and persecutions, writing *The Glorious Kingdom of Christ, Described and Clearly Vindicated*. By this time he has been converted to a radically different view of the possibilities of God's action on mankind; he has become a millennialist. This treatise, which is dedicated to Increase Mather, maintains that there is to be no physical resurrection of saints or visible appearance of Christ before the millennium. It refutes, in particular, the theory of the millenarian Thomas Beverley that Christ is to appear in the air, catching up the living saints to reign with him in an "Airy Humane Kingdom" for a thousand years. God does not work through wonders and marvels, but by the established laws of nature, physical and human. Yet, where before he had doubted that any utopia could ever be discovered on earth, he is now convinced that a righteous earthly kingdom, the holy utopia of the millennium, has been prophesied on the highest authority.

The discovery of that assurance, indeed, is one of the greatest events of the Reformation in general, and of English divines in particular. He notes, however, with regret, that "the chief Writers for the Millennium are Conformists (and men of the greatest Learning and Piety among them) as Jos. Mede, Dr. More, Dr. Twisse (then conformable), Dr. Cressoner, Mr. Beverley." [13] The failure of nonconformists to publish important works on the meaning of

[13] Baxter, *The Glorious Kingdom of Christ* . . . (London, 1691), Dedication.

the prophecies ought to be remedied; the dedication to Mather, who appears to disagree with him in a friendly manner, is a hint that the subject might well occupy dissenting divines overseas. Perhaps Baxter's work helped direct the attention of the greatest of those dissenting theologians—Jonathan Edwards—to this great theme.

This remark, it should be noted in passing, brings out a fact of cardinal importance about millennialist doctrine. Unlike almost every other proposition, it was little involved in sectarian dispute. Anglican and dissenter could and did substantially agree about the significance of the symbols of Revelation, and both could look forward to an earthly kingdom of goodness. There were to be loud and acrimonious controversies among sects about original sin, church government, Sunday schools, awakenings, and such matters; they have occupied the attention of later students probably because they did make so much noise. Yet the quiet but immensely potent idea of millennialist progress has either been ignored or little understood.

Baxter's final opinion is that the Kingdom of God grows by stages. God has not left the conquering of historical and spiritual evil to be accomplished all in a thousand-year period after Christ's personal advent.[14] The Savior's work is comparable to that of "a Physician that hath an Hospital or infected City to cure." As the latter "giveth up that work when it is perfectly finished: So Christ giveth up the Kingdom of Redemption when he hath done that work."[15] The analogy implies that the "cure" of evil can be accomplished *inside* the course of nature. Baxter reminds us that God never works on the soul through miraculous, external changes. By his infinite power, he could certainly "make every Infant a Doctor, that they not stay as Christ, to encrease in Stature and Wisdom."[16] He could wonderfully transform every sinner into a saint, and thus perfectly establish his kingdom instantaneously; but the whole teaching of Scripture shows that this is not the plan of redemption.

[14] *Ibid.*, p. 36.
[15] *Ibid.*, p. 20.
[16] *Ibid.*, p. 69.

As God desires to work with and through human nature to transform the individual soul, so he works with and through men and their institutions to regenerate the kingdoms of this world. To say his ways with the individual soul and those with society must be different is out of keeping with the tenor of the Word. It is wrong, then, to say that there can never be a triumph of Christian principles in the human community, or that it must be introduced by the *deus ex machina* of the millenarians. It is obvious that Baxter's reversal of attitude was induced solely by his reading of Scripture and of commentaries; it was no reflex response to any great change in the political scene.

A little treatise written, apparently late in the 1680's, by one William Torrey, an aged layman in New England, indicates how widely the question of the millennium was being canvassed.[17] Despite a want of formal education—of which he was acutely conscious—he took up the pen to combat what he considered to be a dangerous misunderstanding of the Revelation. Most men, he says, think Revelation 20:4—the vision of the reign of the "souls of them that were beheaded for the witness of Jesus"—is "not to be understood of a bodily Resurrection, but of a spiritual Resurrection in Regeneration." Torrey, however, argues against such Augustinian ideas. There is, he thinks, to be a real millennium. The subject must have been extensively debated in his church to induce a non-specialist to undertake setting forth his own notions.

It would be natural to think that the secular idea of progress, together with the scientific revolution, had exerted an effect on theology, and that millennialism was a way of adapting religion to the new secular optimism. It is true that an amelioration of the conditions of life was going forward. It is also true that the fact of the Reformation gave Protestants an access of confidence in the future. The New Philosophy, moreover, was beginning to stress the point that God operates through the laws of nature even in seeming mira-

---

[17] William Torrey, *A Discourse concerning Futurities or Things To Come* (Boston, 1757). The Rev. Thomas Prince, who published the MS, identifies Torrey as "one of the pious and early settlers of the MASSACHUSETTS COLONY."

cles: in the last quarter of the century, for example, Thomas Burnet (who had many successors) attempted to explain the Deluge and the final burning of the earth in terms of geological processes.[18] And it is true that the "Ancients vs Moderns" controversy reflected a new confidence in the present: the contemporary world, men made bold to assert, had in some fields surpassed even the heights achieved by the ancients.

Yet all this is far short of an "idea of progress." And in fact the idea that progress is the "law" of history, that it is ordained, was religious before it was secular. It has been remarked that the late seventeenth-century champions of the "moderns" lack "at least three essential attributes" of the developed, nineteenth-century faith in progress.[19] These are: universal inclusiveness, inevitability, and infinity. "Total progress in all realms of being—the full-blown theory—is a late eighteenth-, really a nineteenth-century French concept." [20] But all of these three attributes are present in the millennialist commentaries a century before Condorcet and Saint-Simon.

A few major theorists from the late seventeenth and early eighteenth centuries will exemplify the millennialist idea in its pre-American stage. One respected scholar was Daniel Whitby, whose *Paraphrase and Commentary on the New Testament* was published in 1703. It has even been asserted, though inaccurately, that he originated millennialism.[21] Whitby's solid, massive learning helped remove any doubts which might have remained about interpreting the "first resurrection" in the symbolic manner of the millennialists. He shows that the idea that there will be two separate resurrections is inconsistent with the New Testament as a whole. He made it clear, too, that modern millennialism is far from being a continuation of the ancient beliefs: "The

---

[18] See Marjorie H. Nicolson, *Mountain Gloom and Mountain Glory* (Ithaca, 1959), chap. 5; and my *Millennium and Utopia*, pp. 117–126.
[19] Frank E. Manuel, *Shapes of Philosophical History* (Stanford: Stanford University Press, 1965), p. 67.
[20] *Ibid.*, p. 68.
[21] E.g., by Henry Dana Ward, *History and Doctrine of the Millennium* (Boston, 1840), p. 59.

new *Patrons* of the *Millennium* differ in many Things of Moment from the Ancient Asserters, and have indeed scarce any Suffrage of Antiquity for that *Millennium* which they so stiffly maintain." [22] There is an implication that there has been remarkable progress in understanding of the Scriptures' true meaning. The new ideas, of course, have no stigma of "enthusiasm," no association with messianic radicalism—a standard disclaimer from eighteenth and nineteenth century writers. Whitby, like Baxter, points out that the trend is toward millennialism. Such scholars as Mede and Thomas Burnet, who started out as millenarians, "expressly have renounced their Doctrine" of Christ's personal reign on earth.

Finally, Whitby expresses by implication the change of viewpoint in religion which the newer ideas were causing. God's plan is not to reward the martyrs in a sumptuous, "carnal" manner, but to work through human interactions to accomplish what we might call "social progress," which will eliminate the ancient injustices.

In a Word, to foretel Times of Peace and Plenty to succeeding Ages, to raise the Expectation of a People whose Backs are bowed down, and have been long enslaved and afflicted, is very suitable to this divine Oeconomy; but, to promise Plenty, and the Goods of Fortune, as the Reward of Christian Piety and Patience, and let them know that if they suffer for the sake of Christ, he will be sure to raise them up to plentiful Enjoyment of the Goods of Fortune, this is too mean, too much beneath the sublime Spirit of *Christianity*, to be one of her great and precious Promises. [23]

All is aimed at the future. A major part of Christian duty is to prepare for the good time certain to come—for posterity. This theme is a common and important one with millennialists. In this spirit Timothy Dwight, later, dedicated his work on the millennium to those who were to enjoy it hereafter. And Samuel Hopkins' dedication to *his* discourse on the millennium rises to heights of emotion rare with him:

[22] Whitby, *Paraphrase and Commentary* . . . (London, 1760), 2:689.
[23] *Ibid.*, 2:713.

To the People who shall live in the Days of the Millennium.
Hail, ye happy people, highly favored of the Lord! Though
you have yet no existence, nevertheless, the faith of the
Christians in this and in former ages, beholds you 'at hand to
come'; and realizing your future existence and character, you
are greatly esteemed and loved; and the pious have great joy
in you, while they are constantly, and with great earnestness
praying for you. They who make mention of the Lord, will not
keep silence, nor give him any rest, till he establish, and till
he make Jerusalem a praise in the earth. For you they are
praying and labouring, and to you they are ministring; and
without you, they cannot be made perfect. And you will enter
into their labours, and reap the happy fruit of their prayers,
toils and sufferings.[24]

This is the spirit of Blake:

> I will not cease from mental fight,
> Nor shall my sword sleep in my hand
> Till we have built Jerusalem
> In England's green and pleasant land.

Hopkins' millennium, as we shall see, was a utopian world of
justice, benevolence, and prosperity. Without its realization
redemption is incomplete.

What might be termed a normative interpretation of the
prophetic system was provided by the English non-
conformist minister Moses Lowman, in his *Paraphrase and
Notes upon the Revelation* (1737). Of it, the hymn-writer
Doddridge said, "I have received more satisfaction with
respect to 'the difficulties' than ever I found elsewhere, or
expected to find at all." Many preachers agreed, and a large
number—perhaps the majority—of commentators for over a
century relied on Lowman. His notes on Revelation were
part of a compendium of commentaries on the whole Bible
that was reprinted several times by both English and American publishers down to the middle of the next century;
from it, we may suspect, innumerable sermons were mined.[25]
Since Lowman's millennialist scheme represents the kind of

---

[24] Hopkins, *A Treatise on the Millennium* (Boston, 1793),
Dedication.
[25] Simon Patrick *et al.*, *Critical Commentary on the Old and
New Testaments and the Apocrypha* (Philadelphia, 1844).

consensus that emerges only after many authors have labored over a subject, and since it became standard with conformists and dissenters alike, it will repay some detailed investigation.

His central point is that the reign of the saints predicted by St. John is figurative in the same way as the statement that the redeemed soul is "crucified with Christ." (This analogy was common.) He quotes Burnet's *Sacred Theory of the Earth*: "Happy days of peace and righteousness, of joy and triumph, of external prosperity and internal sanctity, when virtue and innocency shall be in the throne, vice and vicious men out of power and credit, are prophesied of in Scripture, and promised to the church of God." [26] This patently is a political and social utopia and requires no supernatural transformation to bring it in. The prophecy, Lowman asserts, "seems to suppose such inhabitants of the earth, during the millennium, as were the inhabitants of the earth when the beast was destroyed, or men in the usual state of natural succession; not persons raised out of the grave, or fetched from the separate state of departed souls." The descent of the heavenly Jerusalem, in Revelation 21:2, signifies a "state of heavenly original and constitution." The statement that there will be "no more sea" (Rev. 21:1) means, in prophetic symbolism, "that in this happy state there will be no turbulent, unquiet spirits, to be managed by the ambitious; and therefore no fear least any beast [i.e. the Roman church] should again rise out of the sea." [27] This glorious state without political factions is no mere ideal which just possibly may come to fruition, for "the time and way of the church's deliverance is everywhere represented, as appointed and directed only by the orders of God and Christ." [28] We need not, like philosophers of the Enlightenment, rely on the amorphous "laws of nature." Yet even in these interpretations there was always an ambivalence, for preachers constantly reminded the faithful that God's people can fail in their duty.

[26] *Ibid.*, pt. 4, p. 106.
[27] *Ibid.*, pt. 4, p. 1109.
[28] *Ibid.*, pt. 4, p. 1019.

The pattern of world history comprehends seven "periods of prophecy," after the Redemption. The first stage, ending in 323, when Constantine made Christianity official, was the persecution of the primitive church. The second was the persecution by idolatrous northern tribes, followed by the division of the empire and the rise of Islam. It ended with Charles Martel's defeat of the Moslem invaders of France. The third was the darkest of all—the time of the witnesses' prophesying in sackcloth for 1,260 "Days" (each day being a year in temporal chronology), and their slaughter. This will be recognized immediately as the reign of the Antichrist, of the revived "Rome," also called the "mystical Babylon." Its exact beginning is hard to determine—a most important fact, for the time-schedule of the advance to the millennium depends on when this era will be fully terminated. The fourth period is the millennium itself, following the last actions against the "beast" in all his forms. After the millennial age, there will be a short renascence of the satanic powers; then the short but terrible final battle; and last the general resurrection and judgment, and the beginning of the "endless sabbath." The millennium is not to be confused with the true heavenly order. Nor is the first "binding of Satan" the end of his strength; the whole millennialist hypothesis depends on the point that evil men will be repressed, not annihilated. For this reason the millennium is utopia, not heaven.

Another characteristic must be emphasized. It will be noted that each defeat of the Enemy is followed by another resurgence of his power; his last great era, "mystical Babylon," is, indeed, his strongest. This fact might at first seem to make for pessimism. Is there to be a constant cycle of dark age, defeat, another dark age, and so forth? But, the prophetic interpreters maintained, each *form* of evil, in each period, is *sui generis*, and when it has been crushed, is permanently out of the way. So the course of history is the progressive destruction of the various kinds of control Satan has possessed. Thus a major American commentator, Enoch Pond, expresses it: "But ordinarily, when great evils are put down, in the providence of God, they are down forever. . . . Other forms of wickedness may be tried, but the exploded form is to be revived no more." [29] Because they understand this fact, the Christians are not as those without hope. Barrier after barrier is to be removed, so that eventually the operation of grace will be uninhibited. As the "vials" are poured out, one source of woe after another is extirpated by a kind of cauterization, as in the work of the surgeon, which Baxter employs as an analogy for the Christian mission.

Every commentator worked out his own arrangement and time scheme for the seals, the trumpets, and the vials. The most responsible denied that any certain date for the end of Satan's kingdom can be set, but most were convinced that we are in the final stages, and that the millennium is not many generations in the future. These terminal victories were thought to be symbolized by the "pouring out of the vials" by seven angels (Rev. 16), and so most of the discussion centered on their possible historical references. It would be infinitely tiresome and largely profitless to enter into the many variations on this theme, for their resemblances much outweigh their differences. To illustrate the method, one example may be representative, and again Lowman is probably the best choice. He arranged the seven final periods of history as follows. The character of each, he assumed, was indicated by the nature of the action associated with the "vial" which destroys that particular province of the satanic kingdom.

The first angel pours out his vial in the form of a "noisome and grievous sore upon the men which had the mark of the beast and upon them which worshipped his image." Since the "beast" was one with the papacy, this is interpreted as a first blow at papal supremacy; Lowman thinks it prophesies the "commotions" following the death of Charlemagne, who had received his crown at the hands of the pope.

The second bowl of God's wrath is poured out upon the sea, "and it became as the blood of a dead man." Here we see the bloodshed of the expeditions across the seas to conquer

[29] Pond, *The Kingdom Given to the Saints* (Andover, 1843), p. 9.

the Holy Land. (The Saracen was usually considered as a kind of auxiliary to the "beast.")

The third, from 1200–1371, typifies the bloody civil wars of the Guelphs and Ghibellines; it is, the Revelation says, upon the "rivers and fountains of the waters"—apparently in contrast with "sea," civil as contrasted with foreign war.

The fourth angel "poured out his vial upon the sun; and power was given him to scorch men with fire." The time is 1378–1530, characterized by the Great Schism and the fall of Constantinople. Both events are taken to be preparatory to the downfall of the "antichristian usurpation."

But it was on the fifth vial that most interest centered, for there was general agreement that it symbolized the Reformation, that second Redemption. It was, as I have indicated in the first chapter, considered to be the pivot of all Christian history, and in a real sense of all history; its occurrence both anticipates and guarantees the final triumph of true Christianity. This angel "poured out his vial upon the seat of the beast; and his kingdom was full of darkness; and they gnawed their tongues for pain, and blasphemed the God of heaven because of their pains and their sores, and repented not of their deeds." The fact that the monster's minions "gnawed their tongues" forecasts the post-Reformation conditions. Severely wounded, exacerbated and incited to more desperate measures than before, the nations and institutions still under his control are temporarily menacing in the extreme; and hardly any commentator thought that peaceful progress alone would prove sufficient to destroy so great a force.

The elusive sixth vial is poured out "upon the great river Euphrates, and the water thereof was dried up, that the way of the kings of the east might be prepared." It gave commentators more trouble than did the others. Many thought it must refer to the destruction of the Turks. Perhaps, Lowman speculates, there will be an invasion of the Papal States. Last comes the climactic seventh angel, who "poured out his vial into the air; and there came a great voice out of the temple of heaven, from the throne, saying, It is done. And there were voices and thunders, and lightnings; and there was a great earthquake, such as was not since men were upon the earth, so mighty an earthquake, and so great. And the great city was divided into three parts, and the cities of the nations fell: and great Babylon came in remembrance before God, to give unto her the cup of the wine of the fierceness of his wrath." In unimaginable struggles and terrors the millennium is to be born. The "earthquakes," in prophetic language, were equated with the fall of nations; the thunders and lightnings, with wars.

The last two vials, Lowman recognizes, are largely in the future. To the sixth, he tentatively assigns the dates 1670–1850; and for the seventh, 1850–2016. It will be recognized that these years are mostly a kind of *terra incognita*, like unexplored areas whose boundaries are roughly traced on maps. Yet these periods are crucial. The events of the eighteenth, nineteenth, and twentieth centuries would certainly be unique in both importance and character. Protestants who lived in these centuries accordingly might be expected to live through the most terrible yet the most inspiring days anyone had known since the Resurrection. And it seemed logical that to some nation or nations would be assigned leadership in finishing God's great plan. Sure enough, an age of revolution ensued—in science and technology as well as in government. A hemisphere, hitherto unknown, came into the forefront of history. And bestriding it, was a new nation. The United States hardly needed to identify itself as the appointed agent of the Apocalypse; it seemed as if the stage manager of Providence had summoned the American people from the wings of the stage of history.

2

As the great events began to crowd in after 1776, it seemed the vials were being poured out so fully that they could hardly lead to anything less than the judgment of mystical Babylon. The famous minister and scientist Joseph Priestley, for example, lived through the upheavals of the last years of the century, and the persecutions he suffered himself, with undiminished interest and confidence; for the signs of the times, he was sure, read in the light of prophecy, more and more plainly intimated the approaching millennial dawn. God indeed has provided the prophecies to sustain our faith during these terrifying but sublime days.

It is . . . so suitable a continuation of the prophecies of Daniel, that something would have been wanting in the New Testament dispensation if nothing of the kind had been done in it; for it has been the uniform plan of the Divine proceedings to give a *more distinct view* of interesting future events, as the time of their accomplishment approached.[30]

So he justifies his conviction that the Revelation of St. John belongs in the inspired canon. And how great is this comfort!

Indeed, some of the most interesting parts of this prophecy are, at this very time, receiving their accomplishment, and, therefore, our attention is called to it in a very particular manner. . . . It is, indeed, sufficient for us, and affords us much consolation, that the great catastrophe is clearly announced, and such indications of happy times, as lead us to look forward with confidence and joy. These prophecies are also written in such a manner as to satisfy us, that the events announced to us were really foreseen, being described in such a manner as no person, writing without that knowledge, could have done. This requires such a mixture of clearness and obscurity, as has never yet been imitated by any forgers of prophecy whatever.

It is this very "mixture of clearness and obscurity" that, paradoxically, is most reassuring: God has neither left us without compass and map, nor made us robots of his will. We make history ourselves although we are under the inspiration of grace. The modern world, to a greater extent than we may appreciate, has been motivated by this kind of conviction, whether its form is Christian apocalypticism or Marxist "dialectic"; both set forth predictions and general guides, both call for the most strenuous efforts to destroy

[30] Priestley, *Notes on All the Books of Scripture*, in *Theological and Miscellaneous Works* (London, 1806–32), 14:443.

the opposition and to progress toward the happy time sure to come, by a path marked out in advance.

For we have been told that Satan, who is "no other than the principle or cause of evil in general, natural and moral," will be overthrown.[31] Natural philosopher and dry rationalist though he was, Priestley never doubted that a conspiracy of malign beings had been at work throughout history. Although originally a millennialist, regarding the "reign of Christ" as the "reign of Christianity" only, in the end he came to think that Christ must rule personally in some manner, although human nature will continue. This situation, he speculates, is not unreasonable, since we are told that Christ, Enoch, Moses, and Elijah are all present somewhere on earth; Christ appeared to Paul.

Priestley, like all his fellow Protestants, thinks the tide has turned against the malign conspiracy with the Reformation: "The blasphemy of the beast, of which the papal power was a part, consists in the Pope's usurping the authority of God, setting up other objects of worship besides him, and persecuting his true worshippers, and in all the kingdoms represented by the ten horns concurred."[32] He calmly views the prospect of terrible events present and even more terrible ones to come. God, as the prophets inform us and we can see for ourselves, works in history through a combination of "the sword proceeding out of the mouth of Christ"—the peaceful teaching of the Gospel—and the temporal sword; and Christ is "represented as conducting the armies by which [the adversaries] are defeated."[33] Especially meaningful at the moment is Revelation 14, which Julia Ward Howe was later to apply to the situation in her time. The "reaping of the earth" by the angel of the Lord, which succeeds the announcement of the fall of Babylon, is followed by the treading of the winepress of God's wrath. Priestley analyzes the symbolical application of this prediction as dispassionately as he might observe an experiment in his laboratory. We cannot deny, he concludes, that the

[31] *Ibid.*, 14:487.
[32] *Ibid.*, 14:476.
[33] *Ibid.*, 14:499.

distinction in the text between "harvest" and "vintage" is "an intimation of calamity by war," for the text says that "blood came out of the winepress, even unto the horse bridles, by the space of a thousand and six hundred furlongs." He agrees with the earlier commentators Mede and Bishop Newton that 1600 furlongs is about the extent of the pope's estates.

Assuming the beneficence of calamity, he could accept and rejoice in the French Revolution. For all its destructiveness, it is another step, and a big one, in the progressive defeat of the tyranny and obscurantism which the conspirators have always employed to prevent the development of man to his true stature. Consequently, Priestley believed, the alliance against the Revolution will fail. It is another and late rally of the followers of the Beast. Being late, it is, despite its superficial strength, actually hollow. The English Establishment, too, is an incongruous relic of the system which the Roman Church had set up. The persecution of those who, like himself, oppose it in God's cause, is only to be expected; but where the early martyrs, like the Lollards, had seemingly suffered in vain, the present revolutionaries will prevail. Once the revived Beast has received its wound, it will never—unlike the first one—be healed. Priestley could not, of course, approve the antagonism to all revealed religion which revolutionary leaders so loudly professed; but the great tyrannies and superstitions of the past, in the name of Christ, understandably had led to an exaggerated reaction against all religion. Yet even the campaign against revealed religion was an instrument in God's hand. In 1794, he told the Gravel Pit Meeting, he agreed with an idea Whiston attributed to Sir Isaac Newton, that "the overbearing tyranny and persecuting power of the antichristian party, which hath so long corrupted Christianity, and enslaved the Christian world, must be put a stop to, and broken in pieces by the prevalence of infidelity, for some time, before primitive Christianity could be restored." [34] Calamitous, no doubt, will be the time of the breaking of nations; "but what

[34] Priestley, *The Present State of Europe Compared with Ancient Prophecies* (London, 1794), p. 25.

convulsion in the political world ought to be a subject of lamentation, if it be attended with so desirable an event" as the ending of the "unnatural alliance of the kingdom of Christ with the kingdoms of this world"? But this is not to say the millennium is to be spiritual only; if it were, why does Daniel 7 predict the destruction of the kingdoms preceding that of Christ, "since they would not have interfered with it, but might have subsisted at the same time"? Priestley is a good example of the degree to which the actual wording of the prophecies created the millennialist ideology.

A nonconformist minister, Thomas Howe, who obviously was much influenced by Priestley's commentaries, sets forth the essence of the millennialist attitude toward the meaning of events:

If serious observers of the signs of the times, [students of history] will mark, in those revolutions which have astonished the world, within a few years past, which have been attended with dire calamities, and which the mere politician attributes to second causes, the same designs of providence carrying on for the destruction of spiritual domination, the establishment of the just rights and liberties of mankind, and the promotion of truth, virtue, and happiness.[35]

For "kingdoms and mighty empires are raised up and overturned, with a view to the accomplishment of these predictions." [36] Prophecies are not so much the outlines of history as history the matter of prophecy; it exists to accomplish them.

This kind of theorizing calmly assumes that ends justify means. True, the theorists would justify God's ways—his permitting a long-lasting reign of darkness, and ordaining the wars and revolutions required to overthrow it—by recalling that mankind inherits the consequences of its own original sin. And God's mercy insures the rightness of all. But as the apocalyptic way of thinking becomes divorced

[35] Howe, "Preliminary Dissertation on the Scriptures of the New Testament," to John Taylor's *A Key to the Apostolic Writings* (London, 1805), p. 44.
[36] *Ibid.*, p. 36.

from the underlying theology, the movement of history through wars, slaughters, implacable conflict, comes to appear simply as the iron law of nature. In every situation, for example, we must see a "confrontation" of the righteous and the wicked; the massive conflict is inescapable, and everyone must identify himself wholly with his cause. Indeed, even in Christian apocalyptic there is a tendency to lose sight of the separate soul, even if its salvation is supposedly the end and purpose of all that takes place. The individual is swallowed up in the preoccupation with symbols of states, eras, wars. At times one feels that souls, like history, exist only to accomplish the prophecies. We may recall that Priestley was a theoretical "necessitarian" in philosophy. If there is a noble challenge to sacrifice one's present happiness and even life to attain the millennium which future generations are to enjoy, there is also the risk that man will turn into mass man.

Thus apocalyptic theory, whatever its type, tends to chain men to the wheels of the Juggernaut of history. As expounded even by Priestley, the apocalyptic view is in direct opposition to the ideas of the Enlightenment, which held forth the hope that men at any time, by using their reason honestly and objectively, can solve their problems and make a relatively good society. Edwards' description of redemption as a "machine" is revealing. Millennialism applies predestination to historical as well as personal salvation. The irony of our day is that, while rigid Calvinism has gone out of style, the notion of predestined history has lasted. Marxism, at least in its propaganda, is the secular apocalyptic. It has three leading characteristics of the religious forms—it is deterministic, dualistic, simplistic. It, too, sees a millennial or quasi-millennial state at the end of things, and it, too, sees a continuing conflict between a monstrous "conspiracy" and the party of the innocent and oppressed. It, too, sees every historical problem in simple terms of good and evil. And it, too, regards violence as necessary ultimately to cut the knots of circumstance created by the conspiracy. Eisenstein's great movie *Potemkin*, if the labels were changed, could serve admirably as a model for an epic of apocalyptic doctrine. It was no accident, perhaps, that Marx was writing when millennialism was particularly strong in both Britain and the United States.

III

The Politics of Providence and the Holy Utopia

It is a commonplace that the nineteenth century was dominated by the "idea of inevitable progress." Thus the Saint-Simonians formulated the faith:

The law of perfectibility is absolute. . . . Today everything leads to the conclusion that with the cessation of wars, with the establishment of a regime that will put an end to violent crises, no retrogression, not even a partial one, will ever again take place. There will be continuity and acceleration of the progressions among the whole of mankind, for peoples will teach one another and will sustain one another.[1]

It was believed that the laws of human nature bring about a constant upward movement, whereby man increases his control over nature, overcomes ignorance and selfishness, and moves steadily onward into a utopian future. Little recognized so far, however, is the fact that there was also a religious "idea of progress," which, although resembling its secular counterpart in many respects, and equally confident

[1] *Doctrine de Saint-Simon.* Exposition. Première année, 1829. Quoted in Frank E. Manuel, *Shapes of Philosophical History* (Stanford: Stanford University Press, 1965), p. 102.

that utopia was at the end of the road, nevertheless differed profoundly from it in assumptions about man, about the nature and means of advancement, and about the purpose of history.

We have seen how the religious idea of progress began and how much it antedates the secular doctrine. It is now in point to examine it in more detail. How, precisely, is progress achieved? And what kind of order is this New Jerusalem which the Scriptures seem to promise mankind? These questions are important, for it is startling to realize how widespread was this religious version of the belief in progress. Especially in the United States, the millennialist interpretation of God's Word did much to shape attitudes toward contemporary problems.

The most telling evidence for the strength of millennialism is the number of treatises, tracts, and sermons on the subject that appeared during the nineteenth century. A long bibliography has been compiled—still, however, not complete; I have merely sampled some of the most important works.[2] Yet this sampling gives, I think, a fair indication of the ideas of the movement, and a fully comprehensive account would be largely repetition. A roll-call of names of authors who wrote on aspects of the doctrine testifies to its ubiquity. The list includes: Jonathan Edwards; his student and associate, Joseph Bellamy; Samuel Hopkins (the principal founder of the "New Light theology," which carried the day in the Presbyterian churches); Joseph Priestley; the "apostle of the American Revolution," Richard Price; Timothy Dwight; the principal founder of the Disciples of Christ, Alexander Campbell; Henry Boynton Smith, an early professor in the Union Theological Seminary, who moved against the current, from Unitarianism back to moderate orthodoxy; Lyman Beecher; the famous educator

[2] For an extensive bibliography of technical treatises on the millennium, see Leroy Froom, *The Prophetic Faith of Our Fathers* (Washington, D.C., 1954), vol. 4. I have necessarily covered some of the ground traversed by C. G. Goen in his article "Jonathan Edwards: A New Departure in Eschatology," *Church History*, 28 (1959), 33 ff., but I have attempted to place Edwards in a wider perspective, both backward and forward.

Mark Hopkins, who was to ascend into the Hall of Fame; the very influential theologian Horace Bushnell; Enoch Pond, who was said to have educated, at the Bangor Seminary, some 700 clergymen; Josiah Strong, one of the founders of the Social Gospel movement; and many more. The pillar of Federalist conservatism, Dwight, agreed in fundamentals about the millennium with the radical Priestley; the suspected heretics Bushnell and Beecher concurred with Edwards—such facts indicate the sweep of agreement. But most important of all is that this kind of thinking about history reached the common man as, it is safe to say, that of Herbert Spencer or Henry Thomas Buckle never did. The opinions of the commentators could hardly have failed to filter down in some form, through sermons and "Bible study" classes as well as magazines, to the congregations of a strongly religious and Protestant nation. They provided the ordinary citizen with a historical philosophy, continuing the work of John Foxe's *Book of Martyrs*.

In 1840, during a discourse delivered to a Boston conference on the question of the Parousia, Henry Dana Ward complained that the doctrine "of a spiritual millennium in this world's flesh before the Lord's appearing," though (he thought) but a little over a century old and a complete novelty in Christendom, had become supreme, "and so firmly planted has this new faith become in all the churches of America, that never a religious newspaper of high standing with its own sect can easily be found, in New York or Boston, to admit an article into their columns, boldly questioning this proud Philistine, which has seized the ark of our faith, and now defies the hope of Israel." [3] Reading such prestigious religious journals as the *Presbyterian Review* will bear out this observation. For it is hard to find any other attitude toward Revelation than the confidence in "a spiritual millennium in this world's flesh,"—a holy utopia—as the end of redemption; and one evidence of intellectual and religious enlightenment, it is assumed, is the discovery that Augustine was wrong about the two Cities.

---

[3] Ward, *History and Doctrine of the Millennium* (Boston, 1840), p. 59.

Ward's objection to the new faith is that it approaches too closely the optimism of the secular progressivists, and he is surely right in saying that it signalizes a revolution in Christian thought. The traditional values associated with the conception of a separate City of God have given way to those of the City of the World. Ward states that Edwards and Hopkins, though tainted by millennialism, did at least stress the expectation of fearful judgments to precede the millennial age—"overwhelming sorrows, which are to cut off the wicked, purify the holy people, and prepare the world for the coming glory." [4] But now, in the hopeful nineteenth century, "all at once Christendom has been furnished with a complete scheme of worldly grandeur, to be attained by a rapid advance in virtue, knowledge, holiness, and the arts, wholly independent of the guarded door of Edwards and Hopkins to the entrance of the millennium." The difference is in fact much less. There is more "hopefulness" in the eighteenth century writers than Ward indicates, and his contemporaries, even the most optimistic, seldom failed to remind their readers that all will not be "smooth" in the advance to the millennium. The real issue is whether the "judgments" to come are purely spiritual means, as Ward says, of purifying the holy people; or, one might say, political means of destroying evil institutions, of purging society rather than men. In general, most writers thought that a combination of the two was possible and likely; but certainly the stress came to be on the political, institutional aspects of the "vials."

Edwards' history of redemption consolidates the theories that preceded him. The powers which for so long have perverted the true Gospel are now rapidly being routed. After the long night of the Middle Ages, and after several previous, abortive attempts to overthrow him, "when God's appointed time was come, his work went on with a swift and wonderful progress." [5] Edwards agrees with Lowman, whom he quotes, that this was the pouring out of the fifth vial. By one dramatic defeat, Antichrist fell halfway toward

[4] *Ibid.*, p. 38.
[5] Edwards, *History of the Work of Redemption*, vol. 3 in *Works* (New York, 1830), p. 368.

utter ruin, and although still valiantly trying to climb back (through such devices as the "Anabaptists, enthusiasts, Socinians, Arminians, Arians, Deists") and although making new gains, he is doomed. The Gospel in "these latter times" has had notable success as evidenced by its spread in America, the last (until recently penetrated) redoubt of paganism. Satan's advances—for example, the prevalence of Deism in Britain, the "principal nation of the Reformation"—are outweighed by the diminishing of the persecuting spirit, which is going out of fashion even among popish rulers.

The sixth vial is about to be poured out; religion will arise, and the Gospel will be universally propagated. The trumpet will sound "and they shall come which were ready to perish in the land of Assyria and the outcasts in the land of Egypt, and shall worship the Lord in the holy mount at Jerusalem" (Isa. 27:13). (This verse Edwards seems to take as referring specifically to the things yet to happen.) Yet we must prepare ourselves for one final, cataclysmic resistance—"the battle of the great day of God Almighty." However great that battle, it is still *within* history. It will conquer, not terminate the City of the World. It is comparable to the other wars of history, for it is carried on not by angels and demons but by human beings then in the flesh and with results that in the first instance are political in nature: the politics, however, of God and not of Satan.

The symbolical "second advent" is in fact only one of four "comings of Christ," each of them "accompanied with a terrible *destruction* of the wicked, and the enemies of the church: the *first*, with the destruction of the persecuting Jews, which was amazingly terrible; the *second*, with dreadful judgments on the Heathen persecutors of the Church; the *third*, with the awful destruction of Antichrist, the most cruel and bitter enemy that ever the church had; the *fourth*, with divine wrath and vengeance on all the ungodly." [6] Edwards' theory of the multiple Parousia, so far as I know, goes beyond any before it in symbolizing the prediction. The "new heavens and new earth," so far from referring to

---

[6] *Ibid.*, p. 327. These "comings" are the accomplishments of Daniel 7:13–14; they bring in "the kingdom of heaven."

a far-off divine event, really signify the stages of these steps in the redemption of society: "Further, there is in *each* of these comings of Christ an ending of the old, and a beginning of new heavens and a new earth, or an end of a temporal state of things, and a beginning of an eternal state." Here there is a hint of a new and radically different interpretation of the Apocalypse—that it applies to history, indefinitely, that "final judgment" and regeneration occur over and over again, that there is to be no literal terminus. (Needless to say, such a conclusion would go far beyond any conscious intentions of Edwards himself; his statement, however, suggests that deep changes in traditional beliefs, deeper than any of which an author may be fully aware, are taking place in Protestantism.)

The first of his successors in the millennial fields was his student and associate, Joseph Bellamy. Although he repeated the essentials of Edwards' theory, he made some changes in emphasis characteristic of later millennialism. One is an even stronger parallel between the Babylon of the Old Testament and mystical Babylon, the medieval world. The experiences of the Israelites in the Captivity are more than analogically repeated by the "remnant" under Rome.

. . . how insupportable would have been the grief of the church of Christ, through the long dark cruel reign of mystical Babylon, while they beheld error and wickedness universally prevail, Satan getting his will in almost everything, and, to appearance, no signs of better times, . . . How great their grief? How almost insuperable their temptations to apostasize, and forsake a cause that heaven seemed to forsake, had not the day of deliverance been expressly foretold, and the glory that should follow opened to view by the spirit of prophecy? [7]

Bellamy comes closer, also, to identifying the whole process of redemption with a long military operation in which, eventually, superior generalship will prevail. The whole Bible is the history of "the glorious and astonishing method that has been entered upon to disappoint all Satan's designs,

[7] Bellamy, *The Millennium* (1758), reprinted in *The Millennium*, a collection edited by David Austin (Elizabethstown, 1794), p. 12.

by the interposition of the Son of God."[8] It follows that true Christians must be "Christian soldiers" in a more literal manner than anyone had quite suggested before. "Nor can the salvation of their own souls, although ever so safely secured, satisfy their minds, without a clear view and fair prospect of Christ's final victory over all his enemies." Redemption is, one might say, increasingly temporalized and secularized. God even appears as a potentate anxious to win *la gloire*. ". . . when things have been ripening these five or six thousand years, and are now so nearly every way prepared for God, to get himself a great name in the total destruction of Satan's kingdom, can we once imagine that God will let the opportunity slip?" How far all this is from Augustine! and from Paul: "Because the foolishness of God is wiser than men; and the weakness of God is stronger than men" (1 Cor. 1:25).

Inevitably, the millennium itself will have a strong this-worldly character. There is, too, an intimation of another idea: that the real root of evil in human nature is ignorance rather than innate sinfulness. Later preachers, notably Alexander Campbell, were to go farther with this notion. ". . . then shall it come to pass that the veil of ignorance, which hath so long spread over all nations, shall be destroyed . . . for Babylon shall fall, Satan be bound, and Christ will reign, and truth and righteousness universally prevail a thousand years."[9] It may even be possible, despite the miserable record heretofore, that the greater part of all men who are to live on the earth will be saved; for in the millennium, when there will be no war, and the conditions of life will be wholly healthful, the earth will support many times more than it can at present. The proportion of the number of souls lost in the past to those who will be saved in the millennium, he figures at one lost to 17,465 and 40/120 saved! It is a sign of the times that the politics of God has expanded to include demography.

There is the suggestion that a moral development occurs

[8] *Ibid.*, p. 10.
[9] *Ibid.*, pp. 35–36.

behind a military campaign. Only God knows "when matters will be all ripened, and every thing in the moral world prepared, so that this glorious day may be ushered in to the best advantage . . . to humble a haughty world, and to disappoint Satan most grievously, after all his wily schemes, great success, and high expectations." Bellamy went farther than did his predecessors, too, in making the true Christians associates of God. They are expected "to exert themselves to the utmost, in the use of all proper means, to suppress error and vice of every kind, and promote the cause of truth and righteousness in the world, and so be workers together with God." [10] Now in prospect are the "crusades" of abolitionists, militant evangelists, prohibitionists, repressors of vice. And there is a concluding, fiery exhortation to participate in the great jehad:

Hail, noble heroes! Brave followers of the Lamb! Your General has sacrificed his life in this glorious cause, and spoiled principalities and powers on the cross, and now he lives and reigns! . . . . Your predecessors, the prophets, apostles, and martyrs, with undaunted courage, have marched into the field of Battle, and conquered dying, and now reign in heaven! Beyond, ye are risen up in their room, are engaged in the same cause, and the time of the last general battle draws on, when a glorious victory is to be won.

Already we seem to hear the far-off strains of the "Battle Hymn of the Republic."

Samuel Hopkins, one of the major theologians the United States has produced, composed *A Treatise on the Millennium*, which perhaps is the most substantial work on the subject ever published in this country. Most treatises had been principally concerned with the approaches to the New Jerusalem and justification of the millennialist theory; the state itself was described in very general terms, often only by negations of the unhappy characteristics of things as they have been. Hopkins' objective, coldly analytical mind saw the need for a detailed description of the holy utopia: he saw that, if the still novel idea of a millennium in the flesh

[10] *Ibid.*, p. 45.

was to gain full credence, it would have to be something envisioned in concrete detail. Hence he wrote his own utopia, and fashioned a part of the American Dream.

First, he succinctly explains the rationale of the termination of history:

> It appears reasonable and desirable, that Jesus Christ, who suffered shame and reproach in this world, and was condemned and put to death as a malefactor, by men, should have this reproach wiped off in the sight of all men, and that the cause in which he suffered and died, should prevail and be victorious in this same world, where he suffered and died.[11]

The millennium will be the age of benevolence, which Hopkins considered to be the essence of all virtue. Holiness and righteousness consist in "piety to God: and disinterested benevolence towards man, including ourselves." [12] This is very similar to the ideas of the followers of Shaftesbury and Hutcheson, the advocates of the "moral sense"; like them, he does not regard reason as truly a moral agency. Like the Shaftesburians, he thinks man is capable of truly "disinterested benevolence," but unlike them he thinks this condition must be made possible by grace, and that a historical transformation, not merely universal enlightenment, will be necessary to establish the ideal society.

Yet, if reason is not properly a moral faculty, it plays a great part in the total illumination of the soul which grace effects. Consequently, intellectual activity of all kinds will be intense during the millennium.

> For knowledge, mental light, and holiness, are inseparably connected; and are, in some respects, the same. Holiness is true light and discerning, so far as it depends upon a right taste, and consists in it; and it is a thirst after every kind and degree of useful knowledge; and this desire and thirst for knowledge, will be great and strong, in proportion to the degree of holiness exercised. . . . Therefore, a time of eminent holiness, must be a time of proportionably great light and knowledge.

[11] Hopkins, *A Treatise on the Millennium* (Boston, 1793), p. 40.
[12] *Ibid.*, p. 57.

Yet there is a Baconian emphasis on "useful" learning:

And great advances will be made in all arts and sciences, and in
every useful branch of knowledge, which tends to promote
the spirit and eternal good of men, or their convenience and
comfort in this life.

Knowledge of the universe does not seem to appeal to
Hopkins as a good, in and of itself. *Welfare*—of soul and
body—is the chief end.

Quarrels among men have resulted from "self love, or
selfishness"; and the fact that they "shall be subdued and
mortified" is represented by the prophets "in a striking,
beautiful light . . . by the most fierce and cruel beasts of
prey, changing their nature, and living quietly with those
creatures which they used to destroy." [13] This kind of symbolism is represented in the most famous of American primitives, Edward Hicks's paintings of "The Peaceable Kingdom."

The millennium will not magically eliminate all the consequences of man's fallen nature; it is, in sober fact, a good
society, and that only. Thus, although there "will then be
no such infinitely miserable objects, which are now every
where to be seen, to excite painful grief and sorrow," there
may still be some want; but

there will be then such benevolent and fervent charity in every
heart, that if any one shall be reduced to a state of want
by some casualty, or by inability to provide for himself, he
will have all the relief and assistance he could desire; and there
will be such a mutual care and assistance of each other that
all worldly things will be in a great degree, and in the best
manner common; so as not to be withheld for any who may
want them; . . .[14]

The ownership of property, it seems, will continue, but the
charity of the primitive church will be revived.

In the golden age of benevolence and useful knowledge,
we can expect immense advances in the arts of husbandry,
"so that a very little spot will then produce more of the
necessities and comforts of life, then large tracts do now.

[13] *Ibid.*, p. 60.
[14] *Ibid.*, p. 73.

And in this way, the curse which has hitherto been upon the ground, for the rebellion of man, will be in a great measure removed." [15] This is the modern, Baconian version of the ancient prediction that the desert will bloom. In consequence, "there will be for all, a sufficiency and fulness of every thing needed for the body, and for the comfort and convenience of every one." In this millennial utopia, it is interesting to see how often the words "comfort" and "convenience" appear; and in this attitude, which also appears in most accounts of the millennium later, we have perhaps one source of the almost religious fervor of Americans for agricultural and technological improvement.

The greatest of the millennial blessings, of course, will be the absence of war, "which has been a vast expence and scourge to mankind in all ages, by which poverty and distress have been spread among all nations." [16] Likewise, "expensive, distressing, desolating pestilence and sickness" will disappear—not miraculously, but simply because of temperance and wise care of the body. Such notions provide one motive for the numerous reform movements of the next century. It was reasonable to ask why, if measures like these, which surely do not require world redemption, produce millennial conditions, humanity should not proceed forthwith to carry them out. Indeed, the story of what might be called secular millennialism is in part an offshoot of the religious one: would not the elimination of eating meat, of alcohol, of tobacco, or the like, of itself produce a state at least partially anticipating the millennial condition itself?

Death will not be absent from the millennial Arcadia, but people then "will be in all respects ready for it, and welcome it with the greatest comfort and joy"; in this way death "will in a great measure loose[*sic*] his sting." [17] This is not to say that death will not finally die—but it will be conquered only in the true heavenly state which will follow the general resurrection, after the end of the millennium.

There will be a universal language—a common theme of

---

[15] *Ibid.*, p. 71.
[16] *Ibid.*, p. 70.
[17] *Ibid.*, p. 75.

millennialists. ". . . when they shall all become as one family in affection, and discerning and wisdom shall preside and govern in all their affairs, they will soon be sensible of the great disadvantage of being divided into so many tongues, which will greatly impede that universal free intercourse which will be very desirable." [18] The use of a common tongue certainly will encourage the dissemination of "useful" knowledge, "and all kinds of intelligence, which may be a benefit to mankind." Improvements of printing will "make it possible for hundreds of thousands of copies of a book to be cast off by one impression." Invention and communication play an important part in creating the millennial conditions.

But, he makes clear, these good things in the last analysis are results and not causes: at this point the millennialist idea of progress diverges from the secular. In the "day of salvation," "the Spirit of God will be poured out in his glorious fulness, and fill the world with holiness, and salvation, as floods upon the dry ground." [19] Yet, as in Bellamy's treatise, there is an organic analogy, which reminds us of Shelley's "Ode to the West Wind": "As winter in the natural world is prepatory to the spring and summer, . . . in the moral world, . . . what precedes the Millennium is as the winter, while the way is preparing for the summer." [20] Grace must germinate, like a seed. Nor, despite the great progress in recent times, can we look forward to a smooth transition all the way; winter's greatest storm often is its last. Hopkins says he agrees with Lowman, that the seventh vial is yet to be poured out. There may be two centuries yet to go; in them will occur Armageddon. "This battle will not be fought at once, so as to be soon finished; but will be carried on through a course of years, probably for more than century and a half." [21] This is a more pessimistic outlook than are other commentators' expectations of a short but terrible struggle.

[18] *Ibid.*, p. 76.
[19] *Ibid.*, p. 81.
[20] *Ibid.*, p. 83.
[21] *Ibid.*, p. 116.

Hopkins wrote at the time when the secular theory of progress was only getting started. In the next century, however, the contrast between it and the millennialist idea of advancement became of crucial importance. Horace Bushnell, in one of the most important works in American theology, analyzes the difference between them, in effect expounding on Hopkins' point about the place of social progress. Bushnell says that the world is just now taken with the idea of the "development, or as it is often phrased, the natural progress of the race."[22]

The human race, it is conceived, exists under laws of progress.
. . . If there are any evils, or bitter woes in society, development is going to cure them, . . . All crime and sin are going finally to be cured in this manner, and character is going finally to blossom, on the broken stock of nature, even as flowers are developed out of stocks not broken, and roots not poisoned by disease.

By contrast,

. . . it may be rightly said, that the whole object of God, in our training, is to develop in us a character of eternal uprightness; developing also, in that manner, as a necessary consequence, grand possibilities of social order and well-being; though, when we thus speak, we include the fact of sin and the engagement with it of a supernatural grace, to lift us from the otherwise remediless fall of nature.

Yet one distinction of Christianity is the setting up of the kingdom of God on earth.[23] It is called the "kingdom of heaven" because "the organic force by which so many wills and finally all mankind are to be gathered into unity, is not in nature, but comes down out of heaven, in the person of Christ the king."

Reform is essential, and Christians should be in the forefront of movements to alleviate the ills of society, but "The conception we have raised of Christianity, as a regenerative work and institution of God, separates it, by a wide chasm,

---

[22] Bushnell, *Nature and the Supernatural, as Together Constituting One System of God*, 5th ed. (New York, 1863), p. 221.
[23] *Ibid.*, p. 384.

from any mere scheme of philanthropy or social reform." [24] Christianity, working outward from the inmost center, "proposes to reform every thing." Even if we could, by "a grand comprehensive sweep of reform," get all sins out of sight, "We should have a race acting paradisaically in their behavior, when they have no principle of good in their life."

The distinction Bushnell makes is an underlying reason for the constant reminders that the transition to the millennium cannot be a "smooth" process of development alone. In the last analysis, the holy utopia *is* holy; it results not alone from improvement, but from the victory of the good in a war between cosmic powers for control over the spirit. An article in the *Presbyterian Quarterly Review*, on the eve of the Civil War, contrasts the development of the natural and of the moral worlds. In the former, growth is in right lines, in obedience to a single force. An acorn becomes an oak, always and naturally. But

in this kingdom of spiritual life, the law is different. It is a law of conflict. The lines of movement are diagonal, from a resolution of contending forces; . . . The disturbing power is moral evil; in secular history, as opposed to law; in sacred history, as opposed to grace. . . . The opposing power in either case is the same: the self-assertion of the finite ego against the infinite Ego sum; the concentrated essence of all the evil in the universe.[25]

The "resolution of contending forces" has nothing like the significance of a Hegelian "synthesis." It is, simply, the absolute triumph of one over the other. The ancient spiritual dualism has taken on new forms and a new terminology, but it is still the same as in the Revelation of St. John. Had the original nature of man continued unchanged, the author of this article says, continuous advancement might have occurred. But the "depravity of man conditions perpetually the kingdom of God on earth." The kingdom, which might

[24] *Ibid.*, p. 512.
[25] "The Historical Development of Christianity," *Presbyterian Quarterly Review*, 5 (1857): 608. The article is unsigned, but probably is by Benjamin Wallace, the editor.

have "grown like a palm-tree," has "wavered like a battle."
Perfect Christianity, as committed by its Founder to the
apostles, is one thing; but "The Christianity of Christendom,
in any or all its periods thus far, as actually making its stand
and unfolding itself in the face of hostile forces, is quite
another thing." Christ indeed brought not peace but the
sword.

Joel Barlow, the disciple of the philosophes, was an elo-
quent spokesman for the naturalistic theory of progress, and
it may be worth while to observe just where and how much
his optimism differed from that of the millennialists. Like
many progressivists, he thought the visions of the prophets
were a kind of intuition of the advances to come, but no
more. He states that he has long believed "that such a state
of peace and happiness as is foretold in Scripture, and commonly called the millennial period, may be rationally expected to be introduced without a miracle." [26] But it will not
be necessary to defeat a powerful, conspiring evil being to
achieve this apex of history. There has been a natural
progression from primitive, selfish isolation to larger and
larger associations. Tyranny is always the natural consequence of the unenlightened selfishness of the strong, and
will disappear as great teachers more and more show men
what their real nature and interest are, and as a kind of
evolution of intelligence takes place. Barlow's certainty
about this mental growth is so strong that he implies there
has been a constant increase from century to century in the
level of civilization. Significantly, where Renaissance historians, Gibbon, and Protestant theologians all took for
granted that there had been an abysmal decline after the
early centuries of the Roman empire, Barlow asserts that
men "were in a much more eligible situation" for universal
civilization in Charlemagne's time than in the Augustan age.
Refinement was spread more evenly throughout the nations;
and the feudal system, despite its faults, laid the foundations
of the balance of governmental powers, thus discouraging
would-be despots.

[26] Barlow, *The Vision of Columbus* (Baltimore, 1814),
footnote to bk. 9, line 68.

As might be expected, Barlow gives the Renaissance (which apocalyptic commentators generally ignore) a part in progress equal to and joined with that of the Reformation. We have seen how even a man humanistically trained, like John Adams, could ascribe the beginning of enlightenment solely to the Reformation. But Barlow relates how Erasmus prepared the way, deriding the "follies" and dissolving the "charm" of "schoolmen's lore and bigot zeal," restoring "pagan books, and science long unknown." [27] Luther's part was to go to the final point, as Erasmus dared not do, to defy "the rising vengeance of the papal throne"—

> Brave adverse realms, control the papal sway,
> And bring benighted nations into day.
> And mark what crowds, his fame around him brings,
> Schools, synods, prelates, potentates and kings,
> All gaining knowledge from the boundless store,
> And join'd to shield him from the rage of power!

We are in an atmosphere very different from that of the "Beast," the angel of judgment, and Armageddon.

With the nineteenth century the prophets of the millennium multiplied, on both sides of the Atlantic. In 1818, Joseph Emerson, a leading Congregational clergyman and a pioneer in women's education (one of his students, Mary Lyon, founded Mount Holyoke Seminary), published *Lectures on the Millennium*. His hopes for the ultimate destination of mankind are as bright as Barlow's, for it is an "error" to neglect the millennium, to doubt "whether the state of the world will ever be very much better than it is." [28] All these treatises are one long polemic, at least implied, against Augustine. He repeats the main points of Hopkins—that there will be a longer lifespan in the holy utopia, population will be increased, millions of acres now barren will be fruitful. Indeed, he more strongly emphasizes the part of scientific and technological discovery than any predecessor.

Rulers and subjects, philosophers, chemists and cultivators, seem to be uniting their efforts in various countries, for the

[27] *Ibid.*, bk 4, lines 125 ff.
[28] Emerson, *Lectures on the Millennium* (Boston, 1818), p. iv.

advancement of agriculture . . . How little does the chemist
think, while his heart is ready to melt at the very thought of
his crucible, how little does he generally think, how much
his labors may conduce to bring on that happy state of things,
that shall distinguish the Millennial period.[29]

He quotes that favorite text of millennialists, "Many shall
run to and fro, and knowledge shall be increased," as indicating that travel will be easier and knowledge will be
gained at a much accelerated pace during the millennium.
There will be an increase of understanding of the "vast
books of nature, revelation, and the human heart," in the
next 500 years, perhaps matching all that has been achieved
in all preceding millennia.[30] The "reign of Christ" is symbolic of the fact that in "that blessed day," "kings and
queens shall be nursing fathers and nursing mothers to the
church" and will "banish or crush the monster vice." [31] It is
fitting that a cousin of the Sage of Concord should be one of
the most optimistic of millennialists; he does indeed deserve
Ward's strictures for representing the transition to the great
age as "smooth." It seems, moreover, to be accomplished
largely by social reform. Perhaps no other millennialist came
closer to making religious the secular idea of progress. He
implies, in fact, that the curse upon mankind is being rapidly
lifted, and this idea affects his ideas of education: "It is my
decided opinion, that every step of the way to the very
pinnacle of science, may be strewed with flowers—with
flowers of the most fragrant odors and the richest hues—
that children may be made to love their studies and instruc-
tions, better than their toys, or their sports or any sensual
delights." But there is no better proof of the folly of specu-
lating about times than his calculation that the millennium
may begin in 1941.

British writers were among the witnesses to the faith who
published in the first decades of the century. An eminent
dissenter, David Bogue, in *Discourses on the Millennium*,
published in the same year as Emerson's *Lectures*, presents

[29] *Ibid.*, p. 95.
[30] *Ibid.*, p. 76.
[31] *Ibid.*, p. 276.

one of the clearest expositions of the end and the means. The very possibility of a millennial order depends, he explains, on the fact that the Spirit does not suspend, but rather heightens the exercise of man's natural faculties, increasing his rationality. "It renders the judgment sound, and frees it from prejudice and error; it inclines him to dislike only what is evil, and to chuse only what is good; it influences him to love objects on account of their excellence, and it raises the affections according to the degree of their excellence." [32] Such a theory accords well with the "new light" theology, which held that original sin did not make man "demonic," or "criminal," or change his essential moral potentiality in any way; as Samuel Hopkins says, only the "corruption of their hearts" prevents men's proper use of their understanding and the natural power of taste. [33] It would be natural to conclude that, when the "disposition" of the mind is changed in conversion, a great release of all the mental powers would take place. As Hopkins says, the "increase of light and order, in forming the natural material world" is emblematic of a light which "began to dawn directly after the fall of man, and has been increasing ever since." [34]

The Scottish preacher agreed with the general American conviction that the separation of religious from civil matters is a key action in the preparation for the millennium: "Oh that spiritual tyranny may soon have a millstone tied about her neck, and she be cast into the midst of the sea; and that religious liberty may be invited to sit down on the empty throne, and sway her sceptre over the whole of Protestant Europe." [35] But, the Americans pointed out, religious liberty in America has already sat down on the empty throne, and it

[32] Bogue, *Discourses on the Millennium* (London, 1818), p. 335. Bogue, who left the Church of Scotland to become an Independent minister, was a founder of the London Missionary Society. The close ties between American Protestants and English dissenters are indicated by the fact that Yale College, in 1815, conferred on him the D.D.

[33] Hopkins, *The System of Doctrines Contained in Divine Revelation* (Boston, 1793), 2:335.

[34] *Ibid.*, 2:229.

[35] Bogue, *Discourses on the Millennium*, p. 371.

was the American people who invited her; what nation, then, is the leader in the world procession?

Yet in the midst of all this excitement about natural and spiritual advancement, Bogue recalls that, although spiritual change is the essential element in the transformation of the world, Antichrist is so well dug in, so closely allied with still great temporal rulers, that his overthrow will be "violent": "the mass of the Antichristian people will be subjected to grievous distresses; . . . the kingdom of Antichrist shall endure dreadful national calamities, and be torn in pieces with horrible convulsions." A reader might well ask whether the Protestant nations—not entirely purged, even yet—will be entirely exempt from those distresses.

An important figure in the Church of England joined the millennialist chorus, although, compared with the others, he sounded a rather uncertain note. Samuel Waldegrave, later Bishop of Carlisle, delivered the Bampton Lectures (1854) on the general subject of millenarianism. After one of the most comprehensive and learned reviews of the history of the doctrine that had appeared in English, he came out in favor of a qualified millennialist view. Papal Rome is certainly the mystical Babylon, and, although its fall has not yet truly taken place, it is shortly to be expected.[36] Prophecy, rightly interpreted, does not mean that there will be any complete incarceration of Satan short of the final judgment, and the first resurrection refers, not to a literal raising up of bodies, but to "the revival of the principles of which those persons were once the representatives." [37] The millennium is often interpreted as a period of "such unmixed, such long continued terrestrial blessedness, as the world has certainly never yet beheld"; Waldegrave is not entirely sure that this definition is required.[38] The holy utopia may or may not be yet to come. But he agrees fully with the other commentators on such matters as the progressive defeat of Satan, and the fact that "a great crisis is near at hand."

[36] The Hon. and Rev. Samuel Waldegrave, *New Testament Millenarianism* (London, 1855), p. 347.
[37] *Ibid.*, p. 359.
[38] *Ibid.*, p. 377.

"Even now is the trumpet sounding. Who is preparing for the battle? Yes! and on which side are we ranging ourselves, we who are here present before God today?" [39]

A work of this kind, with higher credentials of scholarship than any of the American commentaries could boast, would reinforce the confidence of Protestant writers that their great break with all the traditions of past interpretations was justified. And one remark of Waldegrave in particular would serve to strengthen a suspicion which, as we shall see, was growing among Americans. He thought the heightening intensity of the struggle for the world "may bring together the hosts of evil in one concentrated effort to crush the nation, whatever that nation be, which keepeth the truth." Within a few years, many Americans came to believe, such a thing happened. The rebellion of the slave states and their support from abroad would seem to be the great concerted effort to crush the nation that had kept the truth as none other.

One more foreign witness deserves mention. A book by David Brown, Professor of Divinity and Church History at the Free Church College in Aberdeen, had a considerable vogue, and went through several editions in the late 1850's. The millennial resurrection, he holds in the familiar phrases, is simply "the full development of the kingdom of grace in its earthly state," and is not without sin.[40] This Presbyterian quotes the authority of the Anglican Mede—for example, that the millennium is represented by the stone cut out without hands, which is to grow into a great mountain and fill the earth (Dan. 2). The new order, therefore, is to be only the expansion, in purified form, of the old. Civil government will not be ended in the millennium, since it is a divine ordinance. The mission of the church is not to supplant but to impregnate and pervade it with a religious character, thus rendering it subservient to God's glory.[41]

[39] *Ibid.*, p. 398. Among those on the wrong side are the Anglo-Catholics, who are usually considered to be an offshoot of the old Rome.
[40] Brown, *Christ's Second Coming: Will It Be Premillennial?* 5th ed. (Edinburgh, 1859), p. 315.
[41] *Ibid.*, p. 319.

If we think the emphasis on a high standard of living in the millennium is somehow an exclusively American notion, Brown will correct us. He asserts the point that "great temporal prosperity" will prevail, more strongly than almost anyone else; and he bases his speculation on the connection between covenant and reward to which I have alluded before. "If all temporal blessings, . . . are expressly and in numerous prophecies represented as coming in the train of the new covenant blessings, can it for a moment be doubted" that God will materially bless the fruition of his work? [42] He cites a key text in this doctrine, from 1 Timothy 4: "For bodily exercise profiteth little: but godliness is profitable unto all things, having promise of the life that now is, and of that which is to come." Plenty accompanies righteousness, by a natural law, since despotism in government, anarchy among the people, and the devastations of war—all of which destroy the produce of the earth—will be ended. There is no need for the kind of fertility miracle Papias of old expected in the millennium. "Universal righteousness" takes care of economic problems.

Progress is by no means an uninterrupted series of improvements. In fact, a kind of cyclical theory of history is set forth. "It seems . . . to be a law of the moral kingdom, that all the great powers—civil and ecclesiastical, of light and of darkness—that have borne sway among men, shall both rise and fall by degrees." [43] So with the fall of the mystical Babylon. "For three hundred years—from the time when that dark, and withering, and accursed power seemed to get its death-blow at the glorious Reformation, until now—how often has the tide, to human appearance at least, rolled back, and how plausibly has it been asserted that not an inch of solid ground has since that day been gained!" What a great work remains to be done! Contemporary soldiers of the cross need not envy the glory of their ancestors. Brown, finally, adds the intriguing suggestion that the sun of the millennium will set gradually, as it rose. The large number of unconverted who will remain, although exter-

---

[42] *Ibid.*, pp. 411–12.
[43] *Ibid.*, p. 336.

nally held in check, will mount up once again. He recalls what happened in Northampton at the time of the Great Awakening, as Edwards described it. For a time Northampton "seemed to be full of the presence of God." This is the type of the world state in the millennium. For a time there was an "ascendancy of truth and righteousness in human affairs." But in time the spell faded; so it will be when the thousand years has passed.[44]

2

Mark Hopkins, at the mid-point of the century, pointed up the nature of the great revolution that had taken place in the conception of the character and mission of the Christian religion.

Christianity has, indeed, always proposed to herself the subjugation of the world; but she had practically fallen back from her undertaking, not knowing the extent or character of her field. Gradually these were opening upon her, until about the commencement of the present century, when the command of Christ, interpreted by modern discoveries, began to work in the heart of the church. This, though as yet far from assuming the place and creating the movement it ought, is still to be regarded as the central idea. Everything tends to show that this is to be the ultimate result of God's plan.[45]

The real importance of the elements of secular progress is that they have stirred up and made possible the militancy of Christianity in this world, which is to produce the holy utopia. Among these elements are "the idea of the subjugation of the powers of nature to the use of man." The discovery of "this new inheritance of the race," comparable in importance to the discovery of North America, makes it possible for "vast states to be but a single body, pervaded by one sympathetic nerve, and capable of being simultaneously moved by the same electric flash of thought." Hence the

[44] *Ibid.*, pp. 404, 412–13. Citation from Edwards is the *Narration of the Revival of Religion in New England.*
[45] Hopkins, introduction to Emerson Davis, *The Half Century* (Boston, 1851).

enthusiasm about the telegraph, transoceanic cables, and transcontinental railroad. A fair example, from many instances, is a sermon on the last-mentioned event. Discoveries and inventions are "taken up in the Divine plan as means to a spiritual end." [46] They come at appointed times. "We must see a Divine adaptation and harmony in all this—a fitting together of means and ends, a playing of material instrumentalities over into the objects of the spiritual kingdom. Not a railroad is swung by God into its orbit, that he does not put to work on this upward mission."

The second means of millennial grace Hopkins lists as the assertion of the "liberty and rights of the individual," which originate in "the value which Christianity puts upon the individual, and fully carried out, must overturn all systems of darkness and mere authority." Everything in the way of this ideal must be "overthrown," if necessary by violence, as happened in the revolutions so conspicuous in the first half of the century.

Finally, there are the new "benevolent and reformatory" movements, designed to "bring human conduct and institutions into conformity with the idea of right." But, Mark Hopkins warns, only as "quickened by Christianity" can natural conscience move individuals "into organizations, and . . . lead to systematic, protracted, and self-denying effort." More and more, the activities of such organizations were to move into the central position as the means of grace for the world. All of these movements ultimately prepare mankind for "that triumph of Christianity in which alone the perfection of society is involved." Hopkins emphasizes that they do not perform their work by irresistible force, of themselves, but that they fit the human being to "receive those influences of Christianity through which alone our perfect manhood can now find its consummation." [47] A better summary of the temper of probably the majority of

[46] Rev. J. Downell, Sermon in the Congregational Church, Sacramento, 9 May 1869. The text, from Isaiah, is a fulfilled prophecy: "The voice of him that crieth in the wilderness, Prepare ye the way of the Lord, make straight in the desert a highway for our God." Isa. 40:3.
[47] Hopkins, introduction to *The Half Century*.

people both in the United States and Britain could hardly be found.

The idea of the millennium is central in the thinking of major pioneer of the "social Gospel," F. D. Maurice, who was one of the most influential theologians in the Church of England. The advance of knowledge of the Scriptures, he states, has brought about the regeneration of the church; for

the revival of it [the doctrine of the millennium] in our day
has been one great means of removing the clouds which had
hindered us from looking at Christ's church as a Kingdom,
and from connecting all individual blessings and rewards with
its existence and its establishment in that character. The
wretched notion of a private selfish Heaven, where
compensation shall be made for troubles incurred, and prizes
given for duties performed in this lower sphere—this
unnatural notion, clothing itself in the language of Scripture
. . . but severing that language from the idea with which it was
always impregnated, and connecting it with our low, grovelling,
mercantile habits of feeling, had infused itself into our
popular teachings and our theological books.[48]

But, Maurice emphasizes, in the true spirit of progressive millennialism, this is not to be a wholly *new* order, but rather "the full evidence and demonstration of that which is now." And he warns that the enemy is headed by Rome; some commentators on the Revelation "do not seem to see that popery is continually undermining the Church. . . . The serpent at the Reformation was scotched, not killed." [49] Maurice, then, sees the Christian horizon as having been expanded to include the whole of society; like the millennialists generally, he feels that the greatest progress in these stirring times has been the exposure of the Augustinian idea of the City of God.

From the American side came one of the most thoughtful considerations of the whole subject, an article, "Laws of Progress," in 1853. It begins by defending the proposition that a grand, general progress of mankind is the great fact of history.

[48] Maurice, *The Kingdom of Christ*, 2nd ed. (New York and Philadelphia, 1843), p. 511.
[49] *Ibid.*, p. 516.

. . . we ask, what preceding age can compare with ours, in general knowledge and enjoyment of the rights of man, the principles of representative government, the true theory of social happiness, embodied, for example, and held in trust for all mankind, in the British and American constitutions, the true landmarks of progress? In physical science, not merely abstractly, but in practical applications universally familiar, but not the less wonderful, by which the comfort of all is greatly increased, and abridgments of labor are multiplied, leaving more time and energy to be devoted to nobler purposes the pre-eminence of this period is almost universally allowed.[50]

There are some highly interesting implications. The statement that the principles of representative government embodied in British and American constitutions are "held in trust for all mankind" suggests that those principles are providential in origin, and intended to be spread by a sort of missionary effort not unlike the propagation of the Gospel which so preoccupied the churches; they are not merely good, or even the best solutions to the problems of political organization, but *the* ones God has designed as a means of realizing his purpose. And we see why the millennialists so consistently emphasized the "practical applications" of science; perhaps it is one source of the diligent American effort to reduce the necessity for human labor, an effort which in its concentration has been unique. And, as we should expect, there is emphasis on the unprecedented "principled, impartial and wide-reading beneficence" of the century.

All this could well be only the secular idea of universal advance. But soon we hear of the "old adversary." It is suggested that the true idea of progress is the prophetic one, and that Satan, who hates progress more than anything else, has put into men's heads a "shadowy vision of self-produced perfectibility and a sensuous Paradise on earth." It is a dangerous error to think that improvement will continue indefinitely, in accord with some natural law; this notion is the principal device by which Satan now hopes yet to

[50] *Presbyterian Quarterly Review*, 2 (1853): 416 ff.

frustrate the divine plan, for he intends to lull people into a somnolent acceptance of things as they are. Among the millennialists there is something like a cult of revolution. Only by "overturning" can the major obstacles on the road to the kingdom be removed. And, since the course of events follows a pre-established sequence, these often terrible events have their place in redemption, as Priestley also thought, even when the participants have no wish to aid God and the saints.

And in the end, all great revolutions founded in right and truth do succeed. They 'never go backward,' though begun and managed by wrong hands and at wrong times; marred by excesses, and retarded by folly and madness; mixed up with fanaticism, and called by bad names; such as charlatanry in religion, radicalism in politics, ultraism in social reforms.[51]

For, seen in the perspective of revelation, these uprisings really are directed against spiritual evil, not simple political wrong, however little religion itself may seem at the time to be involved.

Whenever and wherever the rights secured by everlasting charter, and sealed by the blood of the Covenant, alike to every human being, are withheld or monopolized; whenever institutions, obviously obstructing general happiness, are sustained by force or appeals to passions and interests; revolutions will occur as light increases, marked with more or less violence, in proportion to the resistance offered, or the wisdom employed, till human rights are all properly employed, till human rights are all properly guaranteed, and wrong principles and institutions are swept away.

There is this striking prophecy, and exhortation:

Overturn, and overturn, and overturn, till he come, whose right it is, is the great annunciation. If the times of restitution of all things are to be reached instrumentally, it will be by subsequent revolutions like the past, the greatest at the close. The last of the apocalyptic vials is cast into the air, and consequent upon it, there are voices, and thunders, and

[51] *Ibid.*, p. 430.

lightnings, and an earthquake such as was not seen, since men were on the earth, so mighty an earthquake and so great.

The "air" upon which the last vial is to be imposed may represent the universality of intelligence: ". . . after men are universally intellectualized and free, these storms and convulsions may be necessary to purify the mental and moral atmosphere, and fit men for universal equality and Christianity." For, however enthusiastically the millenni-alists speak the language of natural progress, most of them come back in the end to the apocalyptic warfare.

When the visions of the far distant future pass before the
ancient seers like panoramic processions, almost invariably
scenes of terror and desolation, falling dynasties and crumbling
thrones are precursive of the glorious close. Along the strings
of the harp of prophecy swept by the Almighty, there is a wail
almost like agony, preceding the Hallelujah of consummation.
These views do not accord with the usual tone of uninspired
prophecy that peals out perpetually from the press, grounded
on the wonderful physical and mechanical triumphs of these
last days.

"Natural development" is the operative term for the disci-ples of Condorcet, Comte, Fourier; the millennialists are inclined to stress terms from drama—"crisis," "reversal," "climax." But, more than anything else, the end of history is not the establishment of things new, but the restoration of the very oldest—the primeval heritage of mankind, of which man has been defrauded by a superhuman Enemy. The process can hardly be peaceful throughout, and least of all at the end. The expectation of terror and desolation, of the "wail" preceding the "Hallelujah of consummation" created what might be called a psychological readiness for the Civil War and the First World War. The author of this article in fact anticipates something like the latter event, and American intervention: "On the fields of Europe, among the rotten systems, reeking with lies and oppression, and in re-gions red with the blood of saints, the lines may be closed up, and we of the western world be forced to take sides, or let the issue for another long cycle go by default. The battle of Armageddon is yet to be fought." We are prepared for the language of the "Battle Hymn," and Wilson's final addresses.

3

One of the most dramatic confrontations of ideas in the first decades of the century occurred in the epitome of an American city, the then Western Cincinnati. For eight days in April 1829, the English reformer Robert Owen and the American church leader Alexander Campbell debated the validity of Christianity. They were not much concerned with such old favorites as whether revelation was a deliberate deceit, whether science had replaced religion, and so forth; the critical issue was the question of progress, and how it is to be accomplished permanently. And the most curious fact is that both contenders were passionate believers in the necessity and indeed certainty of indefinite advancement; at times the debate seems to be a bout of straw-men, the agreement is so close. Yet, underneath, the disagreement is there.

Owen might be said to represent a third view of the question of progress, distinguished from both the Christian and the natural-developmental schools. In some respects, his was closer to the religious than to the naturalistic hypothesis. Like the millennialists, he believed that the task was to regain what mankind has lost, to bring the human being back to his true nature. But, like such philosophers as Rousseau, he believed that man has been blinded by foolish and vicious opinions, resulting in baneful institutions, which have warped him out of all resemblance to his real self. "After much reading, and calm reflection early in life, . . . I was deeply impressed with the conviction that all societies of men have been formed on a misapprehension of the primary laws of human nature, and that this error has produced disappointment and almost every kind of misery." [52] The root of the misapprehension is the notion of

[52] *Debate on the Evidences of Christianity: Containing an Examination of the 'Social System' and of All the Systems of Skepticism of Ancient and Modern Times* (Bethany, 1829), 1:9. (Stenographic report of impromptu speeches.)

original sin: "I was also equally convinced that the real nature of man is adapted, when rightly directed, to attain high physical, intellectual, and moral excellence, and to derive from each of these faculties, a large share of happiness, or of varied enjoyment." The three "most formidable prejudices" he discovered on further rumination to be: false ideas taught by religion; the principle that marriage is indissoluble; and excessive regard for the rights of private property. Together, they "form a chain of triple strength to retain the human mind in ignorance and vice, and to inflict every species of misery, from artificial causes, on the human race."

For all religions are "directly opposed to the divine unchanging laws of human nature." The ideal towards which we must work will be achieved "when the circumstances which surround [an individual] from birth to death are of a character to produce only *superior* impressions; or, in other words, when the circumstances, or laws, institutions, and customs, in which he is placed, are in unison with his nature."

We should "no longer consider man formed to be the ignorant, vicious, and degraded being, that, heretofore, he has been compelled to appear, whether covered by the garb of savage or civilized life." [53] It is society, then, not man that is fallen; and man is man, whether he live in the woods or in Cincinnati.

Campbell, as we should expect, insisted in response that utopia can be attained only by radical changes in the human spirit. "It is called the Reign of Heaven, because down into the heart it draws the heavenly feelings, desires, and aims. From heaven it came, and to heaven it leads. I will shake the heavens and the earth, says the Lord. I will revolutionize the world; and how, my friends, but by introducing new principles of human actions?" [54] But this is to be a change in the world as it is, not reserved to a transcendent order; Christianity "contemplates the reformation of the world upon a new principle." Campbell characteristically speaks in the idiom of the democratic state, and insists that the ancient

[53] *Ibid.*, 1:24.
[54] *Ibid.*, 2:106.

language of divine kingship is outmoded and misleading. God has given men a "new constitution" and promised to every "citizen" of the divine order all "constitutional privileges." The nations of this world are to become the City of God, as "the religion of Jesus Christ melts the hearts of men into pure philanthropy." [55] Campbell goes even farther than most other millennialists in implicitly transferring the focus of redemption from the individual soul to the "world." The purpose of God in his dealings with men is to bring about a peaceful and just democracy in which they may dwell. The biblical story as a whole reveals spreading comprehensiveness of divine grace and illumination. There have been three stages: "the Patriarchal, Jewish, and Christian religions, as we call them"—although they are but books in one history. "The first formed good individuals; the second, while held sacred, made a happy nation, and comparatively a moral people; but the third fills men with heavenly influences; . . . and can make, and will terminate in, a pure and happy world." [56]

Campbell, as I have remarked, agreed in spirit with many of Owen's opinions. In the Prospectus to the first issue of his publication, appropriately named *The Millennial Harbinger*, he declared its purpose to be "the developement and introduction of that political and religious order of society called THE MILLENNIUM, which will be the consummation of that ultimate amelioration of society proposed in the Christian Scriptures." [57] Of the six general subjects to be treated, at least three are social problems. Among them is the "inadequacy of all existing systems of education, literary and moral, to develope the powers of the human mind, and to prepare man for rational and social happiness." Another is the "injustice existing even under the best governments, as contrasted with the justice of the millennium." Social reform is both means and end. Campbell could condemn most of mankind's religious history almost as vehemently as Owen; he proclaimed "the incompatibility of any sectarian estab-

[55] *Ibid.*, 2:105.
[56] *Ibid.*, 2:107.
[57] *The Millennial Harbinger*, January 4, 1830.

lishment, now known on earth, with the genius of the glorious age to come." So bad has the record been, he says, that only the knowledge that the false teachings of the sects were prophesied by Paul prevents him from joining Owen and opposing all religions.

The core of Campbell's opposition to Owen was his realistic appraisal of human nature. To him it seemed impossible that we can, as Owen seemed to expect, lift ourselves by our own boot-straps. We are the victims of our own weakness, ignorance, and the diabolical conspiracies against us. Only a mighty power of love, working from without, could remake society, by giving us the capacity and understanding to do what we cannot do with our own resources. The change is wrought completely within history, however, and, as all nature demonstrates, it must occur in rising stages. No religious doctrine, perhaps, could be more acceptable to a man responsive to the spirit of the times. In the Appendix to this book, I try to show how much of Campbell's attitude is reflected, many years later, in *A Connecticut Yankee*.

Samuel Harris, for a time president of Bowdoin College and later Dwight Professor of Systematic Theology in Yale College, was one of the most prestigious spokesmen for millennialist ideas. He was, moreover, to be a link between the "dialectical" theology and the "modern," which stresses action over systematic completeness. Harris asserts, in his classical book *The Kingdom of Christ on Earth*, that "The idea of a kingdom of God on earth and the prophecy of its realization are present in modern thought and among the forces that determine modern progress and civilization." [58] He condemns the millenarian theory as contrary to the central meaning of God's teaching, since it assumes that all efforts to spread the kingdom, by missionary activities, by overcoming evils, and so on, are hopeless. On the contrary, Christ taught that the kingdom "will gradually grow till it will pervade the world with its life." [59]

---

[58] *The Kingdom of Christ on Earth* (Andover, 1888), p. 19. (Originally, lectures to students in Andover Seminary, 1870.)
[59] *Ibid.*, p. 221.

True, that growth was to be peaceful, and yet has been accompanied by disasters. But we must remember that

Christ's kingdom is not responsible for the violence and revolution which are incidental to the epochs in its progress, and are occasioned by the opposition of the kingdom of darkness. The kingdom of darkness is always in antagonism to the kingdom of light. It is founded and perpetuated in selfishness, and therefore powerful interests become enlisted in perpetuating its abuses, and in resisting the progress of the truth. Hence any epoch in the progress of Christ's kingdom is liable to encounter violent and bloody opposition, and the advancement of Christ's kingdom may be in the midst of revolution and convulsion. In reference to this our Saviour said: "I came not to send peace, but a sword." [60]

Thus the end justifies the means, because the whole plan is a theodicy. And Harris warns that putting off reforms often leads in time to more violent resistance than would otherwise be necessary, from the interests which have been allowed to dig themselves in. Finally, he says of the present time that "no preceding age has presented conditions so favorable to the advancement of Christ's kingdom and so encouraging to faithful Christian effort." [61] So strong was this impression that Harris was constrained to warn against thinking that "the overturn of what has been established is in itself progress to something better," with the consequent danger of falling into "insatiableness of reform." [62] And, as we shall see, like probably a majority of his fellow countrymen, Harris was convinced that the larger part of the obligation and the honor has fallen on the English-speaking nations, for to them "more than any other the world is now indebted for the propagation of Christian ideas and Christian civilization." [63]

These exalted aspirations had long been carried out in missionizing activities. The work of the American Home Missionary Society, for example, was motivated by the

[60] *Ibid.*, p. 190.
[61] *Ibid.*, p. 255.
[62] *Ibid.*, p. 192.
[63] *Ibid.*, p. 255.

knowledge that preparation for the millennium was an urgent and supremely important duty. Thus a communication from a missionary in the Iowa Territory, in 1845:

The past history of the world has been that of wars and animosities. When converted to God, it will be the unfoldings of Christian love. The transforming process is going on. Who would not be an actor in it? If our lives can enter in, as the least of those threads that are to compose the golden cord, which shall at last bind together a redeemed world, it is enough.[64]

The editors of *The Home Missionary* expressed a common impression that events are moving even faster than the most optimistic students of prophecy had anticipated, and that the good time is very near:

And our most sanguine expectations, with respect to the future developments of the divine economy, may fall as far behind the reality. Great events are succeeding each other, in the day in which we live, with a rapidity unparalleled in all time. The vast designs of Providence are fast being accomplished. The end of all things is drawing near. The destiny of our country, and the part which it is to act in the work of a world's redemption, will soon be a matter of unalterable record.[65]

Yet there is the warning, as always, that Satan's greatest efforts have been reserved for these last days, and for the last country of history. In the Iowa Territory, it is to be feared, "every inch of ground, that is here to be won for the Savior, is yet to be contended for, fact to face, with the great adversary of God and man, as if this were his *last hold*, and here his *last hope* of this country." (In fairness, it should be remembered that Texas and California were not yet parts of the national territory.)

One result of this complex of ideas was a conception of religious liberty in which freedom of worship was intimately combined with a kind of national Protestantism. This point has been little understood, and deserves far more study than I can give it here. One editorial statement, from the

[64] *The Home Missionary*, 18 (1845): 45.
[65] *Ibid.*, p. 46.

New York Recorder, however, will indicate how far from wholly secular was the conception of religious liberty during the years before the Civil War:

Thus far the advancement of popular liberty in the Anglo-Saxon race, has been regulated by the more than equal progress of the Gospel, and hence its triumphs have been more those of opinions, than of swords. . . . Our churches and our schools are the true conservators of American liberty, and the best friends of progress. The triumph of Christianity is the triumph of popular liberty, and the school teachers, the tract distributor and the home missionary will do more for liberty than troops of vaunting politicians.[66]

It may be well to end this summary survey of what was in fact a great body of publications with one statement that possesses a greater resonance than perhaps any of the others. One of America's more profound theologians, Henry Boynton Smith, in his inaugural address as a professor in the Union Theological Seminary (1855), places the divine plan of history at the heart of the redemption:

The most diligent investigation of Christian History is one of the best incentives to the wisest study of Christian Theology. The plan of God is the substance of both; for all historic time is but a divine theodicy; God's providence is its law, God's glory its end.[67]

Two years earlier, in his Phi Beta Kappa Address at Yale College, Smith set forth in more detail what he meant by the idea that "historic time is but a divine theodicy." Here he emphasizes that what seems secular history is, in the light of revelation, religious in reality, for "battles fought in the material, are renewed in the spiritual sphere." [68] The greatest progress of insight in modern times is the recognition that human life is communal, that the individual's real importance is his part in the onward movement of the City of God to encompass the City of the World. No less than

---

[66] Quoted in *The Home Missionary*, 19 (1846): 117.
[67] Smith, "The Idea of Christian Theology as a System," 1855, p. 22.
[68] Smith, "The Problem of the Philosophy of History" (Philadelphia, 1854), p. 4.

Marx, Smith stresses the paramount function of the inter-working and conflicts of "powers" rather than of persons. The preceding century, he says, erroneously regarded mankind as the sum of separate, autonomous entities. The rejection of that hypothesis is one of the distinctive marks of the nineteenth century, perhaps the most important.

The atomic theory of the race is superseded by the dynamic. . . . It is studied not as an aggregate of atoms, but as a complex of powers. The race is viewed in the Christian aspect of its unity, and not in the infidel aspect of a mere flock of individuals. [The unity of history] is imaged forth, now, as the life of one man, in its successive periods of youth, of manhood, and of maturity; now, as a growth, through all its stages, like that of a tree with its blossoms and its fruit; again, as a constant ascent in a spiral, steadily aspiring, in spite of alternations, to a high consummation; or, yet again, as the orderly development of one consecutive plan, embracing all nations and races in their progress towards some adequate ultimate end.

But none of these theories, whether of Herder, Comte, Buckle, or whomever, is right, however well the authors may see parts of the truth. The key to history is the advance of the "kingdom of Redemption."

. . . the progress of this divine economy has been a perpetual growth through perpetual conflicts, of which the highest moral antagonism, that of sin and holiness, has been the elementary source, and into which all other conflicts may be resolved. And though states and nations have often been retrograde, and even, to borrow a striking figure, almost literally condemned to death, because sinful, yet still has advanced both by them, and in spite of them, in immortal vigor, that one kingdom of our Lord." [69]

The end of this great process Smith describes in one of the most illuminating descriptions of the millennial age:

. . . a grand and glorious consummation, in which the natural and the moral interests, while *retaining their integrity*, and themselves fully developed, are also made subordinate to the spiritual and eternal welfare of mankind; . . . and in this way does this divine kingdom set before the whole human race

[69] *Ibid.*, p. 26.

an adequate destiny, comprising the highest purposes of infinite justice and benevolence. [Italics added]

It is the unique privilege of the nineteenth century to realize fully what the great American theologian perceived a hundred years before; now we can recognize that "the whole of human history, according to Edwards' unrivalled scheme, becomes one body of divinity, presenting to us an untroubled mirror of the wisdom of God, and the image of his goodness." [70] There is an implication that the unfolding events are not only fulfillments of prophecy, but additions to revelation in themselves. For history is "the spectacle of the building up of the City of God." Christianity, being "in its inmost spirit and highest sense, . . . historical," presents "a grander apology for the Christian faith than the wisdom of a Butler, or the genius of a Pascal, ever framed." Bishop Joseph Butler's *Analogy of Religion*, which defended Christian morality and the ways of God by attempting to demonstrate they are largely paralleled in the system of the external world, was an implied recognition of the primacy of natural philosophy in the eighteenth century; God's book of revelation is sustained and interpreted by the book of nature. But by 1850 the book of nature has been replaced by the book of history; this is the time of Hegel and Carlyle. In the actions of nations, rather than the static design of nature, is to be found the proof of a divine and supremely wise and merciful Mind: for nature shows nothing beyond a kind of engineering perfection, whereas history reveals movement and ends in human terms. And, Smith continues, if we read the book rightly, we discover that "All the great crises in human history have been judgments upon a corrupt or superstitious faith and the inauguration of a purer worship." The "supernatural order" has "always gleamed through and presided over the natural in the actual faith of the race." In every event, especially the greatest ones, we are to look for the part of true faith, and for the part of error; every crisis demonstrates the natural supernaturalized. And great events were already gestating; in them it would be easy to find the

[70] *Ibid.*, p. 29.

meanings and the warnings Smith called for in the study of history.

A question that inescapably comes to mind after a survey of this type is: Did these ideas become viable? Abstruse and radical views in theology may be mooted in seminaries and canvassed in journals read mainly by preachers, without reaching congregations in anything like their pristine forms. In what form was millennialism brought to the everyday American, the pew-holder, the Sunday School teacher? We can get at least an intimation, perhaps, from a sermon preached in 1849 by the pastor of the church at West Milton, New York, to the Albany Synod. Although the listeners were clerical, the atmosphere was not academic, and the choice of subject and the approach must have been influenced by the actual pastoral interests and needs of the body of ministers.

The sermon as a whole is a précis of the doctrines I have described, set forth generally in even more uninhibited terms than usual. There is no doubt that "Henceforward, till time closes, we live under the dispensation of the Spirit." [71] Here, in the New World, is a last echo of the theories of the eleventh-century Joachim of Flora. Joachim thought there would be three eras—of the Father, of the Son, and of the Holy Spirit, respectively; but, where Joachim believed the third would be the age of the perfect Franciscan ideal, supplanting the period of the popes, the nineteenth-century preacher sees what might be called the age of the activist. A fairly long passage deserves quotation *in extenso*, for it epitomizes the vision of the millennium and the means of realizing it as the American preacher was expounding them:

Hand in hand with [the Spirit's] work the conveniences of the present life have ever gone; and it is quite inconceivable that such a result could ever be reached, without carrying along with it the reduction of the miseries of our earthly lot to their minimum and the highest improvements of every name which properly belong to it. Relieve the mind of its

[71] Rev. R. H. Beattie, "A Discourse on the Millennial State of the Church. Discourse Prepared by Appointment and Delivered before the Synod of Albany" (Albany, 1849), p. 29.

errors, the will of its depravity, and the affections of their worldliness; impress upon the soul the views furnished in the Scriptures, produce faith in Christ, shed abroad the love of God abundantly, overthrow the dominion of selfishness, and turn the earth into a scene of busy activity in the service of God, where the rivalry of men shall be rivalry in well-doing, . . . and you have reached the highest degree of progress which our race, yet in the clogs of mortality, can make. . . . Thus, in fact, the kingdom of Christ on the side of holiness, answering to Satan's kingdom on the side of sin, is advancing to the preeminence.

It is a perfect example of the union of material advancement, the Baconian ideal, with the ancient apocalyptic dualism—a union of great importance in the formation of the American mind.

There is a kind of common-sense impatience with the literal interpretations of millenarianism. It is absurd to think of the saints as sitting on shining thrones, or of Satan as a monster bound with real chains, and there is even a hint of unnecessary obscurantism in the inspired book itself: ". . . we are constrained, by the absurdities which gather upon us, to have recourse to those spiritual views the gospel furnishes, ere it exposes such enigmas to our eyes." [72] The supernatural elements are all superfluous. "Nothing more is needed than the power now at work, under Messiah the Prince, to put the world back into its proper place, and enthrone Jehovah in the affections of our disenthralled race." [73]

Common sense likewise dictates our idea of the promised millennium. "We forget not that imperfections shall mark this, like every preceding dispensation." The voice of the pastor is heard in the remark that "prosperity may prove the greater trial." Most treatises on the millennium had separated the sheep from the goats: the saints would continue to the end, the wicked finally rousing themselves to one final effort. But here we find the very practical observation that worldly flourishing may prove a temptation which the saints themselves cannot wholly resist. The millennium is com-

[72] *Ibid.*, p. 43.
[73] *Ibid.*, p. 31.

pletely fused with utopia and its continuity with the previous ages of history is unbroken. Even in the "new heavens and the new earth," we "may expect death to be continuing its ravages, and sin to be multiplying its victims." Although sin is finally to be eliminated, after the millennium, and the dead are to rise, these great mysteries receive only a sentence. Millennialists more and more relegated the Last Things which had so obsessed Christians in most previous centuries—the Last Judgment, the transformation of the earth, the ending of the temporal—to some far-off, dimly envisioned place. It would be unfair to say they gave only lip service to the final transformation and Judgment, but increasingly their real interest, their thought, their preaching, was taken up with the millennium in this world's flesh. The age of Bosch and Brueghel was tormented with visions of the portents, the terrors, the revelations of the Great Day of Judgment; the nineteenth century was, at least in much of the Protestant world, absorbed by the prospect of "thrones rocking to and fro, earth and heaven shaken, chains of superstition and tyranny and error rending, the old foundations giving way." [74] Political and social changes, not graves opened and secrets revealed, dominate the idea of the Day of the Lord; and beyond these events is the Good Time, not the heavenly life which had so long inspired the Christian world. No wonder then that we have this concluding exhortation: "What labor can be accounted too great, what sacrifice too costly, that may be demanded by that Redeemer, who now is on the throne, whereby we may contribute to his glory, and to the fulfillment of his purpose to save."

[74] *Ibid.*, p. 49.

IV

When Did Destiny
Become Manifest?

A vast complex of ideas, policies, and actions is compre-
hended under the phrase "Manifest Destiny." They are not,
as we should expect, all compatible, nor do they come from
any one source. The element most neglected hitherto in the
many studies of this subject is the conception of the "chosen
people" with a millennial mission of the kind I have described. The idea that the United States has been called to be
a chief means of world-wide redemption, and that as a
chosen people it was assigned a new promised land—
obviously, a large part of the continent—has been described
as "apocalyptic"; but this tends to be a rather vague metaphor, and the ideological basis has not been understood. The
suggestion usually is that the notions of a grandiose American destiny look rather like those of apocalyptic prophecies—Hebraic predictions of the triumph of God's people,
for example; it has not been fully realized that they are
literally apocalyptic, that they were regarded as the continuation of the biblical prophecies themselves. Manifest Destiny has been described as a "nationalistic theology."[1] The
statement implies that simple nationalism, the pride of a new
and ambitious nation, with many virtues and advantages,

[1] Albert K. Weinberg, *Manifest Destiny* (1935; reprinted
Chicago: Quadrangle Books, 1963), p. 17.

spontaneously generated a religious justification for its desire to acquire new and rich territories.

The process, however, was not so simple. The American apocalyptic prophets inherited rather than created much of their ideology, and, as we have seen already, millennialism was no American invention. It was a logical development of premises, begun long before in Britain, about God's plans for universal social salvation through history, the revealed will being interpreted in the light of successive world events. Unless we know the detailed intellectual origins of the American hope, we fail to appreciate it properly. In one sense, indeed, Manifest Destiny was thrust upon the United States, and it has been an inheritance by no means welcome to all Americans at any time. It is worth while, therefore, to investigate in some particularity just how and when the religious belief in American Destiny came into being.

First, it will be useful to make some distinctions. Almost everyone thinks first of Bishop George Berkeley's celebrated "Verses on the Prospect of Planting Arts and Learning in America." This poem seems to be clearly millennialist, perhaps even one cause of American ambitions. But just how does it fit into the ideology which we have been analyzing? To what degree is it really something new? We shall find, I think, that, despite the bright hopes Berkeley had for the future of American culture, he was no proper millennialist; he illustrates, perhaps, what American optimism might have been had there been no millennialist doctrine at all.

The real inspiration of the poem—unlike that, for example, of Price's enthusiastic tract on the promise of the American Revolution—is the prospect of a renovated Old World civilization. Berkeley, like Swift, Pope, and many others of his time, was profoundly pessimistic about the decadent condition of Western Europe.

> The Muse, disgusted at an age and clime
> Barren of every glorious theme,
> In distant lands now waits a better time,
> Producing subjects worthy fame:

The close of Pope's *Dunciad*, in the final version, depicts the return of the Dark Ages as a fact, not merely a dire possibility. Unlike Pope, however, Berkeley sees a ray of hope that the classical tradition may be rejuvenated and even improved, for there is a great new land, far removed from those where civilization seems to have grown old.

> In happy climes where from the genial sun
>> And virgin earth such scenes ensue,
> The force of art by nature seems outdone,
>> And fancied beauties by the true:

> In happy climes, the seat of innocence,
>> Where nature guides and virtue rules,
> Where man shall not impose for truth and sense
>> The pedantry of courts and schools:

The complaint that "pedantry," scholastic philosophy, has taken the place of "truth and sense" is of course a common theme with Baconians and Protestants.

> There shall be sung another golden age,
>> The rise of empire and of arts,
> The good and great inspiring epic rage,
>> The wisest heads and noblest hearts.

> Not such as Europe breeds in her decay;
>> Such as she bred when fresh and young,
> When heavenly flame did animate her clay,
>> By future poets shall be sung.

In these first five stanzas there is no hint of apocalyptic ideas. Berkeley is simply restating the common Renaissance historical philosophy, which held that cultures go through life cycles: like them, have youth, maturity, and old age, the final stage being caused by moral and intellectual decay, ending in barren subtleties and artificial refinements that, like weeds, crowd out the flowers of genius and reason. It was inevitable that the discovery of a great, almost uninhabited, rich land would inspire visions of another "golden age," which could rise in it as Europe sank into old age. It was, one might say, the idea or at least hope of the future for the colonies that would have been expected. Thus his conception of the "good and inspiring epic" is that of the Renaissance critics: epic is the work of a learned, accomplished, moral poet, embodying the best wisdom and insights accumulated through human experience. The models would surely be Homer, Virgil, Milton. By contrast, Thoreau looked for a new "heroic age" of poetry in the American West, precisely because the truest and noblest poems are spontaneous and come from an early stage of civilization.[2] To Berkeley the New World should be the pupil of the Old World, even, perhaps, surpassing its teacher. To Thoreau the strength of the New World lies in its lack of contamination by the Old, in its newness and difference.

The great reputation of the poem as a harbinger of *millennial* expectations for America rests, then, solely on the last stanza.

> Westward the course of empire takes its way;
> The four first acts already past,
> A fifth shall close the drama with the day;
> Time's noblest offspring is the last.

Here there is indeed an echo of apocalyptic commentators. The conception of history as a drama, rising to a climactic, ordained, fifth act is something one can hardly find in classical, Renaissance, or Augustine philosophy. Yet this is a pattern only. For one thing, there is no expectation of a universal millennium. The golden age is to be in the Western Hemisphere only, and there is no hint that a renovating influence will go forth to the world. Again, no apocalyptic commentator would characterize the millennium merely as "Time's noblest offspring," implying that it is only one, albeit the best, product of natural historical process. Even if natural forces are the immediate causes of the millennial age, they are directed by Providence, and a holy utopia is more than a cultural golden age. And there is no suggestion of a continuing warfare between good and evil in the apocalyptic manner; moral and intellectual decay is very different from the great conspiracy. Berkeley in fact adapts the ancient idea of *translatio imperii* to the prophetic "image" in Daniel, and the book of Revelation has no place whatever in his poem.

If something like Berkeley's ideal had been realized, the nation to be would have been a better Europe. There assuredly would have been nothing like the cult of newness, of rejection of the traditional, of which we shall see more.

---

[2] See Thoreau's essay, "Walking."

Nor, presumably, would there have been the call for militancy in American missionizing and liberating. It may be speculated, too, that the "humanistic" values might have held a higher place than they have in a large part of American society. This is not to say, however, that ideals of this kind have had no influence; such movements as "Young America" have much in common with Berkeley's vision. And even such a professed millennialist as Timothy Dwight wrote according to neoclassical forms, and borrowed liberally from the great English masters; it was not his fault if he was not, in the art of poetry, the American Alexander Pope.

Translatio imperii assumed that in any given period one nation or people will exercise the *imperium* of civilization, culturally and politically (although Berkeley is concerned only with the cultural aspect). After some centuries, "empire" will move to another state. From the viewpoint of Western Europe it seemed that the *translatio* had always been westward; from the Near East to Greece, from Greece to Rome, from Rome to Western Europe. That a final step should take place, across the Atlantic, was an idea so obvious that it would be impossible to find any definite point of origin. By the middle of the eighteenth century, certainly, it pops up everywhere. Galt, in 1816, gives an *ex post facto* account of the meditations of the young Benjamin West on his first sight of Rome, in 1759. The contrast with Gibbon's reminiscences of his meditations in the Forum is instructive.

. . . he could not but reflect on the contrast between the circumstances of that view and the scenery of America; and his thoughts naturally adverted to the progress of civilization. The sun seemed, to his fancy, the image of truth and knowledge, arising in the East, continuing to illuminate and adorn the whole earth, and withdrawing from the eyes of the old world to enlighten the uncultivated regions of the new.[3]

Although, like Gibbon, "touched with sorrow at the solitude of Decay" of Rome, West "was cheered by the

---

[3] John Galt, *The Life and Studies of Benjamin West* (London, 1819), p. 92. On the subject of America as the land of sebisht, see R. W. B. Lewis, *The American Adam* (Chicago: University of Chicago Press, 1955), chap. 1.

thought of the greatness which even the fate of Rome seemed to assure to America." For there seemed to be "some great cycle in human affairs," and the westward movement of arts and sciences demonstrated "their course to be neither stationary nor retrograde"; the splendor they had attained in their sunset in Europe, exceeding anything before, was "the gorgeous omen of the glory which they would attain in their passage over America." These are, then, the same arts and sciences of the Old World, awaiting only improvement. This idea of manifest cultural destiny contemplates only another, and higher stage in the spiralling, upward progression. But there is no sense of a unique quality in the new country, nothing that would move anyone to say, as Wilson would, it is "a spirit among the nations."

The expectation that the chariot of the cultural sun was about to move over the ocean, West found, had penetrated even the seat of what Protestants still considered to be the Antichrist, even though the colonies were so little known that Cardinal Albani thought the young man must be an Indian. The famous improvisator, Homer, composed an ode for West, expounding the cyclical theory:

But all things of heavenly origin, like the glorious sun, move Westward; and Truth and Art have their periods of shining, and of night. Rejoice then, O venerable Rome, in thy divine destiny, for though darkness overshadow thy seats, and though thy mitred head must descend into the dust, . . . thy spirit, immortal and undecayed, already spreads towards a new world, where, like the soul of man in Paradise, it will be perfected in virtue more and more.[4]

Nothing could have shocked a true millennialist more than a prediction that the spirit of (modern) Rome would "spread towards a new world."

"Manifest Destiny" may, then, refer to either of two kinds of expectations for the settlements in North America: that they may become a New Rome, or that they may be the new Promised Land of a chosen people. The ultimate effects of these ideas are widely divergent. The first would bring the new country into the cultural and historical zone

[4] *Ibid.*, p. 117.

of past cultures: America would enter into competition, on their own terms, with the past and present poets, painters, and scientists of the Old World. The new society would build its own, perhaps noble wing on the ancient Palace of Civilization, in a style consonant with that of the venerable building. Millennialist ideas, on the contrary, necessarily imply a separateness and unique quality in the new country. It would build a new structure which would be the nucleus of a new and a genuine Palace of Civilization. Its affinities with the past would be largely with the ancient people of the promise and with the countries of the Reformation, but only insofar as the latter have separated themselves, too. "Behold, I make all things new" could be the motto.

When did settlers in New England begin to suspect they and their descendants had been summoned to perform a mission of world redemption? The idea seems to have developed, like millennialism itself, out of the Protestant theology. In 1662, Jonathan Mitchel stated that the cause for what Increase Mather later termed "Our fore-Fathers pious Errand into this Wilderness" was "REFORMATION; that is, the avoiding of some special Corruptions, and the vigorous and more Exact Profession and Practice of the contrary Truths and Rules, according to *Scripture-Pattern*." [5] Yet the forefathers were motivated, Mitchel says, by more than a determination to establish a church governed according to what they thought the New Testament commanded. They considered themselves in fact as advancing to the next step beyond the Reformation—the actual reign of the spirit of Christ, the amalgamation of the City of the World into the City of God. John Robinson, in his parting address to the Pilgrims, had expressed his faith "that God hath more truth

[5] Mitchel, "The Great End and Interest of New England," in Increase Mather, *Elijah's Mantle: A Faithful Testimony to the Cause, and Work of God, in the Churches of New England* (Boston, 1722). See Larzer Ziff, *The Career of John Cotton* (Princeton: Princeton University Press, 1962), pp. 160–61, and 170 ff., for an account of millennialist ideas in early New England. John Cotton, unlike later commentators, believed that the "vials" began to be poured out at the time of the Reformation. See also, Charles L. Sanford, *The Quest for Paradise* (Urbana: University of Illinois Press, 1961), pp. 74 ff.

yet to break out of his Holy Word." Perhaps something of this kind was what he meant. In effect they rejected the Augustinian attitude toward history; it was a momentous change. ". . . as the *Prophetical* and *Priestly* Office of CHRIST, was completely Vindicated in the First Times of *Reformation*, so now the great CAUSE and WORK of GOD's *Reforming People*, is, to set up His *Kingdom*." It may seem that the establishment of the kingdom on earth is now a "Fanatic Notion" (this was written just after the failure of the Commonwealth), "Yet the True KINGDOM of CHRIST, (as the Scripture states it) is Glorious, and Divine, and that for which GOD will *Overturn, Overturn, Overturn,* until it be Erected in it's Glory; and (say Men what they will) I will still Pray, *Thy Kingdom Come*." The reiterated "Overturn" is characteristic of millennialist writings until well into the nineteenth century.[6] The Puritan fathers were intent on establishing what might be called the prototype of the millennium.

The Latter Erecting of CHRIST's *Kingdom* in whole *Societies* (whereby CHRIST is seen Ruling all in a Conspicuous and open, in a prevailing and peaceable manner), was OUR DESIGN and is OUR INTEREST in this Country. . . . And this also is CHRIST's Design in these Latter days; To set up His Kingdom in a Public and Openly prevailing manner, in all the Parts and Ways thereof.

Here we find what seems to be an allegorical interpretation of "Christ's reign": the Christian spirit, not the Lord in person, is to rule openly. The great advantage of the wilderness is its remoteness. Here prelacy, and other remains of the apostacy can be finally eliminated; and "In the Common Wealth, CHRIST's Kingdom is set up, when all things therein are so ordered, (Laws and all Civil Administrations) as doth

---

[6] Thus, for example, Enoch Pond: "And he will overturn, and overturn, and overturn,—till intemperance and war and oppression of every kind, Popery, and Mahometanism, and Judaism, . . . all those multiform evils which now afflict the earth and insult the heavens, shall be taken out of the way." *The Kingdom Given to the Saints* (Andover, Mass., 1843), p. 10. Millennialism could be called the doctrine of "overturning."

most fitly and effectually tend to advance, promote, and maintain *Religion* and *Reformation*." It seems to me there is implied here something more than the state Calvin sought to establish at Geneva. Calvin himself, we know, was little impressed by apocalypticism and certainly had no faith in a literal millennium; he remained, apparently, with Augustine. Calvin's vision extended to protecting the City of God against its enemies only, not to the transformation of the City of the World. But, although Mitchel's idea of the holy commonwealth definitely is a stage beyond the early reformers' expectations, he does not anticipate that this pioneer kingdom of Christ in one locality is to be the stone not cut by human hands which will become a mountain and crush the kingdoms of this world. The holy utopia is a real possibility, but not a certainty. The idea seems to be intermediate between the still Augustinian Calvinist eschatology and developed millennialism.

Increase Mather, in the Foreword to *Elijah's Mantle*, refers to "our ISRAEL"; coming from one who knew the Bible so well, this designation clearly indicated that the New England congregations have been called a special people to do God's work, as was Israel of old. There is the implication that the pioneers of New England were separated out from the pioneer nation of the Reformation to advance that Reformation; as the millennialist doctrine developed, it came to seem "manifest" that this separated community, especially after it attained independence, was not only *a* special instrument in God's plan, but *the* agency he had ordained.

Edwards' famous speculation that the discovery of the New World and the Atlantic settlements may prove to be the final events in preparation for the beginning of the millennial transition points in this direction, but still falls short of envisioning the colonies as the peculiar millennial people. Edwards, in fact, calls for an ecumenical cooperation between Protestants, or at least dissenting churches on both sides of the ocean, to further the general redemption Yet the New World has a unique part to play, largely because of its place in the apocalyptic timetable. For the Americas, until recently, have been the last great territories where the Gospel has never been heard. Edwards thought that the Prince of Darkness, in his own uncanny prescience, had established in the Western World a last redoubt against the spread of Christianity. The Enemy had subjugated the unhappy aborigines; and the missionary work among them was a certain proof that the last days were come. Hence

I think we may well look upon the discovery of so great a part of the world, and bringing the gospel into it, as one thing by which divine providence is preparing the way for the future glorious times of the church, when Satan's kingdom shall be overthrown throughout the whole habitable globe, on every side, and on all its continents.[7]

As the Scottish commentator Brown indicated (see chap. 3 above), the Awakening at Northampton could be considered a kind of rehearsal, as it were, of the advent of the millennium. It could also be the spark of the spiritual conflagration which, Edwards thought, was likely to occur in the last times; for several prophecies "speak of an extraordinary Spirit of Prayer, as preceding and introducing that glorious Day of Revival of Religion, and Advancement of the Church's Peace and Prosperity, so often foretold." [8] It is especially important that the Awakening will reach those "that are in the *highest Stations*"; it is by this truly miraculous revolution at the top that the kingdom of righteousness is to be established. In England at this time, Lady Huntingdon was energetically working to evangelize the upper classes, even tackling such unlikely prospects as Chesterfield and Bolingbroke.

It is the more fitting, Edwards thinks, that the Awakening should begin in New England, because other fulfillments of

---

[7] Jonathan Edwards, *History of the Work of Redemption*, vol. 3 in *Works* (New York, 1830), p. 376.

[8] Edwards, *An Humble Attempt to Promote Explicit Agreement and Visible Union of God's People in Extraordinary Prayer, For the Revival of Religion and the Advancement of Christ's Kingdom on Earth Pursuant to Scripture-Promises and Prophecies concerning the Last Time* (Boston, 1747), p. 5. Edwards' own account of the Northampton Awakening strongly implies that it followed the course of the millennium: "And thus Satan seemed to be restrained, till towards the latter end of this wonderful time, when God's spirit was about to withdraw." *A Narrative of Many Surprising Conversions*, in *Works*, 3:28.

prophecies seem to be taking place in the New World. He agrees, he says, with Lowman's opinion that the fifth vial of Revelation refers to the Reformation, and that it is not yet all poured out. There was "almost miraculous taking of *Cape-Breton,* in the year 1745, whereby was dried up one of the main sources of the Wealth" of the chief papist nation, France. And in the destruction of Lima by earthquake, in 1746, "all the ships in harbor were dashed in pieces as it were in a Moment, by the immediate Hand of God." [9] Commentators of the next century were to see not "the immediate Hand of God" but natural causes at work in fulfilling the prophecies; but probably they were more or less of Bushnell's opinion, that the "supernatural," including the human mind, intervenes to act as an element in the chain of cause and effect.

Yet this falls short of any notion that the English settlements are to be the principal and decisive actors. But that idea was germinating, as the English clergyman Andrew Burnaby, who visited the middle colonies in 1759–60, testifies. He reports, with distaste, that "An idea strange as it is visionary, has entered into the minds of the generality of mankind, that empire is travelling westward; and every one is looking forward with eager and impatient expectation to that destined moment, when America is to give law to the rest of the world." [10] Surely this mood reflected an expectation that America as law-giver would be something different from anything the world had known before; already some anticipation of the "ideal" which, Wilson was to say, foreigners thought to find in the new land.

2

It seems that in the 1760's, in the nascent nationalism that followed the French and Indian War, there began to emerge

[9] *An Humble Attempt,* p. 169.
[10] Burnaby, "Travels in the Middle Settlements in North America in the Years 1759 and 1760," 2d. ed. in *A General Collection of the Best and Most Interesting Voyages and Travels,* ed. John Pinkerton (London, 1812), 13:750.

a conception of the colonies as a separate chosen people, destined to complete the Reformation and to inaugurate world regeneration. Adams, as we have seen, appeared to be on the verge of some such idea in 1763. His diary relates how a group of young men gathered to read works on the feudal law, and naturally they discussed what may have been the causes for the feudal system. In February, just before the Stamp Act agitations, Adams had formulated his conclusions in the first draft of his *Dissertation*. The sequence in the title—"Canon and the Feudal Law"—is indicative; for Adams differed from the other members of the group, who regarded feudalism either as a useful expedient in a time of constant invasion, or as a system imposed by conquest. In contrast with these sociopolitical theories, Adams thought the first cause of the still powerful evils of the medieval world was the "Constitution of Policy" framed by "the Romish Clergy" to benefit themselves. Thus Adams saw the question in ecclesiastical, and apocalyptic terms.

Although in England there had been a partial reform, the great importance of the American colonies, Adams began to perceive, was the fact that they, for the first time in history, had resolved to extirpate the canon, and with it feudal law for good and all. Further, they were intended to do this, it could be assumed, as part of a great movement to liberate men from the consequences of their own nature. So, in a sentence I have quoted, he sees the settlement of "America" (now not only colonies) "as the Opening of a grand scene and Design in Providence." The use of the word "scene" hints that it is part of a drama, and it is not unreasonable to assign such an idea to an eschatological source, for no other philosophy of history in the Western World saw the historical process as one dramatic action. (Berkeley speaks of "acts," but the dramatic confrontations of good and evil, leading to a climax, are lacking.) To give the colonies, now advanced to their grander title, such a crucial part would seem presumption indeed. For, however noble their origins, they were, as Adams certainly knew, a very small and, even to well-informed Europeans, very obscure part of the world; they had not yet even effectively asserted their constitutional position within the British system. The notion of

their climactic importance, occurring to so sensible a man as
Adams, must have come from an ideology; and Adams'
references to providential purpose betray the background of
that ideology, now intermingled with Whiggism.

If there can be identified any moment when America's
position in the millennialist pattern becomes "manifest," it
may be the publication in 1771 of Timothy Dwight's anonymous *America: or, A Poem on the Settlement of the British
Colonies: Addressed to the Friends of Freedom, and Their
Country.* The work is described as having been written by
"a Gentleman Educated at Yale-College." Dwight had just
become a tutor at this institution, and the poem appears to
have been the product jointly of the pre-Revolutionary
political agitation and the discussions of prophecy which
seem, from Edwards' time on, to have been conducted at
New Haven.[11] Trumbull thought the poem proved Dwight
was to become "our American poet." The confidence was in
some manner justified, not by its poetic quality, but by the
fact that here is not merely a grandiose vision of future
"glory" but a developed historical myth, in fact the kernel
of the idea of American millennialism.

First is a description of the beginning of the Dark Ages,
with "Tartars in millions, swarming on the day," and of the
sinister, savage epoch itself:

> Sunk in barbarity, these realms were found,
> And Superstition hung her clouds around;
> O'er all, impenetrable Darkness spread
> Her dusky wings, and cast a dreadful shade;
> No glimpse of Science through the gloom appear'd;
> No trace of civil life the desart cheer'd;
> But furious Vengeance swell'd the hellish mind,
> And dark-ey'd Malice all her influence join'd. . . .
> Age after age rolls on in deepening gloom,
> Dark as the mansions of the silent tomb.

With Columbus, who would be surprised to know he was
being adopted as a hero of the Reformation along with

---

[11] See Leon Howard, *The Connecticut Wits* (Chicago:
University of Chicago Press, 1943), pp. 83 ff., for an
account of the origins of this poem.

Wycliffe and Luther, light begins to penetrate the night of religion and civilization.

> At length (COLUMBUS taught by heaven to trace
> Far-distant lands, through unknown pathless seas)
> AMERICA's bright realms arose to view,
> And the *old* world rejoic'd to see the *new*.

But persecution, initiated by Charles and Laud, continued the old evils and frustrated the beneficent colonizing begun by "blest Eliza." New England, as we should expect, became the refuge to which "our fathers came." There is a description of the Indian wars; "sons of Gaul" and "Priests, cloath'd in Virtue's garb," "fir'd the painted bands." But, after the campaigns of Wolfe and Amherst, this danger is over, and the way is clear for the settlements to enter upon their great work; hitherto refuge only, they now can rise to their appointed, paramount place.

> O Land supremely blest! to thee 'tis given
> To taste the choicest joys of bounteous heaven;
> Thy rising Glory shall expand its rays,
> And lands and times unknown rehearse thine endless praise.

So far, this is all very grand but vague. The substance of the emerging myth is expounded in a vision at the end of the poem, which occurs "in a lonely vale, with glooms o'erspread," where the poet encounters a white-robed figure, bright as the mid-day sun, bearing a scepter "blaz'd in gold" with the word "FREEDOM." Although the vision is a conventional literary device, there are elements of the prophetic visionary experience in this one. It apparently is not a dream. Freedom has angelic attributes: she has a "radiance," she is bright as "mid-day sun," and her "heavenly limbs" are enclosed in pure white robes. She presents a series of tableaux of world-encompassing events in the manner of the angels of St. John's vision.

First is an apocalyptic battle, whose participants are indistinctly identified:

> Behold! my Heroes lead the glorious way,
> Where warring millions roll in dread array,
> Awful as Angels, thron'd on streams of fire,
> When trembling nations feel the thund'rer's ire;

> Before them, Terror wings the rapid flight,
> And Death behind them shrouds whole realms in night.

These personifications are in the conventional eighteenth century tradition, but they have some of the demonic quality of the actors in Revelation. There ensues a reign of "white-rob'd Peace," and there is a description of the utopian land, blessed with philosophy, and the arts of sculpture, literature, painting. Then the vision expands to include the world as we see

> Religion lead whole realms to worlds of joy,
> Undying peace and bliss without alloy.

Destiny has awarded the *imperium* in the New World to Columbia. The first two lines contain the essence of Manifest Destiny.

> Hail Land of light and joy! thy power shall grow
> Far as the seas, which round thy regions flow;
> Through earth's wide realms thy glory shall extend,
> And savage nations at thy scepter bend.
> Around the frozen shores thy sons shall sail,
> Or stretch their canvas to the ASIAN gale.

Thus there are prophecies, seemingly of clipper ships and of the American passion for exploration; her sons will venture into "worlds unfound beneath the southern pole," "where no ship e'er stemm'd the untry'd way."

This is empire, the sway of a blessed people over great and wealthy territories, not the agrarian, limited utopia Jeffersonians might prefer:

> Round thy broad fields more glorious ROMES arise,
> With pomp and splendour bright'ning all the skies;
> EUROPE and ASIA with surprize behold
> Thy temples starr'd with gems and roof'd with gold.

This, needless to say, is classical and not medieval Rome. "APPIAN ways" and canals will join the far-separated parts of the great realm. Here, five years before the Declaration, is the prophecy that the farthest parts of the continent await their time of becoming parts of Columbia.

The culmination of the vision demonstrates that all this glory is not simply empire for empire's sake. After the great battle, and after the "Land of light and joy" has firmly established its position, by a seemingly shockless transition, the millennium will begin:

> No more on earth shall Rage and Discord dwell,
> But sink with Envy to their native hell.

With this final subsidence of the ancient kingdom of darkness, the Savior will display his power:

> Then, then an heavenly kingdom shall descend,
> And Light and Glory through the world extend.

Fraud, malice, discord will disappear,

> And every region smile in endless peace;
> Till the last trump the slumbering dead inspire,
> Shake the wide heavens, and set the world on fire.

This maiden effort set the theme of Dwight's whole prophetic-poetical work (which, it must regretfully be noted, failed to improve in literary value). His most ambitious work, the epic *The Conquest of Canäan* (1785), is an extended lesson for Americans. Its point resembles that of Price's *The Importance of the American Revolution* of the previous year, however much the politics of the two authors differed. Since history is the record of one long conflict between the party of good and the party of evil, the experience of the first chosen people is of vital concern to the latest one. The epic tells the story of how the hero Joshua, after Israel had repented of the misdeeds of one family that broke the divine covenant, led his people to victory:

> The chief, whose arm to Israel's chosen band
> Gave the fair empire of the promis'd land,
> Ordain'd by Heaven to hold the sacred sway,
> Demands my voice and animates my lay.[12]

The historical types are plain. In the first draft, Dwight even interspersed a number of parallels between biblical figures and their counterparts, American soldiers who fell in defense of liberty. God has given the land—a continent—to the new republic as he did the promised land to the Israelites of old; and it is "Ordain'd by Heaven to hold the sacred sway" in generations to come.

---

[12] Dwight, *The Conquest of Canäan* (Hartford, 1783), Book 1, lines 1–4.

The traditional epic prophecy of the future revealed to the hero gives the poet the opportunity to point up his warning to the new chosen nation. There is the vision of the desolation of Judah, a part of the people of God which failed in its mission and became corrupted:

> Where once the palace raptur'd eyes descried,
> And the tall temple rear'd its splendid pride,
> Round mouldering walls the nightly wolf shall howl.

Joshua is vouchsafed a vision, finally, of the last epoch of the redemption:

> Far from all realms this world imperial lies;
> Seas roll between, and threatening storms arise;
> Alike unmov'd beyond Ambition's pale,
> And bold pinions of the venturous sail;
> Till circling years the destin'd period bring,
> And a new Moses lifts the daring wing,
> Through trackless seas, an unknown flight explores,
> And hails a new Canäan's promised shores.
>
> [X, 501 ff.]

It really is regrettable that the new Canäan was not named Columbia.

In this world reserved to the last days, a new Eden is to be created. And as the shadows of slavery darken over the Old World, a great union is formed in the New World; it is the fifth kingdom, or "empire" predicted in Daniel.

> Here Empire's last, and brightest throne shall rise;
> And Peace and Right, and Freedom, greet the skies.

The time scheme of the vision is the apocalyptic division of history into seven "days," like Edwards': the first two under the "law divine"; two of preparation for the Messiah; and two under the Gospel. Then the Lord's Day of history will dawn,

> . . . o'er yon favourite world, the Sabbath's morn
> Shall pour unbounded day, and with clear splendour burn.
>
> [X, 573 f.]

Like his grandfather, Jonathan Edwards, Dwight thought the millennium would spread from the American continent; but he went much farther in giving central importance to that land, and to its inhabitants as the direct inheritors of the promise. Columbia is to be not only the first in the transition, but the source of grace to all mankind.

> Hence o'er all lands shall sacred influency spread,
> Warm frozen climes, and cheer the death-like shade;
> To nature's bounds, reviving Freedom reign,
> And truth, and Virtue, light the world again.
>
> [X, 577 ff.]

There are all the familiar features of the millennial utopia. War and famine will cease; waste places will bloom; universal commerce will bless the happy time.

> Unnumber'd ships, like mist the morn exhales,
> Stretch their dim canvas to the rushing gales.
>
> [X, 674 ff.]

There is a scene forecasting those Edward Hicks painted in his allegories of "The Peaceable Kingdom": the wolf will retire with the lamb—and without ulterior motive.

> New hymns the plumy tribes inraptur'd raise,
> And howling forests harmonize to praise.

The millennial era merges into God's great final miracle:

> See tombs, instinctive, break the sleepy charm,
> And gales divine the dust imprison'd warm;
> From finish'd slumbers changing patriarchs rise.
>
> [X, 695 ff.]

Already the final battle, intervening between the millennium and the resurrection, is being "smoothed" away.

The mission of the new republic as the agent of the millennium was Dwight's great subject, and he represented it again and again, with little imaginative variation. His poem "Columbia," for example, appeared in one of the earliest collections of poetry of the United States—significantly, the millennialist theme being present in a majority of the poems.

> Columbia, Columbia, to glory arise,
> The queen of the world, and child of the skies:
> Thy reign is the last, and the noblest of time,
> Most fruitful thy soil, most inviting thy clime;
> Let the crimes of the east ne'er encrimson thy name,
> Be freedom, and science, and virtue, thy fame.[13]

---

[13] *The Columbian Muse* (Philadelphia, 1794), p. 48.

If these lines give an impression that the "reign" is to be, as in Berkeley's hymn, simply a cultural and moral pre-eminence, a later passage indicates that the final cause is the redemptive mission.

> As the day-spring unbounded, thy splendour shall flow,
> And earth's little kingdoms before thee shall bow;
> While the ensigns of union, in triumph unfurl'd,
> Hush the tumult of war, and give peace to the world.

Dwight's best known, and best poem, *Greenfield Hill*, seems at first rather to contradict this general theme. The idyllic description of the Connecticut township in which Dwight was for several years pastor before he became president of Yale College, and in which he conducted a widely-known school, appears at first no more than an American pastoral. As he describes the plain living and high thinking of a community of yeomen, shunning "the lures of Europe," we are reminded of Jefferson's famous dictum that

> Those who labour in the earth are the chosen people of God, if ever he had chosen people, whose breasts he has made his peculiar deposit for substantial and genuine virtue. It is the focus in which he keeps alive that sacred fire, which otherwise might escape from the face of the earth. Corruption of morals in the mass of cultivators is a phenomenon of which no age nor nation has furnished an example.[14]

Jefferson's version of "chosen people," then, is a class, not a nation. If Americans are chosen in any way, it is because they belong largely to this group; it is favored by Providence because of its mores, not because it has been designated to play a historical role. *Greenfield Hill* likewise extolls the "plain and honest manners," the lack of aristocratic distinction, the honest toil of the inhabitants of the new Eden. Dwight is no less aware than Jefferson of the illusory attractions of European courts, cities, and wars. Yet these similarities ultimately accentuate differences of viewpoints. Jefferson's statement (admittedly his most extreme) echoes Rousseau's belief that "dependance," which "begets subservience and venality," is the "natural progress and consequence of the arts." Only the husbandmen, living on their

---

[14] Jefferson, *Notes on the State of Virginia* (Philadelphia, 1825), p. 224. (Written 1781–82.)

own produce, are dependable, sound elements in society. By contrast, *Greenfield Hill* envisions a dedication to arts and sciences.

> See, in each village, treasur'd volumes stand:
> And spread pure knowledge through th' enlighten'd land;
> Knowledge the wise Republic's standing force,
> Subjecting all things, with resistless course.[15]

Following where "Europe's Genius leads the splendid way," American students will investigate chemistry, botany, the mysteries of lightning, and especially the divine science of astronomy. A "rich museum" is to be the crowning glory of every village. Jefferson sees America as blessed in the fact that it has begun again and can, if it makes the hard decision, stop at the point where degeneration usually sets in. But Dwight foresees no ideal state of husbandmen: the millennium is to be the culmination of every human activity; it will be preserved from corruption by the very fact that it *is* the millennium, and Satan is bound.

And the idyll *Greenfield Hill* does, in fact, end with the usual Dwight vision. The Resurrection and the spiritual influence which is to radiate from the new country are paralleled. The "Genius of the Sound," obviously own sister to the figure of "Freedom" in *America*, thus prophesies concerning the ultimate destiny of Columbia:

> Yet there, even there, Columbia's bliss shall spring,
> Rous'd from dull sleep, astonish'd Europe sing,
> O'er Asia burst the renovating morn,
> And startled Afric in a day be born;
> As, from the tomb, when great MESSIAH rose,
> Heaven bloom'd with joy, and Earth forgot her woes,
> His saint, thro' nature, truth and virtue spread,
> And light, and life, the SACRED SPIRIT shed.[16]

Thus Jefferson's theory is based finally on the laws of human nature and history; Dwight's, on the operation of grace. Jefferson's theory, carried to its extreme implications,

---

[15] Dwight, *Greenfield Hill* (New York, 1794), book I, lines 401–4.
[16] *Ibid.*, VII, 303–10.

assumes a static condition as the desideratum; innocence and integrity are to be defended, as if they were besieged; whereas Dwight's message breathes infinite confidence in grace as moral progress. Once a forerunner of the kingdom of God has been established, its effect as will spread like concentric waves. This might be called the "nucleus" conception of the millennium.

> Here Truth, and Virtue, doom'd no more to roam,
> Pilgrims in eastern climes, shall find their home;
> Age after age, exalt their glory higher,
> That light the soul, and this the life inspire;
> And Man once more, self-ruin'd Phoenix, rise,
> On wings of Eden, to his native skies.

Thus the apparently inconsistent version of America as Eden *redivivus* and the prototype of the millennium merge in the "self-ruin'd Phoenix"; reborn in the New World, he will soon be ready to take flight.

Dwight's poems were no passing manifestations of enthusiasm engendered by the Revolution. In 1801, in days that sorely tried his Federalist soul, and in the prose of a sermon, he held firm to his millennialist creed and still applied the biblical prophecies to the dark world situation.

But while we look forward with faith, consolation, and
transport, to rising periods of order, peace, and safety, in which
truth shall triumph, justice preside over the concerns of men,
and mercy pity and assuage the sufferings of this agonizing
world; while we foresee seasons of general happiness
and universal virtue, a vernal growth of moral beauty,
and an autumnal harvest of converts to holiness; . . .
we cannot fail to revert to the 'troublous times' which are
now revolving.[17]

The chief assurance is the "manner, in which God *bare* your fathers to this land *on eagles wings,* and *kept them in the hollow of his hand.*" The analogy here clearly implies that the American colonists were a chosen people, for the reference is to Exodus 19:4, "Ye have seen what I did unto the

---

[17] Dwight, *A Discourse on Some Events of the Last Century* (New Haven, 1801), p. 41.

Egyptians, and how I bare you on eagles' wings, and brought you unto myself."

Seen in the perspective of prophecy, the contemporary upheavals in Europe are a new stage in and a new form of the strategy of the Beast.

The present opposition of Infidels in Europe to true religion, and their persecution of its votaries, is a mere continuation of the general system, begun by the Hierarchy in distant ages.
It has arisen, and been exercised, on the same ground, by the descendants of the original and most distinguished persecutors; it has sprung from the same spirit, been regulated by the same policy, is the same design, and has been pursued with the same, and even greater, zeal and cruelty.[18]

And that conspiracy is a "monstrous system of wickedness, denoted by the Beast of the Apocalypse; and the secular powers, which have been coadjutors in this system, [are] the mass of wickedness denoted by the Dragon." [19] An obvious objection is that the infidels of the French Revolution are persecuting the Roman Church itself; for this reason Priestley regarded them as unwitting agents of Providence. But Dwight explains that their persecution, essentially, is directed against that saving remnant of Catholic priests who, even though deluded, are sincere pastors. The old hierarchy, he says (perhaps having in mind the sometime Bishop of Autun, Talleyrand) has quickly come to terms with the dominant powers.

We have advanced to a new step in the development of the millennialist theory. Hitherto, the Beast had always been identified only with the traditional enemies of the "true" church—primarily, the Roman See and its "satellite" princes, and that general enemy of Christendom, the Turk. But now a very different kind of historical event has occurred. Could the professed enemies of Rome itself, and of all religion, be somehow included in the large dualistic theory of history, which regarded every great event as in some way a confrontation of the same Enemy and the same Sav-

18 *Ibid.*, p. 38.
19 *Ibid.*, p. 55.

ior? It is not hard to extend the theory: Jacobins are only the old Papists writ in different script. It will prove equally easy to fit other menaces, as they emerge, into the same pattern—the slave-trader, the "Hun," the Bolshevist. The aura of supernatural conspiracy and cunning, which even the most secular millennialist usually associated with the Roman Church, will be transferred to these newer antagonists. And the disciples of Marx, who—as I have suggested earlier, shows an apocalyptic strain—logically will return the compliment; the United States will appear to be "chosen," indeed, but by the reverse Antichrist, "imperialism."

A very early expression of the myth of the chosen people, in roughly developed form, lies behind what must be one of the most curious official documents in American history, *Apocalypse de Chiokoyhikoy, Chef des Iroquois*, published under authority of the Continental Congress in 1777. It purports to be a translation from the original Iroquois of a prophecy composed in 1305 and until recently hidden in a cavern. The anonymous translator tells us that he was on a secret mission to the Iroquois when the chief took him to the cavern and gave him the "manuscript" ("deux grandes et belles Ecorces d'arbre, proprement rollées"), since, the chief believed, the time for deliverance of his people had arrived. This piece of propaganda, evidently designed to counteract the operations of such British agents as Sir William Johnson among the Indians, seems to imitate elements from the tradition of the sixteenth-century Huron prophet Deganawída, but with a strong infusion of Christian apocalyptic.

In a modern version, Deganawída, the father of the Iroquois confederacy, is supposed to have had a vision of the dark times which would follow the coming of the white men. A great white serpent, which the Indians would at first accept as a friend, would arrive. But it would fall upon the friendly natives.

. . . when things looked their darkest a red serpent would come from the north and approach the white serpent, which would be terrified, and upon seeing the red serpent, he would release the Indian, who would fall to the ground like a helpless child, and the white serpent would turn all its attention to the red serpent.[20]

In the ensuing sublime battle between these monsters, the Indians will remain neutral, and will see the need for re-establishing the brotherly cooperation Deganawída taught them but which they have abandoned. In their peril, they will summon the prophet to return. Eventually, a black serpent will enter the conflict; the serpents will weaken one another, and the white one will break into two parts, one section joining the Indians "with a great love like that of a lost brother." A great light, which turns out to be Deganawída, will appear in the east, traveling westward; it so terrifies the reptiles that they will slink off, and the Indians will be a greater people than ever before.

In the countermyth of the eighteenth-century propagandist, the valiant Chiokoyhikoy, who is imagined along the lines of the greater prophet of the tribal legend, falls asleep on the shores of the great lake and has what seems to be a shamanistic kind of vision. Pricked on the finger by "a small insect," he soon feels an intense burning sensation and knows fear, which he has never experienced in battle. Soon he sees, in the West, "a fiery cloud," which seems to be divided into five parts; it appears to be "a new world, a new land." It is inhabited by a multitude of animals rather resembling men; outstanding are "five human monsters." [21] They descend to earth, and savagely attack the Indians, who are enslaved. A Prophet-bird, a parrot, interprets this disaster. The five mysterious beings of the clouds have come from

[20] Edmund Wilson, *Apologies to the Iroquois,* new ed. (New York: Farrar Strauss and Cudahy, 1966), p. 164. Mr. Wilson got his version of the legend from an informant, and we cannot, of course, know what form it may have had in 1777; but the modern version would seem to suggest that an earlier one may have been employed by the author of the *Apocalypse.*
[21] *Apocalypse de Chiokoyhikoy, Chef des Iroquois, Sauvages du Nord de l'Amérique.* Ecrite par lui-même vers l'an de l'Ere Chrétienne, 1305. Traduite en Français sur l'Original Iroquois. Publié par ordre du Congrès-Géneral. (Philadelphia, W. Roberdson, Imprimeur ordinaire des Colonies Conféderées, 1777), p. 3. English translation mine.

another world, beyond the great lake. For a long time, they will be masters of the land; but in the end a brave minority among them will overthrow the rest. The saviors of the Indians "will be enemies of injustice; your brothers will become their brothers; they will unite, and live in good accord." [22]

The five animals, obviously counterparts of the great Beast of the Revelation, are, of course, the various European conquering nations. The worst of all will be the English; but from them, in the course of generations, will separate itself a new community: "this foreign Blood finally will purge itself; it will bring forth a new people." [23] This seems to be a conflation of the break-up of the white serpent in the Indian legend, the idea of a new people chosen from the old Anglo-Saxon nation, and the Declaration of Independence. This people is destined to conquer the conquerors, and, despite early defeats (this is 1777), to introduce a New World millennium. "They will be righteous and peaceful. They will neither kill nor rob; they will venerate the great OKA." Here is one of the most explicit statements of the American mission, even if the name of the supreme Deity is Oka:

[they] are destined to become, in the hand of the great OKA, the agent of a blessed revolution, which is to bring peace, prosperity, innocence to the new world, and to restore all their rights to the true masters of that world; the savages [or aborigines].[24]

Propaganda though this be, it has an underlying pattern of vastly greater significance; extended to the whole world, the mission of establishing all peoples "in all their rights" is not unlike what Wilson undertook after the First World War. How much all this has been shaped on the model of millennialism is strikingly revealed by the final events of the prophecy. After this millennial age, the Prophet-bird goes on, there will be a period when the evil peoples again will rise up against the just. After their final defeat, and only

[22] *Ibid.*, p. 23.
[23] *Ibid.*, p. 27.
[24] *Ibid.*, p. 88.

then, will the supreme god return, and the happy times return, for good. "Thus decrees the great OKA; so it will be; treachery and cruelty will have ruined your brothers; the oppressors' own envy, hostility, and greed will destroy them; your brothers will gain thereby; the good times will return." The most interesting fact about this conclusion is that it is gratuitous and even confusing. For the purposes of the propaganda, it is enough that the republic is destined to introduce peace and justice and to save the Indians. Its addition suggests that the author (perhaps a missionary) is conscientiously following the lead of the Revelation. A millennium *must* be followed by the temporary release and victory of the dark powers.

A comparison of the Indian legend (which may, of course, have been influenced originally by Christian teachings) and the anonymous "translation" points up significant features about the millennialist doctrines. Although in the legend there are "bad" and "good" animals, and although there is at least a rough form of symbolism, the structure is loose. It exhibits no sense of a consistent dualism, nor of an action moving purposively to a climax. The separation of the white serpent into a good and a bad part is episodic, as is everything else; there is no sense of a "purification," or of an ordained sequence of actions. It is, one perhaps might conclude, the crude form of apocalyptic.

One of the most extreme forms of the millennialist myth of the American people is that of David Austin. A graduate of Yale, he had considerable prestige as a biblical scholar and preacher until he caused a commotion by predicting that the transformation was to occur in 1796. Before he went over the edge, however, he was one of the most important successors in the millennial fields to Edwards and Bellamy, whose works he edited.

In *The Downfall of Mystical Babylon; or A Key to the Providence of God, in the Political Operations of 1793-1794*, he laid out the most complete program for American millennialist function that had yet appeared, and found the new republic more specifically designated in the prophecies than had anyone else before him. Like all his predecessors he located the key to all modern history in the decline and ultimate ruin of mystical Babylon, of which the type was Nebuchadnezzar. The papacy "hath made the world a wilderness by her bloody persecutions; but much more hath she made the Christian Church a wilderness, by with-holding from it the spiritual nourishment of sound doctrine, the ministration of the word and the ordinances of God, in their purity, spirituality, and power." [25] Like Priestley, he regards the Jacobins and their like as unknowing agents of Providence: "are they not, in the hand of God, as well chosen instruments for the execution of threatened vengeance upon mystical Babylon, as the heathenish kings of the east were, for the same design, upon Babylon of the Chaldees?" [26] But their work is only preparation. There must soon come the "regnum montis," which will fill the whole earth (Dan. 2). The stone not cut by human hands, we can now see "was begun on the Fourth of July, 1776, when the *birth* of the MANCHILD—the hero of civil and religious liberty—took place in these United States." [27] Scripture predicts that he is "to rule all nations with a rod of iron"—something more than simply moral influence; and he is to carry out a literally heroic function of liberation. Austin sketches something like the plot of a Blakean prophetic poem.

Behold, then, this hero of America, wielding the standard of civil and religious liberty over these United States!—Follow him, in his strides, across the Atlantic!—See him, with his spear already in the heart of the beast!—See tyranny, civil and ecclesiastical, bleeding at every pore! See the votaries of the tyrants; of the beasts; of the false prophets, and serpents of the earth, ranged in battle array, to withstand the progress and dominion of him, who hath commission to break down the usurpations of tyranny—to let the *prisoner out of the prison-house;* and to set the vassal in bondage free from his chains—to level the mountains—to raise the valleys, and to prepare an highway for the Lord! [28]

[25] Austin, "The Downfall of Mystical Babylon," in *The Millennium,* ed. David Austin (Elizabethtown, 1794), p. 353.
[26] *Ibid.,* p. 365.
[27] *Ibid.,* p. 383.
[28] *Ibid.,* p. 392.

One could see the American intervention in the First World War as the accomplishment of this prophecy.

Austin gives us a lesson in the way the symbols of the prophecies were riddled out, and a brief summary may be instructive. Revelation 12 relates how the great Dragon will seek to devour the child the "woman clothed with the sun, with the moon under her feet, and on her head a crown of twelve stars," is to bring forth. She will flee to the wilderness, where she will find refuge. After the Dragon has been cast out of heaven, a loud voice has warned the dwellers of earth and sea, "For the devil has come down to you in great wrath, because he knows that his time is short." The Dragon will pursue the woman; but she will be given "the two wings of the great eagle that she might fly from the serpent into the wilderness." In seeking the historical equivalents of these mysterious happenings, the interpreter first looks for the generalized significances. The Dragon, it becomes evident, represents the persecutors of the true church, who are inspired and guided by Satan. The woman is the "sufferings of the true church in every age"; the wilderness is "a state of spiritual dearth and barrenness"; the wings of the eagle are the "special providence and agency of Almighty God in conquering the enemies of his people." [29] The man-child is to be the spiritual result of persecution, just as papal "tyranny" brought forth the "glorious reformation," beginning with Wycliffe, Huss, and "Jerom."

The particular identities of the symbolic creatures, however, become evident only as history unfolds. So we can now recognize that the further sufferings of the woman, after the man-child is brought forth, represent the revival of tyranny under Mary, Charles, and James. In response to the "solemn appeals, and reiterated cries" of the woman, she is wafted "on the wings of a bounteous Providence" across the Atlantic, and settled in "these peaceful American abodes." "In a word, behold the hero of civil and religious liberty born in these western climes!" And the mystery of the eagle is now solved:

[29] *Ibid.*, p. 409 ff.

She hath taken her station upon the broad seal of the United States; and from thence has perched upon the pediment of the first government-house, dedicated to the dominion of civil and religious liberty, where she is still to be seen, an emblem of the protection of Providence towards our present government, and towards this our happy land.

Dwight also, it will be recalled, saw a connection between an eagle—the type of the one in Revelation—and the heraldic eagle of the United States. And, we might add, the fact that the latter eagle carries in one talon the arrows of war and in the other the olive branch of peace might symbolize the two ways in which millennialists thought the way was prepared for the earthly Kingdom—by violent "overturning and breaking" of evil, and by peaceful progress. The motto on the reverse of the Great Seal, "Annuit Coeptis Novus Ordo Seclorum," could with no difficulty be given a millennial significance.

Austin was certainly an enthusiast, but his theories were by no means only eccentric products of an odd mind. They resemble those set forth, for example, in the poems of Colonel David Humpreys, a member of the Connecticut Wits, aide and protégé of General Washington, and subsequently minister to Spain and Portugal. In the Advertisement to "A Poem on the Future Glory of the United States of America," he asserts that "America, after having been concealed for so many ages from the rest of the world, was probably discovered, in the maturity of time, to become the theatre for displaying the illustrious designs of Providence, in its dispensations to the human race." [30] Recalling that the functions of poet and of prophet have ever been "intimately blended together," he aspires to celebrate what might be called millennialist nationalism.

If the past is to furnish any criterion for forming a judgment of the future, we are undoubtedly destined, as a nation, to advance with large and rapid strides towards the summit of national aggrandisement. Fully persuaded of the

---

[30] Humphreys, *The Miscellaneous Works* (New York, 1804), p. 48.

magnitude of the blessings which await us there, the writer wishes to impress the same conviction on the minds of his fellow citizens.

He believes, with Edwards, that the millennium is to dawn in the West, which for him is the Northwest Territory.

> Beyond these glooms what brighter days appear,
> Where dawns on mortals heav'n's millennial year!
> In western wilds what scenes of grandeur rise,
> As unborn ages crowd upon my eyes;
> A better area claims its destin'd birth,
> And heav'n descending dwells with man on earth.[31]

The expedition to subdue the pirates of Algiers has its place in the apocalyptic timetable and its type from the Old Testament:

> Thus hath thy hand, great God! through ev'ry age,
> When ripe for ruin, pour'd on man thy rage;
> So didst thou erst on Babylon let fall
> The plagues thy hand inscribed upon the wall.[32]

Humphreys is another witness to the seemingly incongruous fact that millennialism, in America, despite its theoretical glorification of revolutionary overturning, had in general a Federalist tone; the Democrats, followers of Jefferson, by and large were less likely to see the United States as the pioneer of a world utopia. Thus Humphreys, unlike Priestley but like Dwight, sees the new "monster-pow'r" (revolutionary France) as an avatar of the Enemy, and not an instrument of Providence.

> No beast more fell, with rage and vengeance swell'd
> Th' Apocalypse in Patmos' isle beheld.[33]

On the young, weak republic (which, many observers predicted, could not last) is placed the whole burden of bringing perfect order out of discord; it is to establish a world confederation which Austin almost calls the League of Nations.

---

[31] "A Poem on the Future Glory of the United States of America," lines 15–20.
[32] *Ibid.*, lines 454–57.
[33] *Ibid.*, lines 515–16.

> From disappointed hope, the baffled plan
> That promis'd bliss with liberty to man:
> From tyrant force too strong to be withstood,
> Corruption, terror, ruin, fire and blood;
> A Pow'r shall rise to bid the Discord cease,
> And join all nations in the leagues of Peace.[34]

And he asks his countrymen: "What but disunion can our bliss destroy?"

Humphreys' most original contribution is his consistent combination of the westward and the millennialist mystiques. In "The Future State of the Western Territory," he foresees a virtuous race, sent by heaven to establish the last and fairest empire. This is not to be a new Eden, simply a pastoral paradise set up in the wilderness, free from the old corruptions of advanced civilization; it is to possess all the glories of the greatest metropolis together with the true Christian integrity.

> Then cities rise, and spiry towns increase,
> With gilded domes, and ev'ry art of peace.
> Then Cultivation shall extend his pow'r,
> Rear the green blade, and nurse the tender flow'r;
>
> . . . .
>
> Then shall rich Commerce court the fav'ring gales,
> And wond'ring wilds admire the passing sails,
> Where the bold ships the stormy Huron brace,
> Where wild Ontario rolls the whit'ning wave,
> Where fair Ohio his pure current pours,
> And Mississippi laves th' extended shores.[35]

Humphreys is a very early exponent of the mystique of the Middle West. Addressing the visionary empire, he says that as "Thy beauties ripen, and thy pomp ascends," blessings will roll out over the whole earth, "To southern oceans and the northern pole." The present wilderness, on the authority of the prophets, is to "blossom as the rose," "Like Salem flourish, and like Eden bloom." There is the exaltation of the pioneers, in whom the greatness of their race reaches its apex in some highly romantic exploits:

[34] *Ibid.*, lines 531–36.
[35] *The Columbian Muse*, p. 162.

A band of heroes and a patriot race:
. . . .
Healthful and strong, they turn'd the virgin soil,
The untam'd forest bow'd beneath their toil:
At early dawn, they sought the mountain chace,
Or rous'd the Indian from his lurking place;
Curb'd the mad fury of those barb'rous men,
Or dragged the wild beast struggling from his den:
To all the vigour of that pristine race,
New charms are added, and superior grace.

3

Humphreys' conviction that the then western regions were to be occupied by Americans and to become the seat of a great community was, of course, by no means unique. Freneau's poem "On the Migration to America, and Peopling the Western Country," also published in *The Columbian Muse*, says of the "sire of floods" and his tributary streams:

No longer shall they useless prove,
Nor idly through the forest rove.

But if Freneau foresees that the land will be settled and cultivated for human benefit, his expectations are significantly different from those of Humphreys. The West is to be an Arcadia realized, a refuge for mankind, presumably because of its perpetual isolation. We do not hear of "pomp" of architecture and of bold ocean-going ships on the stormy Huron.

While Virtue warms the gen'rous breast,
    Here heav'nborn Freedom shall reside;
Nor shall the voice of War molest,
    Nor Europe's all-aspiring pride;
Here Reason shall new laws devise
    And order from confusion rise.[36]

There is no apocalyptic fervor. The hope for the future of the great unsettled lands, and for the nation, consists in the

[36] *The Columbian Muse*, p. 173.

right application of "reason"; this is the voice of Enlightenment. Europe, it would seem, will always retain her pride and her wars. There is none of Dwight's confidence that "fair Columbia" will eventually see

> Her genial influence thro' all nations roll,
> And hush the sound of war from pole to pole.[37]

In an "epistle," Dwight warns Humphreys, who was then (1785) setting out for Europe, to remember that the fulfillmen of God's great plan depends on people of his kind. He is not going from the back woods to the seat of every social grace, but

> From realms, where nature sports in youthful prime,
> Where Hesper lingers o'er his darling clime,
> . . . .
> Where rising science casts her morning beam,
> Where empire's final throne in pomp ascends,
> Where pilgrim Freedom finds her vanish'd friends,
> The world renews, and man from eastern fires,
> Phoenix divine, again to Heaven aspires.

The frequency of the phoenix image in Dwight is not merely self-quotation; it so exactly epitomizes the basic millennial idea that it could hardly be spared. The reverence paid to travelers who have visited the fashionable world of London is one of the tricks the Old One uses to frustrate the hopes not only of America but of the world. Dwight prays Humphreys may return "to add new glories to the western morn" and

> Bid o'er the world her constellation rise,
> The brightest splendour in the unmeasur'd skies.

Dwight's position is that, if old Europe has much to teach us about the arts and the sciences, she in her turn must in the greatest things learn from and be inspired by God's people in the New World.

There is a contrasting view of American destiny in the oration Joel Barlow delivered, on Independence Day, 1809,

[37] Dwight, "Epistle to Colonel Humphreys" in *The Columbian Muse*, p. 63.

before an audience that included the President and members of his cabinet. The necessity for complete separation, in politics, philosophy, and even ways of life, from the rest of the world, is the burden of Barlow's prophetic message.

The form of government we have chosen, the geographical position we occupy, as relative to the most turbulent powers of Europe, whose political maxims are widely different from ours; the vast extent of continent that is or must be comprised within our limits, containing not less than sixteen hundred millions of acres, and susceptible of a population of two hundred millions of human beings; our habits of industry and peace, instead of violence and war . . . all these are circumstances that render our situation as novel as it is important.[38]

Destiny would appear manifest, already, in 1809; sixteen hundred million acres is nearly five sixths of the present area of the conterminous United States. But this great country, with its future two hundred millions of citizens, is not to hush the sound of war from pole to pole. It is a new creation, protected by its ocean moat, and should seek as its national goal containment within its own integrity. Barlow at this time of wars has no faith in a future of unlimited world commerce, which he himself earlier had foreseen in *The Vision of Columbus.* "The greatest real embarrassment we labor under at present, arises from our commercial relations; the only point of contact between us and the unjust governments of Europe. We cannot overwhelm them by sheer force; alliances for defense are highly unsatisfactory." [39] He suggests that "the means of submarine attack, invented and proposed by one of our citizens, carries in itself the eventual destruction of naval tyranny." These are not counsels of despair; on the anniversary of independence, "Minds of sensibility accustomed to range over the field of contemplation that the birth of our empire spreads before them, must expand on the occasion to great ideas, and invigorate their patriotic sentiments." But what should be

---

[38] Barlow, *Oration, Pronounced on the Fourth of July, 1809* . . . (Newburyport, 1809), p. 5.
[39] *Ibid.,* p. 14.

the role of "our empire" in the world? Barlow and the millennialists would agree that "there has been no nation, either ancient or modern, that could have presented human nature in the same character as ours does." But does this fact suggest that our proper course is to maintain our distinction by purging ourselves of feudalism and keeping ourselves always a separate people, using our inventive gifts to find new and unconquerable weapons to reinforce the uniquely great moat which nature has given us? Is intercourse with the rest of the world a blessing or an insidious temptation? Or are we destined to extend the new character of human nature throughout the whole world?

When the phrase "Manifest Destiny" actually was invented, in 1845, it was so far from being a novelty that the only wonder is that it had not appeared somewhere decades earlier.[40] It represented the effect of an ideology, in which millennialism had a substantial part, working in conjunction with the unparalleled circumstances of the formation of the new state. Self-interest and chauvinism were involved, but to attribute the whole conception to them alone is misleading. What happened was that the possibilities for territorial expansion in the years just after the Texan revolt came into a kind of chemical combination with the general Protestant theology of the millennium, and with the already old idea of the destined greatness and messianic mission of "Columbia."

In 1846, a year after the phrase first appeared, an article by J. Sullivan Cox, in *The United States Magazine and Democratic Review*, exhibits the amalgamation of ideas.

There is a moral sense—a soul in the state, which longs for something more than the tariffs, the bank, and the bankrupt bills of a temporizing present; which looks for some celestial beacon to direct the course of popular movement through the eternal future![41]

The moment has come, the author asserts, when the prophetic longings of the "soul in the state" are to be satisfied. The biblical imagery in the following paragraph is indica-

---

[40] See Weinberg, *Manifest Destiny*, pp. 11–12; 144–45.
[41] "Imaginary Commonwealths," *United States Magazine and Democratic Review*, 19 (1846):184.

tive, for it recalls the divine guidance of the first chosen people as they were conducted through Sinai:

Something of the same spirit now glows in the bosom of every member of this western commonwealth in America. Call it what you will, destiny, or what not; it is leading us as a cloud by day and a pillar of fire by night. It beckons to us from the dim and shadowy distance, and bids us, All Hail! It illumines our faces with hope, lights our eye with enterprize. Who can define it? As well define infinity, space, eternity; yet who so heartless as not to feel it. It has been called manifest. Its effects *are* manifest. They are seen in the throbbing pulse of America. It whelms and controls us, yet who would stem its rushing stream.

As we might expect, the calling of the Anglo-Saxons is mentioned: "And is there no energy in this our Saxon race, no elements of perfection in this our human nature, by which to dare that destiny? [42] The scriptural prophecies are confirmation of the hopes obscurely represented by secular utopias through the centuries; these latter are, as it were, intuitions of the divine plan.

. . . to him who feels that there is a universal conscience which will never cry peace while impurity exists; to him, the Republic, the Utopia, and the Oceana, embody an earnest feeling and a congenial faith, in the *summi gravissimi fines* of social existence, which has ever been sung by the prophetic harps of the earth, and uttered by the elect oracles of heaven.

Essentially, this restates the rationale for the expectation of a millennium in this world's flesh as Goodwin expressed it, nearly two centuries before. And all these rays of hope seemed, as the rays of the sun concentrated by a magnifying glass, to focus on the American West.

That such outpourings were no simple reflex reactions to the current political situation is shown by one of earlier date, and two later. Cooper, in 1832, while still in England, set forth a vision of history, which

embraced the long and mysterious concealment of so vast a portion of the earth as America, from the acquaintance of

[42] *Ibid.*, p. 185.

civilized man; the manner in which violence and persecution, civil wars, oppression and injustice, had thrown men of all nations upon its shores; the effects of this collision of customs and opinions, unenthralled by habits and laws of selfish origin; the religious and civil liberty that followed; the novel but irrefutable principle on which its government was based, the silent working of its example, in the two hemispheres, one of which had already imitated the institutions that the other was struggling to approach, and all the immense results that were dependent on this inscrutable and grand movement of Providence.[43]

In 1858, an article in *Harper's New Monthly Magazine*, entitled "Providence in American History," recapitulated the elements of the faith in the American destiny. The author asserts that the fundamentals of American democracy have developed from the idea of a Kingdom of God on earth. Although the separation of church from state is essential to the American idea, that idea has, in essence, been created by the pure religion of Protestantism. The author epitomizes what, I think, was the dominant contemporary attitude in a striking sentence: "A national Church is one thing, a national Religion is quite another; and in nothing are they more unlike than in their capacity to awaken the sense of Providence in the breast of a people." [44] It is not exaggerated to say that there was a "national Religion," which included millennialist beliefs, even if part of that religion was the exclusion of an established religion. The author undoubtedly expresses a widespread conviction when he says that "the American Constitution has a moral meaning, a sacredness, over and above what political science and civil compacts can ever give to the organic law of a commonwealth." [45]

In America, moreover, the chosen people has found the appointed theater. The physical features of the North American continent, in sharp contrast to those of the Eastern Hemisphere, show that

[43] James Fenimore Cooper, *The Heidenmauer* (1832), Introduction.
[44] "The Editor's Drawer," *Harper's New Monthly Magazine*, 17 (1858):697.
[45] *Ibid.*, p. 697.

It is strikingly adapted not only to greatness of empire, but to that peculiar form of greatness which seems to be reserved for our inheritance. . . . Taken in its whole, it is a wonderful provision for the intelligence, sagacity, energy, restlessness, and indomitable will of such a race as the Anglo-Saxon—a race that masters physical nature without being mastered by it—a race in which the intensest home-feelings combine with a love of enterprise, advent, and colonization— a race that fears nothing, claims every thing within reach, enjoys the future more than the present, and believes in a destiny of incomparable and immeasurable grandeur.

No wonder, then, that "every thing connected with our position, history, progress, points out the United States of America as the land of the future"; and it is true of our land as of Horeb: "Put off thy shoes from thy feet; for the place whereon thou standest is holy ground." (Ex. 3:1)

And in 1890, Washington Gladden, who was associated with Josiah Strong as a founder of the "social gospel" movement, in preaching a centennial sermon on the founding of Gallipolis, Ohio, again expounded the essentials of the doctrine. History, Gladden says, is the working out of God's plan; and the central fact is the westward movement. Although hunger, fear, love of liberty, greed, and many other immediate reasons have led men to the West, "Yet all over these conflicting motives, harmonizing them all and bringing order out of them, is the plan of the all-wise Ruler of the world, who makes the wrath and the folly and the greed of man to praise him." [46] The movements of population were essentially "spontaneous rather than deliberate; prophetic more than economic." And, it would seem, it has been by divine ordination that "the great mass of these inhabitants of the New World belong to that Aryan race, whose teeming millions have been hurrying westward ever since the dawn of time." [47]

This sermon was preached in the year when the census was to indicate that the great tracts of free land had been

[46] Gladden, "Migrations and Their Lessons," *Publications of the Ohio Archaeological and Historical Society,* 3 (1891):184.
[47] *Ibid.,* p. 180.

largely exhausted, and that the end of the western migration was in sight. Gladden reminds his audience that "those great currents of migration from east to west, . . . are stayed upon our western shore and can no further go. For number-less centuries, they have been flowing westward; and the slow tides of time have brought them to the final barrier." [48] At the Golden Gate, "the pilgrims stand and gaze afar to that Asian continent from which in the dim twilight of history their fathers set forth—to countries crowded with a decadent civilization." Whitman, thirty years before, in "Facing West from California's Shores," had likewise re-flected, as a child of the migration, upon the completion of the circle, and had concluded by wondering:

(But where is what I started for so long ago?
And why is it yet unfound?)

Gladden, although no strict fundamentalist (he was a disciple of Bushnell), finds the key in the promises of revela-tion: ". . . here, upon these plains, the problems of history are to be solved; here, if anywhere, is to rise that city of God, the New Jerusalem, whose glories are to fill the earth."

Thus far we have been considering two kinds of optimism about the American destiny. One sees the hope for America in its separation from the Old World; the other believes, in Gladden's words, that here "the problems of history are to be solved." There was, however, a third attitude toward the new country and the westward movement. The real signifi-cance of the emergence of the new people is that they represent a new and vital spirit; it is not the empire they are to create, the final achievement of their work, but the very fact of their strenuous lives that is important. They neither consciously reject the past in favor of a new order, nor aim to transform the race; they simply turn their backs on the Old World, absorbed in the exhilaration of escape, pioneer-ing, conquering. Whitman expresses this attitude in his marching song "Pioneers! O Pioneers!"

All the past we leave behind,
We debouch upon a newer, mightier world, varied world,

[48] *Ibid.*, p. 195.

> Fresh and strong the world we seize, world of labor and the
>   march,
>   Pioneers! O pioneers!

It is the exuberance of a youthful people in a youthful
world that is all-important; youth is the meaning of it all.
There is no debating about the kind of world to be built.

> We to-day's procession heading, we the route for travel
>   clearing,
>   Pioneers! O pioneers!

>   Not for delectations sweet,
> Not the cushion and the slipper, not the peaceful and the
>   studious,
> Not the riches safe and palling, not for us the tame
>   enjoyment,
>   Pioneers! O pioneers!

There is no vision of the future, of what all this is to
achieve; the poem ends with a call to action, to the supreme
joy of the hard and absorbing, unending march, ever westward:

>   Has the night descended?
> Was the load of late so toilsome? did we stop discouraged
>   nodding on our way?
> Yet a passing hour I yield you in your tracks to pause
>   oblivious,
>   Pioneers! O pioneers!

>   Till with sound of trumpet,
> Far, far off the daybreak call—hark! how loud and clear
>   I hear it wind,
> Swift! to the head of the army!—swift! spring to your
>   places,
>   Pioneers! O pioneers!

Such an attitude is consonant with the late nineteenth century cult of *élan* as a mystique, and end in itself; the process,
the beginning, are more important than the end. Much of
the popular romanticism of the frontier, of the precivilized
history of the West, may well reflect this mood.

It has long been recognized that a factor of central importance in American history is the sense of "mission." Professor Merk describes it as "idealistic, self-denying, hopeful of

divine favor for national aspirations, though not sure of it. It made itself heard most authentically in times of emergency, of ordeal, of disaster." [49] It should be remarked, however, that "mission" is not one idea, but a complex of ideas, with different origins and, despite many similiarities in results, fundamentally different purposes. The sense of mission, says Professor Merk, could motivate such diverse kinds of action as programs of public welfare and the "national sense of responsibility for saving democracy in Europe," in 1917–18. He is inclined to feel, however, that Manifest Destiny—the conception that the nation was assigned dominion over most of this continent—was essentially opposed to the "self-denying" nature of mission *per se*, even if the two could on occasion be confused. Here I must disagree. The idea of the chosen people, one form of the conviction of American mission, implies that this people is to establish a great territorial "empire," even though much of it, like the Promised Land, might at first be under the Philistines; indeed, several authors I have quoted vaguely suggested there would ensue a kind of righteous dominion over the entire world, in which the political would be mixed with spiritual and moral elements. Yet this expectation of empire was part of an ideal of world regeneration. Still, it is true that many leaders opposed the expansion of the United States in the 1840's, the imperialism at the end of the century, and similar movements, also in the name of America's special calling to serve. The explanation is that mission itself can be divided into at least two really antagonistic forms.

One, as we have seen, holds that the United States is to be a new Eden. Its example may and should inspire others to carry on their own revolutions against ancient tyrannies and injustices; but the Americans' first duty is to develop and protect their own land as a refuge, and to demonstrate true benevolence by giving material assistance without political involvement. Barlow, nevertheless, demonstrates that the acquisition of territory was not inconsistent with these views;

[49] Frederick Merk, *Manifest Destiny and Mission in American History: A Reinterpretation* (New York: Alfred A. Knopf, 1963), p. 261.

but the territory would be part of an area contiguous with the original thirteen states. As Professor Merk observes, both Republicans, like Thomas B. Reed, and Democrats, like Cleveland, opposed *imperalist* expansion, as would Barlow. Cleveland, indeed, expressed the essence of the isolationist view of mission.

The annexation of the Hawaiian Islands seemed to Grover Cleveland in 1898 'perversion of our national mission. The mission of our nation is to build up and make a greater country out of what we have instead of annexing islands.' Animating all defenders of the old faith was the sentiment of Daniel Webster admonishing expansionists of his day: 'You have a Sparta; embellish it!' [50]

In contrast with the new Eden-Sparta was, of course, the new Israel. The millennialists would fervently agree that the chosen people must be on guard, and must take action to destroy without mercy the corruption the Enemy tries to introduce; but this protection was intended not only to make a greater country out of what we have but to form the kind of nation that would save the world. The word "empire"—understood in the sense of the prophecies of the "kingdoms"—was never an evil one to the militant millennialist. A race destined to "out-populate" the decadent areas, to bring up the old nations, to end wars, could hardly be satisfied with embellishing its homeland.

The danger in all this is evident. To assume that what is good for America is good for the world, that saving the United States is saving mankind, is to open up a large area of temptation. Manifest Destiny, under the cloak of what was often a very sincere belief in the great beneficent calling of the United States of America, undoubtedly often concealed selfish and sordid motives. "Americanization" of the world can easily become mercenary rather than messianic. But it has seemed to many people that the two purposes could be harmonized. I think it would be unfair to Humphreys, for instance, to deny him a very real idealism about the West, even while recognizing that he had interests in western

[50] *Ibid.*, p. 263.

lands. The consequence has often been that the United States has seemed inconsistent, and consequently probably hypocritical in many actions. The record in the Philippines is a case in point. The original purpose of the Spanish War, to free oppressed colonies still under the control of the mystical Babylon, was not basically a hypocrisy. The "pacification" of the islands in the first decade of the twentieth century, which so outraged Mark Twain, Finley Peter Dunne, and others, seemed nothing more than the old familiar colonialism of the European powers. It was his high sense of mission that led Mark Twain to thunder: "I pray you to pause and consider. Against our traditions we are now entering upon an unjust and trivial war, a war against a helpless people, and for a base object—robbery." [51] Yet the same nation, in 1934, guaranteed ultimate independence to the Philippine republic, and the United States played a large part in assisting the territory to develop its own democracy. For the first time it seemed as though the white man had really carried his burden to the finish, and that some of the millennial ideal had been realized. In fact, the original pacification probably was not quite so completely "unjust" as Mark Twain had thought, nor was the Tydings-McDuffie Act quite so altruistic as it might appear. The apocalyptic view of history tends, unrealistically, to categorize nations and actions as wholly bad or wholly good; this fact has encouraged Americans to judge history even of this nation by the same standard.

The myth of American millennialism is undoubtedly an example of nationalist ideology, but, as I have suggested, it has qualities unique among religious forms of nationalism. We may better appreciate those qualities if we contrast the conception of the new chosen people with another powerful nationalistic myth, that of the nation which, Tocqueville foresaw, was to become the rival of the United States for

---

[51] Mark Twain, "Two Fragments from a Suppressed Book Called 'Glances at History' or 'Outlines of History,' in *Letters from the Earth*, ed. Bernard De Voto (New York, 1938), p. 97. Copyright, Mark Twain Co., President and Fellows of Harvard College.

world leadership. Late in the fifteenth century was composed the "Tale of the White Cowl," which has been called
"the cornerstone of Russian national ideology." [52]

The "Tale" relates how Constantine, after his conversion,
had the White Cowl (symbolizing supremacy of the spiritual power) made for Pope St. Sylvester. In the ninth century, after the schism between the Eastern and the Western
churches had developed, a heavenly vision directed the then
pope to send the sacred garment to the patriarch of Constantinople and the pope complied. Later, the pope
wickedly demanded its return to Rome, but the patriarch
replied that the Roman bishop was the precursor of Antichrist because he asserted his right to rule over the whole
church. In time, however, as the condition of the Eastern
empire became more and more insecure, Sylvester in another
vision instructed the patriarch as follows:

. . . you must send this Holy White Cowl to the Russian land,
to the city of Novgorod the Great. . . . And when you send
it to the Russian land, the Orthodox Faith will be glorified
and the Cowl will be safe from seizure by the infidel sons
of Hagar and from the intended profanation by the Latin
pope. And the grace, glory, and honor which were taken
from Rome, as well as the Grace of the Holy Spirit, will be
removed from the imperial city of Constantinople after its
capture by the sons of Hagar. And all holy relics will be
given to the Russian land in the predestined moment. And
the Russian tsar will be elevated by God above other nations,
and under his sway will be many heathen kings. And the
power of the patriarch of this imperial ruling city will pass
to the Russian land in the predestined hour. And that land will
be called Radiant Russia, which, by the Grace of God, will
be glorified with blessings. And its majesty will be
strengthened by its orthodoxy, and it will become more
honorable than the two Romes which preceded it.

In both American and Russian ideologies, there is a *translatio imperii* from a mother country to one that had been in

---

[52] S. A. Zenkovsky, *Medieval Russia's Epics, Chronicles, and
Tales* (New York: E. P. Dutton, 1963), p. 265. I have
quoted from the translation of the "Tale of the White Cowl"
included in this collection.

a form of colonial status, both politically and culturally. There is the implication in each case that the new state is a purified offshoot of the older one; as Britain, although the pioneer of the Reformation, has failed to fulfill its task, so Byzantium, although preserving the true faith and spreading it, has become corrupt. Each myth suggests that the *translatio* is to be the decisive event in history before the last days, and each is grounded in apocalyptic prophecies; each, finally, implies that the new dominant people will have world power to an extent previously unknown. But the "Tale of the Cowl" owes most of its religious sanction to the predictions in Daniel, and not, unlike American millennialism, to the St. John Revelation. Hence in the Russian version there is no millennial utopia, no confidence that history is moving upward and that the future of the human family on this earth is brilliant. The role of "radiant Russia" is to preserve the true religion like a treasure, unchanged, and to bring the other nations into the fold of the church in preparation for the sequence of eschatological events, all of which are yet to happen. It is to be a soldier in the cause of Christ, but not, in the sense of the hymn, a "Christian soldier." The Russian program is static, dedicated to maintaining a faith already completed, as contrasted with the dynamic expectations of the millennialists. Nor, obviously, does the "Tale of the Cowl" have any thought of a radically new kind of society; the older Romes are to be recreated, but more splendid and more virtuous. The ruler is to be another Caesar—a "tsar"—and the spiritual head is to be the direct successor of the patriarch, and to hold the same title in the hierarchy. Things are not to be made new; the past is accepted in principle, although judged for its faults.

Yet in both countries ideas with an apocalyptic foundation undoubtedly made for a sense of nationalism among many loosely confederated states. Both stories rationalize and justify what in fact has happened: thus Byzantium has fallen, and if its culture and religion are to survive, a new land on the periphery of the old empire will have to take up the torch. And a religious explanation is given to the political and economic separation of the British colonies from the motherland. Yet there is a difference. Byzantium, at the time the Russian story arose, was gone; but the American ideology was formed when Britain was reaching the zenith of her power. Now it is hard to realize how ludicrous the predictions of America's supreme mission appeared even in 1845. Clearly, only a powerful idea, something going far beyond contemporary history, was at work. There is, too, the fact that the idea of a millennium was developed long before anyone had thought of independence for the American colonies; it developed independently of the democratic ideal itself, which was later incorporated into the nucleus of the millennialist interpretation of Scripture.

It is interesting, also, to compare the geographical movements of the two myths of *translatio imperii.* There is no consistency in the Russian story. The sacred garment moves eastward, north and westward; there is nothing comparable to the mystique of the westward course of empire. If anything similar to geographical determinism were to develop in Russia, it might indeed be a notion of an eastward movement. This serves to remind us that the whole idea of the ordained westward movement is oriented to western Europe, and grew up when only a limited part of the history of mankind was real and vital to our ancestors. Thus the Orient is still, in American as in British usage, the "Far East."

But the most important contribution of the millennialist idea was the confidence that mankind can and will climb at last into a Golden Age. That contribution originally was religious, and the idea of progress in English-speaking countries probably has never wholly lost its religious coloration.

V

Chosen Race ...
Chosen People

"Surely, to be a Christian and an Anglo-Saxon, and an American in this generation is to stand on the very mountain-top of privilege." [1] These words came, not from a super-heated Independence Day orator, but from the apostle of the Home Missionary movement, in a highly influential message to the Protestants of America on their opportunities and responsibilities. They were no expression of smug self-congratulation or of chauvinism. Josiah Strong was one of the first to sound the alarm that the churches were ignoring the great problems of the cities and of the working classes. Many a wealthy congregation, he asserted, is provided with every necessity and comfort—"except some Christianity." In the last decades of the nineteenth century he was in fact reviving an old call to Protestants, especially those in the United States, to regenerate the nation and the world in preparation for "the coming kingdom."

The Anglo-Saxon Christians, like the Savior himself, stood on the mountain-top of both privilege and trial. And why had they been given this unique mission? In the past, Strong asserted, the Hebrew, Greek, and Roman peoples each had played its appointed part in making possible the

[1] Josiah Strong, *The New Era, or The Coming Kingdom* (New York, 1893), p. 354.

final world-wide redemption; now the Anglo-Saxons are summoned to combine the peculiar qualities of all three in the last stage of making straight the way. "Privilege" is an ambiguous word: to Strong it was synonymous with the "talent" of the Gospel parable. Study of modern history in the light of revelation teaches us

that the world is evidently about to enter on a new era, that in this new era mankind is to come more and more under Anglo-Saxon influence, and that Anglo-Saxon civilization is more favorable than any other to the spread of those principles whose universal triumph is necessary to that perfection of the race to which it is destined; the entire realization of which will be the kingdom of heaven fully come on earth.[2]

Neither Strong nor anyone else in the century had invented the articles of this doctrine. It was, on the contrary, the climax of the Protestant millennialist interpretation of the prophecies, combined with certain ethnic theories which seemed, as if providentially, to support it. The idea is familiar enough; but we have not understood its nature, since we have not known just how it originated.

The Jewish people, of course, were represented in the Old Testament as the chosen of God. This statement implies, not arbitrary divine favoritism, but a calling: they were chosen and should be worthy, the high prophets taught, to do God's work. Christianity from Paul onward tended to substitute a universal church, composed of persons from all nations, for the old single nation, and to change radically the signification of "chosen." This is not to say, however, that the problem of the unconverted Jews became insignificant. It was generally agreed by all Christian eschatologists through the centuries that the predictions of Christ's second advent could not be fulfilled before the conversion and ingathering of the people of the promise. It was widely believed, too, that the descendants of Israel must return to the Holy Land before the City of God could come into its own. The commentator Whitby, to whom I referred

2 *Ibid.,* p. 81.

earlier, says, for example, that "converted Jews and those who will join them may be dominant in the millennium, although the temple will not be rebuilt." [3] In all the discussions of the causes for "anti-Semitic" feeling, this point seems to have been ignored. The Jews offended Christians in all periods, not only because of their alleged "deicide" but because their obstinate unbelief was thought to be postponing the longed-for time when Satan's reign would be ended. This idea has died out in probably the larger part of Christianity, but the associations of beliefs linger on. As Locke says, fear of the dark remain in many people because of childhood stories about bogies; the stories have been forgotten, but the associated fears continue.

The conception of a specific chosen nation died away as salvation came to be considered the redemption of individual souls, bound in a mystical rather than political or social body. Needless to say, several nations have had a high opinion of their importance, and have regarded themselves as specially designated to extend their dominion in order to spread the blessings of their civilization among the benighted; but the idea that any one state is to "redeem" history is wholly inconsistent with the Augustinian and medieval idea of the City of God, which denies that this world's community and history can ever be transformed. Victories of armies and military extensions of the faith are not in themselves acts of final redemption. But when the Protestant millennialist theory was formed, logically there came with it a need to find a new chosen nation, or nations. If history is theodicy, if redemption is historical as well as individual, if evil is to be finally and decisively bound through great conflicts, God must operate through cohesive bodies of men; there must be children of light and children of darkness geographically, and the City of God and the City of the World should be susceptible of being designated on maps.

Especially is this true if the universal church was dominated by Antichrist, who possessed his own estates. Since

---

[3] Daniel Whitby, *A Paraphrase and Commentary on the New Testament* (London, 1760), 2:696.

there was a dictatorship temporal as well as spiritual, the church could not spontaneously generate resistance strong enough to overthrow its rulers without a most palpable miracle. Some power in the world must at least begin the heroic deliverance, and later defend it. From the start, the reformers were supported by certain princes against pope and emperor; in such accounts as that of Foxe, they were associated with the spiritual reformers as the heroes of the great renewal. Although German rulers first performed this function, Englishmen soon became convinced that the pillar of fire had come to rest over the tents of Albion. It was England that had provided the indispensable support for the reformed churches when the pope and emperor had most gravely threatened them, and God had visibly shown his choice in the wondrous fiasco of the Spanish Armada.

It was believed, moreover, that if the actual effective Reformation began in Germany, it was in England that the saving remnant had preserved the true Gospel faith most stoutly, throughout the dark age of the apostacy. A medieval legend, which originally had bolstered up the claims of the English crown against the pope, became the foundation of the myth of the Anglo-Saxon mission. It was said that Joseph of Arimathea, "who waited for the kingdom of God," and who procured the body of Jesus and laid it in the tomb, had come as the first missionary to England. There he established a branch of the true primitive church. It was still extant when Augustine of Canterbury arrived, and persecuted the people of God, introducing the "Romish service," so that "the souls, bodies and estates of Englishmen were trod by the foul feet of the Roman Antichrist." [4] Thus John Foxe, in the classical formulation of the Protestant myth, *The Actes and Monuments*, relates the story. Perversion of the true Gospel teaching continued apace, until most English people knew nothing of the "liberty of a Christian man" and idolatry replaced saving faith. All Europe was under a

---

[4] Robert Baillie, "A Parallel or Brief Comparison of the Liturgies with the Masse-Book" (1641), quoted by S. A. Burrell, in "The Apocalyptic Vision of the Early Covenanters," *Scottish Historical Review*, 43 (1964):8.

great eclipse of the Sun of Righteousness. Yet in a few places a few martyrs held out, and England most prominently kept up some resistance to the Harlot on the seven hills. "Foxe's telling of the story of English kings down to Edward III is focused upon the struggle of English rulers to maintain the independence of the English crown and the English church against the aggressions of the papacy and its instruments." [5]

This opposition in itself was proof that in England the true church, even though sorely oppressed, had continuously existed in a manner and strength found nowhere else. In the preface to the sixth book of *The Actes and Monuments*, Foxe says that the faith "hathe continually from time to time sparkled abroad, although the flames thereof have never so perfectly burst out, as they have done within these hundred yeares and more." For, although the English preachers honored Luther, Melancthon, and other continental reformers, they insisted that the English Wycliffe was the "morning star of the Reformation." In this fact they read a symbolic message related to the biblical prophecies.

That message burgeoned steadily. Timothy Bright, in 1589, added to Foxe's thesis the extravagant proposition that England was the first nation that "univerallie embraced the Gospel." Wycliffe, Henry VIII, Edward VI, and Elizabeth I all promulgated or forwarded the Reformation. "In brief, England was 'the first [nation] that embraced the Gospel: the only establisher of it throughout the world: and the first reformed.' " [6] Subsequent events seemed to confirm these heady claims: the fate of the Armada, the exposure of the Gunpowder Plot, the succession of a Protestant (and a bigoted one) after Elizabeth I, and so forth. Later, even if the Commonwealth collapsed, Protestantism preserved its basic power; there was, eventually, the "Glorious Revolution" and the deliverance by the Protestant hero, William III. By contrast, much of the German territory originally

---

[5] William Haller, "John Foxe and the Puritan Revolution," in *The Seventeenth Century*, by Richard F. Jones, *et al.* (Stanford: Stanford University Press, 1951), p. 213.
[6] *Ibid.*, p. 219.

won to Lutheranism had been lost again, and the Latin countries produced only abortive Protestant movements. The escape of the Huguenots to England and Holland seemed symbolic. ". . . who could deny that Englishmen held a special place in the favor of the Lord and a special responsibility for the fulfillment of his purposes on earth?" [7]

This conviction was by no means limited to the Puritan factions, nor did it end with the Civil Wars. There is ample evidence that it continued as a presiding idea in English-speaking countries down into the twentieth century. It is the core of the faith in the Anglo-Saxon mission, and an essential component of "the white man's burden." The real beliefs of any religion go far beyond the formal credal statements which usually absorb the attention of historians. Thus in no formal profession of faith will the doctrine of "God's Englishman" be found; but it was, truly, a matter of deep religious conviction, and it produced incalculably great results.

Jonathan Edwards, remarking as a matter of course that "our nation" is "the principal nation of the Reformation," was referring to England and her colonies as one. Milton, a century before, had appealed to this assumption in supporting his arguments for a limited degree of religious liberty.

Nor is it for nothing that the grave and frugal Transylvanian sends out yearly from as far as the mountainous borders of Russia, and beyond the Hercynian wilderness, not their youth, but their staid men, to learn our language and our theological arts. Yet that which is above all this, the favor and the love of Heaven, we have great argument to think in a peculiar manner propitious and propending towards us. Why else was this nation chosen before any other, that out of her, as out of Sion, should be proclaimed and sounded forth the first tidings and trumpet of reformation to all Europe? . . . Now once again by all concurrence of signs, and by the general instinct of holy and devout men, as they daily and solemnly express their thoughts, God is decreeing to begin some new and great period in his church, even to the reforming of reformation itself; what does he then but reveal himself to his servants, and as his manner is, first to his Englishmen?

[*Areopagitica*]

[7] *Ibid.*, p. 220.

For it is in "this vast city, a city of refuge, the mansion-house of liberty," that God is preparing his next great work. The Reformation, as Milton was to assert again and again, was the great turning point at which Antichrist was cast half-way down; its pioneers and most valiant defenders were English; now further battles in the war to overthrow the Beast are preparing, in fulfillment of the prophecies, and again God is calling on his people. The English nation is peculiarly fitted for such a mission because it has preserved the spirit of liberty and has become the strongest aggressor against the power which binds soul and body.

Over two centuries later, the conviction that English-speaking peoples have consistently been the champions against Antichrist remained strong. George Marsh, a pioneer in American studies of Anglo-Saxon language and literature, thus explains in his Lowell Lectures (1861) why these works have special value.

The English nation and its writers . . . were not habitually sunk in that humiliating submission to the papacy which long paralyzed the intellectual energy of other Christian races, and restrained them from the discussion of high and noble themes, nor was the occupant of the Roman see regarded with that abject reverence which so often in Continental history bestowed upon him the name and attributes of the Most High.[8]

He strangely contrasts Charles V, who, during the Great Schism (according to Froissart), commanded that the Pope should be obeyed as God on earth, with Wycliffe, "cheered and sustained by many of the nobility as well as commonalty of England," who said that the Pope and clerks should give up worldly lordship. In consequence, English literature had a "'reality and straightforward naturalness of thought and expession not often met with in contemporaneous writings of Germanic or Romance writers."

An ethnic theory underlay and supported the specifically religious idea. Macaulay, in his *History of England*, expressed what was really an old platitude:

[8] George Marsh, *The Origin and History of the English Language, and of the Early Literature It Embodies,* 3d ed. (New York, 1872), p. 7.

The Reformation had been a national as well as a moral revolt. It had been not only an insurrection of the laity against the clergy, but also an insurrection of all the branches of the great German race against an alien domination. It is a most significant circumstance, that no large society of which the tongue is not Teutonic has ever turned Protestant, and that, wherever a language derived from that of ancient Rome is spoken, the religion of modern Rome to this day prevails.

This notion had begun as early as the seventeenth century. The Germanic peoples in general, it came to be assumed, had throughout their history exhibited qualities of courage, intelligence, and love of liberty that peculiarly fitted them to be the defenders of the "Christian liberty" promised in the New Testament, and to advance the cause of religion and civilization. The most important sources were Tacitus' *Germania*, read in a highly partial manner, and Caesar's *Gallic Wars*. We are not concerned here with the relation of this idea to the conception of the primitive English constitution, as Sir William Temple and others had set it forth, but only with its religious involvements. No better exposition of the belief in its full development can be found than John Lothrop Motley's *The Rise of the Dutch Republic*, which might be described as a prose epic of the Reformation. Its immense prestige is indicated by the fact that Motley was early selected to the Hall of Fame, entering it in the class that included Andrew Jackson, Phillips Brooks, Holmes, and Bancroft. His book describes the heroic resistance of a "Gothic" people, closely related ethnically to the Anglo-Saxons, against a tyranny which owed its life and power to the mystical Babylon—the superstition and idolatry foisted on Europe by the "Romish usurpation."

To all who speak the English language, the history of the great agony through which the Republic of Holland was ushered into life must have peculiar interest, for it is a portion of the records of the Anglo-Saxon race—essentially the same, whether in Friesland, England, or Massachusetts.[9]

The history of the Lowlands shows, almost as in a controlled experiment, the inner character of this "race," for

[9] Preface to *The Rise of the Dutch Republic*, in *The Complete Works of John L. Motley* (New York, 1900).

the area during nearly two thousand years has been inhabited by two contrasting peoples, "Celts" and "Germans." "Of these two elements, dissimilar in their tendencies and always difficult to blend, the Netherland people has ever been compounded." [10] Had the two been able to fuse, no nation would have been "more richly endowed by nature for dominion and progress than the Belgo-Germanic people"; but Motley's thesis is that their apparently preordained mental and moral characteristics made such a result impossible, and the Germanic segment seems to have been preserved intact and uncontaminated through many centuries to advance the liberation of mankind.

Point by point, Motley contrasts the two peoples. In government, "The polity of each race differed widely from that of the other. The government of both may be said to have been republican, but the Gallic tribes were aristocracies, in which the influence of clanship was a predominant feature; while the German system, although nominally regal, was in reality democratic." Whereas among the Gauls there were two orders, nobility and priesthood, "while the people, says Caesar, were all slaves," among the Germans "the sovereignty resided in the great assembly of the people."

To be sure, the Gauls seemed to be superior in some ways. They "were an agricultural people," and thus, in the commonly accepted theory of the development of civilization, a step ahead of the Gauls; they built towns and villages. The Germans preferred gaining wealth by conquest, and "the truculent German, Germann, Herr-mann, War-man, considered carnage the only useful occupation, and despised agriculture as enervating and ignoble." But even this apparent blemish had its final cause. "Thus they were more fitted for the roaming and conquering life which Providence was to assign to them for ages than if they had become more prone to root themselves in the soil. . . . The German built his solitary hut where inclination prompted. Close neighborhood was not to his taste." Here are the ancestors of Daniel Boone; "civilized by Christianity," this truculent independence is to become the virtue of the hero of liberty; and it is

<hr />

[10] Motley, *Dutch Republic*, "Historical Introduction," p. 7.

implied in part of the mystique of the frontiersman, who carries his axe and the ark of religious-political liberty ever westward, securing the continent as the homeland of the chosen nation.

Since the heart of the contrast was religious, we find the most striking differences in this area.

The Gauls were a priest-ridden race. . . . What were the principles of their wild theology will never be thoroughly ascertained, but we know too much of its sanguinary rites. The imagination shudders to penetrate those shaggy forests, ringing with the death-shrieks of ten thousand human victims, and with the hideous hymns chanted by smoke-and-blood-stained priests to the savage gods whom they served. . . . The German, in his simplicity, had raised himself to a purer belief than that of the sensuous Roman, or the superstitious Gaul. He believed in a single, supreme, almighty God, All-Vater or All-father. This Divinity was too sublime to be in-carnated or imaged, too infinite to be inclosed in temples built with hands. . . . Their rites were few and simple. They had no caste of priests, nor were they, when first known to the Roman, accustomed to offer sacrifice.

If, later, the Germans sometimes so far forgot themselves as to offer up an occasional prisoner, they had been corrupted by contacts with their neighbors. In short, according to this fanciful account, the German is an embryonic true-blue Protestant; the Celt, a subject ripe for subservience to the great master of superstition.

Despite their surface crudities, the Germans were much the better adapted to create a holy commonwealth. "The Gaul was singularly unchaste. The marriage state was almost unknown. . . . The German was loyal as the Celt was dissolute. Alone among barbarians, he contented himself with a single wife, save that a few dignitaries, from motives of policy, were permitted a larger number." The funeral pomps of the Celts stood in stark contrast with the burials of the Germans. The former burned, with the corpse, many animals, slaves, and dependents; but "The German was not ambitious at the grave. He threw neither garments nor odors upon the funeral pyre, but the arms and the war-horse of the departed were burned and buried with him. The turf was his only sepulcher, the memory of his valor his only monument." Whatever the opinion of the war-horse may have been, such rites point to a more purely spiritual cast of mind and to a brave humility. These Germans were Batavians. In course of time, they disappear as a people, but we find that "the old Batavian element has melted, not to be extinguished, but to live a renovated existence, the 'free Frisians,' whose name is synonymous with liberty, nearest blood-relations of the Anglo-Saxon race."

The lesson of Motley's work and its contemporaneous applications are explicitly stated in the *Prebyterian Quarterly Review*.[11] Motley's reviewer in this instance associates religious and political revolution against tyranny with racial characteristics. There were, he says, three great migrations into Europe from the east. Under their pressure the "Scythian," or Teutonic race crowded the Celts across the Channel. Eventually, the line between the two was drawn "between the Cheldt and the Straits"—that is, in the Lowlands and Germany. In the Batavian marshes, the Teutonic tribes 'developed together a fixed type of character, of which the great elements were intense love of freedom, indomitable valor, steadiness, sobriety, industry, receptivity to culture, sagacious intellectuality."

The Belgians, to the south, on the other hand,

the bravest of the Gallic tribes, exhibited in excess all the qualities of the Celtic race. Vehement, impulsive, reckless; not without industry in the routine of agriculture, but slow to take on improvement; always superstitious, and the mere slaves of a priesthood; passionately addicted to a sensuous religion; an animal, rather than an intellectual or spiritual people; in short a sort of exaggerated or overgrown children, they were wholly unfitted to march in the van of civilization, and therefore, lining as they did the whole Atlantic coast of Europe, they presented a positive obstacle to human progress.

But "the sword of Caesar was the instrument in the hands of Divine Providence for reducing their dangerous numbers within manageable limits."

If this last seems a sanguinary remark from a writer in a

[11] Vol. 7 (1859):654 ff.

major religious journal, one must remember its matrix in apocalyptic: as we have seen, the overcoming of the power of darkness in its many forms does at times require the sword as well as the Word. For—and this is the real point of the review—all these events were preparations for the ultimate destruction of the mystical Babylon to come. From the beginning, royal and priestly forces were allies. The savage priesthood of the early Celts was part of the Antichristian party, and it anticipated in purpose and method the fullness of the "Romish tyranny." As the Germans resisted contamination in tribal times, so even throughout the height of the Papacy, "the brave Frisian stedigners defended their freedom in the marshes of the Weser, till Gregory IX was obliged to preach a crusade against them, and crush out their heresy and their lives together. In the twelfth century, the Poor Men of Lyons gave the people the New Testament, in rude verse to be sure, but written in their own language."

Since the history of mankind is one, there is a meaning for the present moment in all this. First, the history of the Netherlands, the reviewer contends, confutes the "shallowness" of the theories of Buckle and his fellow positivists, that all national differences are due to differences in soil, climate, and other environmental factors; the great determinants are "religion and race." Even though the two peoples lived side by side for centuries, the Celtic Walloons continued to demonstrate the "low grade of civilization, the Celtic inaptitude for culture, the immature childish mental development, which naturally harmonizes with a sensuous religion and the control of a priesthood." Only by "disintegrating" the Celtic race, "grinding it small, and mixing it liberally with other elements," can it be saved from itself: "a process going on very remarkably with reference to one Celtic people in the times passing under our own eyes." The Anglo-Saxon Americans have been called to redeem the Irish immigrants.

The reviewer, of course, hailed *The Rise of the Dutch Republic* not as a brilliant novelty of thought but as scholarly confirmation of an old and deeply believed idea. If the reader is surprised to find such remarks about the Celts in a Presbyterian journal—is not Scotland supposed to be Celtic?

—an explanation is provided in an article that appeared some two years previously. The population of Scotland, like that of the Lowlands, is divided between two ethnic strains. The "Culdee" people, intermingled Gothic and Celtic, for centuries maintained a bastion against the Roman rulers. They occupied the shores of the "German ocean,"—Solway Firth, the Firth of Clyde; they are "the Scottish men of history." [12] "The purer Celts of the centre and northwest" have had little to do with great events; they were "not included within the domain of civilized life . . . but rested beside it, somewhat as the Indian tribes did in the struggles of our people against French and English domination in this continent." But, like the Indians, they could be manipulated as tools of "despotism," for the popish Jacobites made use of them. All—French, Jacobites, and even, on occasion, Church of England supporters—are, in the large view, under one great commander, fighting many wars in many campaigns; and so, on the other side, are the Germanic peoples wherever they have established themselves.

Ideas of this kind were by no means exclusively American; they influenced even Victoria, as items in her Journal show.

The Catholic Irish, even the upper classes, were 'totally unreliable, totally untrue . . . grievances they really have none.' Only 'a new infusion of race' would solve the Irish problem. She had in fact been infected by the Prince Consort with vague racial theories which attributed Scottish superiority to a mixture of Scandinavian blood.[13]

Bushnell gave this kind of theorizing about the qualities of modern "races" an interesting philosophical foundation. He rejected the generally accepted theory that mankind has

---

[12] "Scotland," *Presbyterian Quarterly Review*, 5 (1857):583.
[13] Elizabeth Longford, *Queen Victoria: Born to Succeed* (New York: Harper & Row, Publishers, 1966), p. 366. The Prince Consort apparently sympathized with Protestant attitudes. Victoria, when it was proposed to disestablish the Protestant Church of Ireland, confessed that she felt herself " 'very much a dissenter, or, even more, Presbyterian.' " Apparently she was influenced by the fact that "Prince Albert used to say that the Reformation was left half finished and some day it would have to be completed." *Ibid.*, p. 361.

developed from "primitive" beginnings, through the "hunting," "agricultural," and other levels, to full civilization. American Indians, African tribes, and other "primitives" are, according to this theory, peoples who for some reason have stuck fast in an early stage; to bring them up through the subsequent steps of development is the white man's burden. Bushnell regarded this view as an example of the errors of a purely secular account of mankind. Savages, he said, "are beings, or races physiologically run down, or become effete, under sin; fallen at last below progress, below society, become a herd no longer capable of public organization, and a true social life." [14] For, Bushnell, like Swift, thought the natural movement of society was deterioration rather than advancement. All races began together in a "stage of crudity, or crude capacity," equidistant from the lowest and the highest stage of culture.

"After that they separate, some ascending, led up by their holy seers and law-givers, and others, not having or giving heed to such, going down the scale of penal deteriorations to become savages." The latter can be elevated, or restored, only from without. The secular idea of progress teaches the self-sufficiency and perfectibility of the natural man; but we know from the revelations that "as all society is under sin, it is of course suffering the retributive action of penal causes, and as all discord propagates only greater discord and can not propagate harmony, it follows that the run of society under sin must be downward, from bad to worse, unless interrupted by some remedial agency from without."

In the setting of this kind of thinking, the mission of the Germanic peoples is obvious. Providence has chosen them, not out of ineluctable favoritism, but to prepare them for their conquering-redemptive work among the "undeveloped" or "fallen" races that surround them. Applications of this conception abound; at critical moments, for instance when expansion of the nation was in issue, it moved into the

---

[14] Horace Bushnell, *Nature and the Supernatural, as Together Constituting One System of God*, 5th ed. (New York, 1863) p. 224.

forefront of national thinking.[15] Instances occur in the debate over the recognition of the Republic of Texas, which occurred at a time when the Protestant millennialist theory was especially strong. Here is Senator Benton's description of the rebellion:

Just in its origin, valiant and humane in its conduct, sacred in its object, the Texan revolt has illustrated the Anglo-Saxon character, and given it new titles to the respect and admiration of the world. It shows that liberty, justice, valor—moral, physical, and intellectual power—discriminate that race wherever it goes. Let our America rejoice, let Old England rejoice, that the Brassos and Colorado, new and strange names—streams far beyond the Western bank of the Father of Waters—have felt the impress, and witnessed the exploits of a people sprung from their loins, and carrying their language, laws and customs, their *magna charta* and its glorious privileges, into new regions and far distant climes.[16]

Senator Preston's speech during the same debate made explicit the connection between Anglo-Saxons, Magna Charta, and redemptive mission.

This invader had come at the head of his forces, urged on by no ordinary impulse—by an infuriate fanaticism—by a superstitious catholicism, goaded on by a miserable priesthood, against that invincible Anglo-Saxon race, the van of which now approaches the *del Norte*. It was at once a war of religion and of liberty. And when that noble race engaged in a war, victory was sure to perch upon their standard.[17]

In the context it appears that victory is sure to take up her perch among the Anglo-Saxons not only because of their innate sublime qualities, but because in the destined course of world liberation from darkness, they are taking the leadership.

---

[15] See Albert K. Weinberg, *Manifest Destiny* (1935; reprinted, Chicago: Quadrangle Books, 1963), pp. 369–70. Although Weinberg, like all other writers on the subject, observes that the idea had a religious coloring, he does not see it in its context of apocalyptic interpretations.

[16] Thomas Hart Benton, *Thirty Years View* (New York, 1854), 1:675.

[17] *Ibid.*, p. 665.

Other accounts of the Anglo-Saxon qualities recognized that, in an absolute moral sense, they are not all desirable; but held that these characteristics are the ones adapted to do the divine work at this particular moment in history. Alexander Campbell pointed out that, as biblical history shows, "the *Most High* . . . always took the world as it was in every period in which he chose to develope himself anew, or his purposes." . . .[18] When the conquest of the promised land was necessary, "he chose to appear as the *Lord of Hosts,* or God of Armies." To accomplish his purposes, "he took one nation under his auspices," and became their cammander-in-chief; needless to say, he chose a warlike people. In modern times, the urgent need appears to be for a chosen people again, to finish off the defeat of Antichrist. Such a people, logically, would be aggressive, courageous, naturally restive under despotism, and gifted with ability to organize and lead. These were the characteristics associated with Germanic peoples from Tacitus on. The half-white George Harris, in *Uncle Tom's Cabin,* expresses this opinion:

"To the Anglo-Saxon race has been intrusted the destinies of the world, during its pioneer period of struggle and conflict. To that mission its stern, inflexible, energetic elements were well adapted. But, as a Christian, I look for another era to arise. On its borders I trust we stand; and the throes that now convulse the nations are, to my hope, but the birth-pangs of an hour of universal peace and brotherhood." [Chap. 43]

The belief in the approaching millennium is an essential element of this book. In the time of universal brotherhood, the "hot and hasty Saxon" will not be the man of the era. Then the "Christian calling and mission of our [Negro] race" may come into its own.

If not a dominant and commanding race, they are, at least, an affectionate, magnanimous, and forgiving one. Having been called in the furnace of injustice and oppression, they have need to bind closer to their hearts that sublime doctrine of

---

[18] *Debate on the Evidences of Christianity: Containing an Examination of the "Social System" and of All the Systems of Skepticism of Ancient and Modern Times* (Bethany, 1829), 2:99. (Stenographic report of impromptu speeches.)

love and forgiveness, through which alone they are to conquer, which it is to be their mission to spread over the continent of Africa.

Thus he is confident "that the African race has peculiarities, yet to be unfolded in the light of civilization and Christianity, which, if not the same with those of the Anglo-Saxon, may prove to be, morally, of even a higher type." But it is important to remember that these noble "peculiarities" will flower only under the influence of Christianity; and to bring that influence is the work of the Anglo-Saxon, even if he has greatly wronged the race also. This ambivalence of relationship between the races is an important element in the whole question of slavery, before and after emancipation.

Theodore Parker likewise thought the Negroes may possess a greater natural aptitude than other races for true religion. As for the Anglo-Saxons, Parker also emphasized that their qualities are the very ones required to conquer a new land and to establish the nation of destiny. The five leading "peculiarities of the Anglo-Saxon tribe," he lists as follows:

its exclusive nationality, hostility to other tribes of men; its intense materialism, and unideal, unpoetic character; its great administrative power . . . ; and its remarkable love of individual liberty, which is practically modified by decorum and love of order.[19]

In sum, not a wholly amiable character: but it recalls the traits of the Israelites in the day of Joshua.

2

Milton's encomium of England as having had the honor to "blow the first evangelic trumpet to the nations" was accompanied by a profoundly important *caveat*. In *Of Reformation*, he wrote: "methinks the precedency which God gave this island, to be the first restorer of buried truth, should have been followed with more happy success, and

[19] Parker, *Centenary Edition* (Boston, 1907), 6:349.

sooner attained perfection." For some reason the nation has stopped short of full reform; it is still partially under the spell of Antichrist, and could yet slip back all the way. Milton referred primarily to church discipline, and corruption; but in later times, as Adams intimated, there were added to the charge the failure to extinguish all the feudal institutions, absence of toleration for the sects, and other faults. In other words, England nobly carried on the great work of the Anglo-Saxons—but only up to a point; it seemed that the completion of the task might be reserved for another offshoot of the "German race."

Bushnell (who, perhaps with prophetic foresight, was to decline appointment as first president of the University of California) explained, in a Phi Beta Kappa address, that the time of the discovery of America, combined with the qualities of the race that settled the Atlantic seaboard, points to a special mission of the new republic which is to arise.

There are too many prophetic signs admonishing us, that Almighty Providence is pre-engaged to make this a truly great nation, not to be cheered by them, and go forth, seeking out the principles of national advancement. This western world had not been preserved unknown through so many ages, for any purpose less sublime, than to be opened, at a certain stage of history, and become the theater wherein better principles might have their action and free development. Out of all the inhabitants of the world, too, a select stock, the Saxon, and out of this the British family, the noblest of the stock, was chosen to people our country; that our eagle, like that of the prophet, might have the cedars of Lebanon, and the topmost branches of the cedars, to plant by his great waters.[20]

The combination of the prophetic and the American eagles indicates that this is "a country where God had ennobled the land itself in every feature, filling it with the signs of his own august nobility, and training the people up to spiritual vastness and force by symbols of his own." There is an amalgamation of ideas here. Romantic aesthetics had long

---

[20] Bushnell, "The Principle of National Greatness," An Oration Pronounced before the Society of Phi Beta Kappa, 1837.

assumed that "sublime" spectacles—vast scenes, the sea, great mountains, and so forth—literally had an "expanding" effect on the mind of the beholder; and the New World had long been recognized as the land of the sublime, *par excellence*. Thus, characteristically, interpretations of prophecy enlist current ideas. We are for the first time in a position to understand what the prophets' visions mean in concrete realities.

Parker, after listing the five leading peculiarities of the Anglo-Saxons, goes on to explain how a special group was chosen out of this energetic but, it would seem, not as a whole particularly religious "race":

This religious origin has marked New England hitherto, and will distinguish her and her descendants for centuries to come. She is the daughter of a great idea, and the mother of yet greater. . . . It was the most spiritual part of the old Anglo-Saxons which came over, the least materialistic, the most ideal, the most devout; a little maddened by oppression, no doubt, but fired too with great thoughts of duty to God and the destination before man.[21]

By a kind of providential selection, a special group within a group was chosen—a group, as the last phrase implies, fired by expectations of the Kingdom.

The notion that the inhabitants of the new republic have been selected to carry on and probably to complete the racial mission was more than an American chauvinism, however naïve and well-meaning. The eminent Prussian historian and administrator Frederick von Raumer, who later represented the Frankfurt Parliament in Paris, visited the United States in 1845. In a book written, it should be noted, in his own language for his own countrymen, he thus describes the world-saving mission of the American Anglo-Saxons:

While there is but little hope of a new and more extended development of humanity in Asia and Africa, how sickly do many parts of Europe appear! If we were forced to despair

[21] Parker, *Centenary Edition*, 6:350.

too of the future progress of the Germanic race in America, whither could we turn our eyes for deliverance, except to a new and direct creation from the hand of the Almighty! [22]

After describing the "cheering sun of liberty" which "is now scattering its effulgent beams over all the habitations of men," confounding "scowling despots" who would persuade them that "it is but a scorching and devouring flame," he tells the Germans:

The Anglo-Saxon offshoot of the great northern family of nations has long basked and thriven in this sunshine of the soul. The glistening eyes of Germans and Scandinavians look upon the success and happiness of their more fortunate kinsmen with feelings, not of envy, but of honest pride and emulation.

To those Europeans who say the Americans "have no antiquity and no monuments, no youth and no poetry, no literature and no art," he replies in language that matches the most extreme hopes of Emerson and Thoreau:

America has no monuments, it is true; but she has a nature which joins all the venerableness of age to the elastic vigor of youth. And do pyramids, and colossusses, and robber-castles exhibit more the value and progress of art, or the misery which tyranny ever produces? The poetry of the Americans lies not in the past but in the future. We Europeans go back in sentiment through the twilight of ages, that lose themselves in night; the Americans go forward through the morning dawn to day! Their great, undoubted, historical past lies near them; their *fathers* did great things, not their *great-great-grandfathers!*

No less a writer than Herman Melville, in the book that preceded *Moby Dick*, summarizes the doctrine in all its implications and ramifications, and his statement deserves quotation at length:

Escaped from the house of bondage, Israel of old did not follow after the ways of the Egyptians. To her was given an express dispensation; to her were given new things under the sun. And we Americans are the peculiar, chosen people—the Israel of our time; we bear the ark of the liberties of the

[22] Von Raumer, *America and the American People*, trans. W. W. Turner (New York, 1846), "Author's Preface."

world. Seventy years ago we escaped from thrall; and,
besides our first birth-right—embracing one continent of earth
—God has given to us, for a future inheritance, the broad
domains of the political pagans, that shall yet come and lie
down under the shade of our ark, without bloody hands
being lifted. God has predestined, mankind expects, great things
from our race; and great things we feel in our souls. The rest
of the nations must soon be in our rear. We are the pioneers
of the world; the advance-guard, sent on through the wilderness of untried things, to break a new path in the New World
that is ours. In our youth is our strength; in our inexperience,
our wisdom. At a period when other nations have but lisped,
our deep voice is heard afar. Long enough have we been
sceptics with regard to ourselves, and doubted whether, indeed,
the political Messiah had come. But he has come in *us*, if we
would but give utterance to his promptings. And let us always
remember that with ourselves, almost for the first time in the
history of earth, national selfishness is unbounded philanthropy;
for we cannot do a good to America, but we give alms to the
world.[23]

The extended parallel between historical Israel and the
United States has vastly important corollaries. As the Israelites were given the land of the pagans, so the last chosen
people has been given a rich continent for its heritage. Since
the past has been largely the record of the rule of darkness,
its wisdom is largely darkness, too; the present bearers of the
ark, therefore, must discover their own wisdom, which will
eventually enlighten the world. Newness is a mark of the
calling; the barbaric yawp may be a sign not of crudity but
of renewal.

Melville could, moreover, draw an extreme conclusion
which must have occurred to theological commentators, but
which they might well have hesitated to express. The ancient Jewish apocalyptic had assumed that a mysterious
hero, the "Son of man," would be the agent inaugurating
the heavenly order (see Daniel 7:13–14). Since, of course,
the millennialists assumed that the Parousia would not occur

---

[23] *White Jacket*, chap. 36. Many years later, in *Clarel*, there
seems to be a profound disillusionment with these high
expectations.

until after the millennium, this apocalyptic figure must be allegorical. But could not a *nation* perform this function? Is the American people to be the "messiah" of the transformation? Certainly the tone of many utterances about the American mission would be consonant with such a conception, bold as it it. Finally, in consequence, the welfare of this "peculiar" people must be identical with that of mankind; what seems "national selfishness" is in the end "unbounded philanthropy."

Indeed, Americans could hardly fail to have exalted ideas of their calling when they heard expressions from Europeans such as this from the great English preacher Richard Price:

It is a conviction I cannot resist, that the independence of the *English* colonies in America is one of the steps ordained by Providence to introduce these times [the last, universal empire predicted in Scripture]. . . . it will be true of them as it was of the people of the Jews, that *in them all the families of the earth shall be blessed.* It is scarcely possible they should think too highly of their own consequence. Perhaps, there never existed a people on whose wisdom and virtue more depended; or to whom a station of more importance in the plan of Providence has been assigned.[24]

But he proceeds to set forth a long list of warnings against the terrible risks and temptations such a peculiar people must experience. The conviction that one is called to play a supremely important and demanding part can result in tensions and even neurosis; and the same thing may be true of nations as well.

For Americans there was always the awful and baffling question, what is the chosen people to *do?* The prophecies might point to them, but were silent, to a large extent, about their exact functions. This problem has constantly been in the background and often in the foreground of the great political debates of our history. In the controversies over expansion, isolation, colonies, entry into foreign wars, aboli-

---

[24] Price, *Observations on the Importance of the American Revolution, and the Means of Making It a Benefit to the World* (London, 1784), p. 7.

tion, even prohibition—again and again it has been at least implied. We must behave, not as just a prudent and well-meaning nation but as a "peculiar people."

In general, the millennial mission could be thought of in two opposing ways. One, by far the more popular, saw it as wholly peaceful (so Melville seems to think of it). Its example, its very existence, could work a transformation in minds all over the world. The decay of mystical Babylon, a process already well advanced, would go forward with increased speed as more and more nations threw off their bonds and followed the democratic path of the pioneer. Wars among the remnants of the lands under Antichrist, which were accounted as among the events predicted by the pouring out of the last vials, would further weaken the old regimes and make the final revolutions easy. The "shade of the ark" will be enough. Two duties are clearly indicated: to expand and perfect a society which is closer to the millennial condition than any before it; and to maintain an integrity unknown previously in any other country, to eliminate remaining vestiges of the old evils, to avoid the temptations which the power of darkness is undoubtedly preparing for us. Added to these was some mission of active enlightenment. For a religious time, this consisted in using American wealth and American energy for world "benevolence," of which the greatest service was to "evangelize the world" right speedily.

On the other hand, it was possible that the United States would have to participate in the destructive events predicted before the millennium. The question had already been asked, as we have seen: can nations so completely under the domination of tyranny, so "subservient" by racial heredity, succeed in accomplishing their liberation by their own efforts? If a great and bloody battle is yet to take place, can the millennial country stay aloof? Or would our attempt to intervene lead us into a clever trap, designed to pull us back into Satan's own game of power politics, and make us forget our mission of world beneficence? Similarly, is expansion of American territory, especially into colonies, is the "white man's burden" a means of extending enlightenment or merely another trap, causing us to disguise mere self-interest under pious professions? The debate over our acquisition of the Philippines perfectly reflected these divergent questions.

One of the most important theories about the American role in future history was set forth in an address Motley gave before the New York Historical Society, December 1868. History, he says, obviously is no pointless sequence of happenings. It is governed by the "law of progress"—"slow, confused, contradictory, but ceaseless development, intellectual and moral, of the human race." [25] It soon becomes evident, however, that this is not the "law of progress" of Buckle or Spencer. The real determinant of historical events and their timing is "destiny," a secularized name for "Providence." The "law of progress" is a theory of history, millennialist in form, expressed in "scientific" terms. The United States appears as the chosen nation, and it is described in language reminiscent of Meville's.

This nation stands on the point towards which other peoples are moving—the starting-point, not the goal. It has put itself— or rather Destiny has put it—more immediately than other nations in subordination to the law governing all bodies political as inexorably as Kepler's law controls the motions of the planets.

We occupy this foremost position "mainly from the bounty of heaven,"—which consists in our location in the temperate zone, without which circumstance the area might have been inhabited by "wandering savages or broods of speechless reptiles." It appears, however, that this "bounty" is not pointless. The continent, "long hidden in entranced sleep within primeval forest," was discovered at just the right moment. Everything is predestined. "The orbit of civilization"

seems preordained from East to West. . . . China, India, Palestine, Egypt, Greece, Rome, are successively lighted up as the majestic orb of day moves over them; and as he advances still further through his storied and mysterious Zodiac, we

[25] Motley, *Historic Progress and American Democracy* (New York, 1869), p. 6.

behold the shadows of evening as surely falling on the lands
which he leaves behind him.[26]

Anyone familiar with all Motley's work would immediately know why the discovery had come at just the right
moment: for it immediately preceded the Reformation, the
pivot and climax of history. This decisive revolution struck
at the cooperating religious and secular tyrannies. The great
work, however, was balked of much of its proper results,
for even in Protestant countries princes established the formula "Cujus regio, ejus religio" and "Church and State
maintained their incestuous union." The liberation could go
only so far in the Old World; to a new, uncorrupted state it
has been given to complete the emancipation of mankind.
Geography, date of discovery, racial character of the settlers, all have been destined to accomplish this result. Motley's answer to the question, How is world liberation to be
completed? involves a mystical process not unlike the operation of grace. ". . . there is an electric chain by which all
humanity is darkly bound. It is impossible for one nation to
acquire without acquiring for all—for one great member of
the human family to advance or to retrograde without has-
tening or retarding the general march of humanity.[27] Here
the assumption that mankind is a mystical body is given
something like a scientific form. One striking illustration of
the working of this chain is the fact that in Britain a Tory
government, no doubt influenced by American example, has
recently passed an electoral reform bill. England once again
is becoming a partner with her old colony in the liberation
of humanity; both, after all, are "children of the ancient
German mother."

If American democracy is the single most important influence, there are other ways in which the new society is
revolutionizing the world. One is American inventiveness
and initiative. The steam engine, telegraph, free school, and
"that immense instrument of civilization, the daily press,"
although not strictly speaking all American devices, had

[26] *Ibid.*, pp. 21–22.
[27] *Ibid.*, p. 19.

been waiting to appear until the new nation "could show their value on an immense scale." Millennialists, of course, had for decades cited such improvements in technology and institutions as effective means of destroying the superstition on which the mystical Babylon rested, and had recalled the apocalyptic prediction that "many shall run to and fro, and knowledge shall be increased" (Dan. 12:4).

The second contribution of the United States is due to its unique geographical blessing. Where such innovations as the telegraph have made democracy possible on a huge scale, adumbrating the universal state to come, the vast area of the West, waiting to be peopled, makes it possible for this country to exemplify, for the first time, a whole great nation in the shape of a pyramid resting on its base and not on the apex. (Motley assumes that the shape of the pyramid will, however, continue; presumably some kind of aristocracy, of merit and intellect, will endure.) The mission of the United States is now to continue working, harder than ever, to build the largest, most successful, most impressive democratic Protestant state the world has ever seen. And, I think, there is the implication that this great nation will be the monolith not cut by human hands that destroyed the image in Nebuchadnezzar's dream; the great democracy may overwhelm the kingdoms of darkness by its sheer weight, physical and moral.

The United States, furthermore, has earned its position by a great sacrifice—a purging, in its own blood, of its own remaining evil. The generic name of the Enemy is, Motley says, "privilege." Even the new land has been cursed by one remaining form of this evil—slavery. Although its destruction has purified the American people, the effects extend to the whole human race:

The inestimable blessing of the abolition of slavery to the cause of progress, above all to the South itself, can never be exaggerated. The fetters have fallen not from the black alone, but from the white, from all mankind. The standing reproach to Democracy is removed at last, and the basis of our national institutions has become an everlasting truth.[28]

[28] *Ibid.*, p. 69.

The address was not perfervid political rhetoric, but a statement of faith by a famous historian-diplomat to the most prestigious historical society in the United States. It is the more surprising, then, to realize that this idyllic account of the state of the nation—not only as some future possibility, but as existing fact—was delivered at the close of one of the murkiest administrations on record. Motley himself had been summarily recalled as ambassador to Austria because of some disagreement with the reconstruction policies of Andrew Johnson. How, at such a moment, could so experienced a man soberly assert that the United States was the paragon of nations, the high point of history, and that even Mammon, for the first time, had been transformed into a force for good, providing means to save the nation and to "relieve distress, or foster Science and Art"? And indeed an Englishman, one H. Bragg, hastened to ask this very question. He quotes the *New York Herald*, April 17, 1869: " '. . . the administration of the government has become in every department the most corrupt and extravagant one on the face of the earth.' " [29] Sour notes in the millennial symphony are heard from the "whisky ring," the "Pacific Railroad ring," the "National Bank ring," and other quarters. Even the Civil War itself, that apocalyptic conflict, was accompanied by massive profiteering; and, far from being purified by that war, the republic is wallowing in more extravagance and mismanagement than ever before. And, however fair the theory, the fact is that the western utopia is acting strangely like the old, selfish countries. For instance,

. . . the original owner of the soil—the Mohawk, Seminole, or Cheyenne—is dealt with very much after the manner in which Marshal Bugeaud dealt with the troublesome Arab tribes in Algeria; and no better than we have treated the Indoos; . . . (and yet the voice of protest is seldom heard there-against from either New or Old England philanthropist).[30]

Although British leaders, including John Bright and Goldwin Smith, cry "Amen" to this glorification of the Union,

[29] Bragg, *Under Which King, Bezonian?* (London, 1869), p. 3.
[30] *Ibid.*, p. 11.

they too are moved by faith, not observation. For them, it would seem, "there was in fact only one thing wanted to make the Republic an Arcadia, and that was Saint Patrick. If in its early days there had been one to banish human infirmities and their consequences from its area forever the Great Republic would have been, what it is even now, A Wonder." [31] The author is not out to denigrate the United States. The republic, as he observes, does have many virtues and in some respects does represent an advance over anything Europe has attained. But some of the advantages are simply accidents of history, and it is misleading to attribute them to some superiority of American character. Great areas of unsettled land, still existing in the West, have prevented American cities from becoming so desperately crowded as those of the Old World; but this good fortune inevitably will end as population increases, and in time the new nation will have the mass poverty so well known in England and France.

These strictures were at least partially justified. The United States had come to possess, in its own eyes and in those of many Europeans, an unreal image. Since world redemption is approaching, and since the newest great state must be the last in the succession of empires, it *must* represent the closest approach to perfection mankind has yet attained; it must be at least a proto-millennium. Its very real virtues were magnified and given a providential source. Exaggeratedly great expectations, disappointed, always produce great disillusionments. When it came to be realized that this nation, with all its contributions, also had faults like those of other peoples, that it was not a society close to the millennium and the agent of Providence, it came, by reaction, to seem something monstrous. If it did not embody the mystery of redemption, then it must be nothing less than the mystery of iniquity. The apocalyptic conception of history undoubtedly exacerbated the reaction. Even so moderate and sensible a theologian as Henry Boynton Smith regarded the historical process as a series of conflicts between "sin and holiness," into which "all other conflicts may be re-

[31] *Ibid.*, p. 39.

solved." [32] When it became evident that the United States had its quota of rascals and hypocrites (but no more than its share, certainly) there was a tendency to move it, so to speak, from the side of light to that of darkness. And in fact the United States has seldom been realistically evaluated; it has been either fantastically exalted or extravagantly condemned.

3

Josiah Strong, as we have seen, devoted his entire career to arousing the United States to awareness of its unique mission and unique dangers. His magnum opus, *Our Country: Its Possible Future and Its Present Crisis* (1886), was an expansion and rewriting of a manual that the Home Missionary Society had first published in 1842. By 1916, *Our Country* had sold 175,000 copies, and individual chapters had been reprinted innumerable times in newspapers and magazines. As its recent editor says, "The book . . . mirrors the thoughts and aspirations of this dominant segment [Protestant] of American society towards the close of the nineteenth century, and it is therefore a historical document of major importance." [33]

Providence, Strong demonstrated with a variety of instances, is moving to "Anglo-Saxonize" mankind; and the American branch of the "race" is the most fully adapted to perform the work. The American people, however, is not English. It is "the result of a finer nervous organization, which is certainly being developed in this country." Providence has brought forth out of the old German stock a new type, fitted especially to consummate the work of world redemption: ". . . at once more delicate and more enduring, more sensitive to weariness and yet more patient of toil, impressible, but capable of bearing powerful irritation; we are woven of finer fiber, which, though apparently frail, yet outlasts the coarser." [34] It would be interesting to observe

[32] Smith, "The Problem of the Philosophy of History," p. 26.
[33] Strong, *Our Country*, ed. Jergen Herbst (Cambridge: Harvard University Press, 1963), p. ix.
[34] *Ibid.*, p. 208.

how far this kind of paradoxical ideal is embodied in such heroes as Owen Wister's "the Virginian."

Strong, as we should expect, gives a résumé of the racial doctrine. "Greater Britain" has come out of "Great Britain." The Anglo-Saxon, culminating in the American, has developed two related ideas: civil liberty (the Anglo-Saxon has refined the old truculent German love of freedom); and "the idea of a pure *spiritual* Christianity" ("it was no accident that the great reformation of the sixteenth century originated among a Teutonic, rather than a Latin people."). But Strong's conception of the "American" is far from simple or consistent; Americans have, he says, a "mixed origin." Finley Peter Dunne, in his famous Mr. Dooley sketch "On the Anglo-Saxon" satirized the idea: the Hibernians, the "Dagos," even the "Poles" are now beginning to "raise their Anglo-Saxon battle-cry."

But, if the Anglo-Saxon "race" is to comprehend the best from all parts of the earth, the melting pot is not to blend the various native characteristics of these diverse peoples. The "mold" in which they are all to be remade is the perfected form of the Germanic and its outgrowth, Anglo-Saxon. On this people the whole course of history has converged, and Strong's language makes clear that they have a really messianic mission. "It would seem as if these inferior tribes [for example, American Indians] were only precursors of a superior race, voices in the wilderness crying: 'Prepare ye the way of the Lord.' " [35] How carefully all this has been ordained is indicated in Strong's theory of complementary action:

Thus, while on this continent God is training the Anglo-Saxon race for its mission, a complemental work has been in progress in the great world beyond. God has two hands. Not only is he preparing in our civilization the die with which to stamp the nations, but, by what Southey called the 'timing of Providence,' he is preparing mankind to receive our impress. Is there any room for reasonable doubt that this race, unless devitalized by alcohol and tobacco, is destined to dispossess many weaker races, assimilate others, and mold the remainder, until, in a

[35] *Ibid.*, p. 176.

very true and important sense, it has Anglo-Saxonized man-kind?

And, as the following statement indicates, Strong is restating and extending ideas of his predecessors: "Thus, in what Dr. Bushnell calls 'the out-populating power of the Christian stock' may be found God's final and complete solution of the dark problem of heathenism among many inferior peoples." [36] The phrase "final and complete solution" now has an ominous ring, and it hints at the kind of blatant racism that could easily emerge from such theorizing; but it is unfair to call Strong a racist. He did not intend to exalt Anglo-Saxons as ideal and vastly superior beings in themselves; to him they were or should be servants, instruments for the accomplishment of beneficent changes in all men. "I do not imagine that the Anglo-Saxon is any dearer to God than a Mongolian or an African. My plea is not, Save America for America's sake, but, Save America for the world's sake." [37] For, we now can clearly see,

. . . the world is evidently about to enter on a new era . . . in this era mankind is to come more and more under Anglo-Saxon influence, and Anglo-Saxon civilization is more favorable than any other to the spread of those principles whose universal triumph is necessary to that perfection of the race to which it is destined; the entire realization of which will be the kingdom of heaven fully come on earth.

The three great periods, we find, are the Incarnation, the German Reformation of the sixteenth century, and the "closing years of the nineteenth century." [38] The first two have made possible the climactic third. And everything points to the conclusion that the presently world-dominant race is so by design, since it has been "especially commissioned to prepare the way for the full coming of God's kingdom in the earth." [39]

But sounding the trumpet was only part of Strong's purpose; he was just as intent on warning his contemporaries

[36] *Ibid.*, p. 177.
[37] Strong, *The New Era*, p. 80.
[38] Strong, *Our Country*, p. 1.
[39] *The New Era*, p. 69.

that the powers of evil, fully cognizant of the divine plan, were strenuously working to corrupt the millennial people from within; for "both good and evil have a longer leverage in the United States than anywhere else in the world."[40] This menace intensified his awareness of social evils. The most important, threatening not only the nation itself but the accomplishment of the great plan for the world, were "the saloon," tobacco, and the infiltration of "inferior stock." Strong realized also that the rapid growth of poverty in large cities threatened to lower this blessed country to the level of moral degradation that so long had cursed England and France. Satan's power was being more and more concentrated on this peculiar people. Resolute attack on every kind of social wrong was required. But Strong was of the apocalyptic tradition in that he still saw these things as just evils, and not problems; in every situation, there was a force to be defeated, an army to be annihilated. Thus the saloon was not a symptom of an underlying disease, but the work of a diabolical conspiracy, to be put down as an enemy is put down. Strong, like most other Protestant leaders, regarded "Demon Rum" as no mere metaphor: he *was* a demon, with his dark cohorts, as surely as the "Papal usurpation," and in fact there was thought to be a sinister connection between Catholic Irish saloon-keepers, corrupt politicians of the same general allegiance, and the "conspiracy of Rome." "Rum, Romanism, and rebellion" was no chance product of campaign rhetoric, but the epitome of what many regarded as a real alliance.

The redemptive people had responsibilities at home as well as in the world at large. We have seen how the Celtic immigrants, divided into small groups, are to be rescued from their ethnic weakness and assimilated. A further point, as we have seen too, is that by a kind of magnetism the New World will attract the naturally independent elements from all nations. Just as Parker assumed that the "most spiritual" element of the Anglo-Saxons had fled to New England, so the select from other lands will become adoptive Anglo-

[40] *Ibid.*, p. 80.

Saxons. Timothy Dwight, addressing "Columbia," foresaw
such a process:

> To thee, the last refuge of virtue design'd,
> Shall fly from all nations the best of mankind;
> Here, grateful to heaven, with transport shall bring
> Their incense, more fragrant than odours of spring.[41]

There will be an ingathering of the saving remnant, who
will not only seek "refuge" but prepare to perform heroic,
though vaguely specified acts of deliverance:

> To conquest, and slaughter, let Europe aspire;
> Whelm nations in blood, and wrap cities in fire;
> Thy heroes the rights of mankind shall defend,
> And triumphs pursue them, and glory attend.

This Union is destined to reign, in something more than a
figurative sense, over a world on which peace has been
imposed:

> As the day-spring unbounded, thy splendour shall flow,
> And earth's little kingdoms before thee shall bow;
> While the ensigns of union, in triumph unfurl'd,
> Hush the tumult of war, and give peace to the world.

Dwight comes close to intimating that this is the reign of the
saints.

But, as Strong says, the leverage of good and evil is
greater here than anywhere else. How necessary, therefore,
it is for the American people to be brisk and alert! His ideas,
in fact, were old. Lyman Beecher's famous tract *A Plea for
the West*, many years earlier, reviewed both the challenges
and the pitfalls of a chosen people. The text is a verse which
seems to be not only appropriate but specifically intended to
foretell the course of American history: "Who hath heard
such a thing? who hath seen such things? Shall the earth be
made to bring forth in one day? Or shall a nation be born at
once? for as soon as Zion travailed, she brought forth her
children" (Isa. 66:8). The message of Isaiah for both chosen

---

[41] Dwight, "Columbia," in *The Columbian Muse* (Philadelphia, 1794).

peoples is, Beecher says, that "when the time to favor Zion comes, it shall outrun all past analogies of moral causes, as if seed-time and harvest should instantly meet on the same field, or a nation should instantly rush up from barbarism to civilization." [42] The long centuries of maturing which other nations have experienced are denied to this final nation, since its work must be performed so soon and so rapidly. ". . . I consider the text as a prediction of the rapid and universal extension of civil and religious liberty, introductory to the triumphs of universal Christianity." Yet superstition and feudalism are still very strong; not for nothing do we recall that "revolutions and distress of nations" must occur before the reign of peace can begin. But, whatever may be required, the United States is assigned the star role: "It is clear that everything comes to a focus on this republic. It was the opinion of Edwards, that the millennium would commence in America. When I first encountered this opinion, I though it chimerical; but all providential developments since, and all the existing signs of the times lend corroboration to it." [43] Comparison of the nature of the ordained task and the capabilities of the various nations leaves no room for doubt that none in the Old World has what is needed; we cannot avoid destiny.

What nation is blessed with such experimental knowledge of free institutions, with such facilities and resources of communication, unobstructed by so few obstacles as our own? There is not a nation upon earth which, in fifty years, can by all possible reformation place itself in circumstances so favorable as our own for the free unembarrassed application of physical effort and pecuniary and moral power to evangelize the world.

There is that sense of a rapidly approaching paramount crisis which seems to pervade the nineteenth century—due, I think, in some measure to the millennialist theories.

But if this nation is, in the providence of God, destined to lead the way in the moral and political emancipation of the world, it is time she understood her high calling, and were harnessed for the work. For mighty causes, like floods from

[42] Beecher, *A Plea for the West* (Cincinnati, 1835), p. 8.
[43] *Ibid.*, p. 10.

distant mountains, are rushing with accumulating power to
their consummation of good or evil, and soon our character
and destiny will be stereotyped for ever.

The mystique of the westward movement (discussed in
the preceding chapter of this book) is of central importance
in our calling: "It is equally plain that the religious and
political destiny of our nation is to be decided in the
West." [44] Beecher hoped that Ohio, whence this clarion call
emanated, would be a center and symbol of the spiritual
preeminence of the West. Lane Theological Seminary, in
Cincinnati, of which Beecher became president, sent forth a
stream of preachers imbued with this vision of the mission
of the church and of America; Josiah Strong, for example,
graduated from this institution.

How terrible are the penalties if a chosen people fail its
calling, the Old Testament warns us. If, for example, the
nation should break up (like the kingdom of Israel), if the
"great experiment of self-government," which is part of the
preparation for the millennium, should fail, "the descent of
desolation will correspond with the past elevation." [45]
Beecher's vision of that desolation anticipates the peroration
to Webster's Seventh of March speech: "May God hide me
from the day when the dying agonies of my country shall
begin! O thou beloved land! bound together by the ties of
brotherhood and common interest, and perils, live forever—one and undivided!" Unlike Webster, however,
Beecher cries out not only as a patriot but, even more
poignantly, as a minister who believes that God can transform the world and select his own instruments for doing so;
the failure of the United States, the chosen heir of the
Reformation, would call into question the whole prophetic
plan and with it the faith to which Beecher's life was dedicated.

One of the frequent themes of the millennialists, as I have
indicated, was that the perils to the chosen nation are largely
if not entirely internal. Even Walt Whitman stated, in *Democratic Vistas*, that "America, if eligible at all to downfall

[44] *Ibid.*, p. 11.
[45] *Ibid.*, p. 44.

and ruin, is eligible within herself, not without; for I see clearly that the combined foreign world could not beat her down." Such an idea, of course, recalls the common theme of the Old Testament prophets, that when Israel was defeated, it was because of her failure to obey God's will; when she kept her part of the covenant, the God of Battles would certainly keep his. The fear that the republic, still weak as it was in arms, could be defeated by the great foreign powers, hardly figures in the warnings of the modern prophets; but corruption and subversion by papal sympathizers replace Jezebel and Baal of old.

The Anglo-Saxon oneness and determination, triumphantly manifested for so many centuries, may be weakened by infiltration. Mobs of immigrants from the old lands of darkness, Beecher fears, are thoroughly indoctrinated with ideas of double allegiance—to their homeland and old church as well as to the republic. "It is not the *northern* hive, but the *whole* hive which is swarming out upon our cities and unoccupied territory as the effect of overstocked population, of civil oppression, of crime and poverty, and political and ecclesiastical design." [46] It was the political and ecclesiastical design that most worried him. Despotism and feudalism center in the "Roman apostacy," he says in the conventional terms, and such power is always found "contending against the civil and religious rights of man." This apostacy extinguished the remains of Roman liberty, and "warred for thirty years against the resurrection of civil and religious liberty in modern Europe, and holds now the mind in unmitigated bondage wherever its power is unbroken, and is the mainstay of opposition to the efforts of European patriots to break the yoke and ameliorate the condition of man." [47] He refers to the Boston riots. "Has it come to this?—that the capital of New England has been thrown into consternation by the threats of a Catholic mob, and that her temples and mansions stand only through the forbearance of a Catholic bishop?" [48] The spread of Catholic

[46] *Ibid.*, p. 69.
[47] *Ibid.*, p. 71.
[48] *Ibid.*, p. 91.

schools, especially those operated by the old bogies the Jesuits, is alarming. They will indoctrinate many of the immigrants' children in the old notions of the supremacy of church over state, and the old virus will take on new vigor in this new body. Yet we cannot even consider forcibly repressing them; to do so would soon reduce Protestantism itself to the level of the old persecuting church. Perhaps Satan's deep plan is to tempt us to make this fatal mistake. The only safe course is a "medium between denunciation and implicit charity." [49] If this nation is to continue to be both a refuge for the best and the home of a select people, immigration must be controlled, not prohibited. Why, he asks, should the makers of our constitution have been so careful to set up checks and balances to prevent tyranny, if we are to show "such reckless improvidence in exposing [our institutions], unwatched, to the most powerful adverse influence which can be brought to bear upon them from abroad?" But here we come upon the essence of the American dilemma. Its greatest defense is its preservation from most of the old contaminations; but it cannot be a hermit nation, for its mission calls it to save the corrupted world. It cannot rest content in its own happiness, maintaining its integrity by dismissing the Old World with "A plague on both your houses." It must be Zion and not Eden.

Woodrow Wilson was brought up in a manse, where the millennialist ideas must have been heard; and he lived in an atmosphere permeated by such expressions of faith as this, from *The Princeton Review:* ". . . in the book of Revelation the fall of the great Antichristian power is described in terms which are largely borrowed from the Old Testament predictions of the overthrow of Babylon. It is really an old enemy revived in a new dress, and the spirit of ancient prophecy demands its destruction." [50] In 1880, President Noah Porter of Yale College, in a critique of Herbert Spencer, called for a sociology guided by religion and looking forward to a real and expected utopia. It is to be expected because it is no mere construct of unaided human

[49] *Ibid.*, p. 162.
[50] *Princeton Review*, 2d ser., 34 (1862):575.

reason and theory, but the assured end of God's ways with men:

[The sociologist] would also find the amplest reason to believe that in the kingdom of God, which God is even now developing on the earth by natural forces under supernatural guidance, the perfect society will at last be real on the earth, and the science of Sociology will be illustrated in a living example when the tabernacle of God shall be with men, and he will dwell with them, and they shall be his people, and God himself shall be with them and be their God.[51]

In the same issue of *The Princeton Review* was another article on the same subject, by the Swiss philosopher Frederick Godet.

Do we see in thought, advancing upon the theatre of a purified earth, the majestic band of the fellow-workers with God?— here the manufacturers, authors of a world of wonders which shall eclipse these numberless masterpieces which we here behold; there the merchants, who, in the midst of universal peace, will enrich the entire globe with the precious products of every part; . . . organizers of social life, the guides of that public administration which maintains order in all these spheres. . . . All this army of free workers is moving under the influence of a single inspiration, the spirit of a holy love, toward a single end, placed high enough to be the end for all, and low enough to be incarnated immediately in the world of each. . . . Here is the collective destination. It is the kingdom of God in man, or, if you prefer it, of man in God. And, as the result, the earth transformed into heaven—that is to say, heaven realized on the earth.[52]

What greater work could there be than to use the "natural forces" of politics, hitherto usually a curse, to forward the advance toward the promised time! And in the Great War, which seemed spontaneously to be called "Armageddon," it would be logical to see the opportunity Dwight had foreseen so long before, to "Hush the tumult of war, and give peace to the world." I do not, of course, suggest that Wilson fully subscribed to all the articles of faith I have described.

<hr>

[51] *Princeton Review*, 4th ser., 6 (1880):296.
[52] Godet, "The Ultimate Design of Man," *Princeton Review*, 4th ser., 6 (1880):297.

But, in a time when even Roosevelt could speak of standing at Armageddon and fighting for the Lord, it is difficult to think that one with Wilson's background of religion and idealism could have failed to be substantially affected by the atmosphere of American millennialism. I doubt that, if he had not been so influenced, he could have written the following lines; in them his eloquence gave classical expression to the best of the millennialist vision for the United States.

I have no doubt that many a simple soul has been thrilled by that great statue standing in the harbor of New York and seeming to lift the light of liberty for the guidance of the feet of men; and I can imagine that they have expected here some ideal in the treatment that they will receive, some ideal in the laws which they would live under. . . . It is easy, my fellow citizens, to communicate physical lessons, but it is very difficult to communicate spiritual lessons. America was intended to be a spirit among the nations of the world.[53]

A Note on The Millennial Beliefs of the Latter-Day Saints

One of the most conspicuous American religious groups holding a belief in the literal fulfillment of prophecies regarding the millennium is the Church of Jesus Christ of Latter-Day Saints. It is difficult to fit the Latter-Day Saints into the pattern of millennialism, as I have defined it, for essentially they maintain a millenarian doctrine. (See chapter 2, part 1 above, and footnote 11 thereto.) Yet, if they fit awkwardly into the full movement I have described, they cannot, like the Millerites for example, be completely excluded, either. For the setting of the ideas Joseph Smith and his disciples promulgated reflects in many important ways the kind of optimism, the confidence in the progressive defeat of evil by God's power in this world, and the convic-

---

[53] Wilson, Address, 13 July 1916, in *The New Democracy, Presidential Messages, Addresses, and Other Papers*, ed. Ray S. Baker and William E. Dodd (New York, 1926), 2:248.

tion that the American republic has been called to do a
unique work, that their contemporaries displayed. Theirs is
a uniquely *American* form of millenarianism. Unlike the
common run of those who expect the return of Christ in
person, they surround the Parousia with hopeful expectations about world progress; they certainly do not think that
the course of history is one of increasing decline, which can
be ended only by the personal intervention of the Lord.
And their belief that "Zion" is to be located somewhere in
the American West is a segment of our continental
thinking.

The tenth of "The Articles of Faith of the Church of
Jesus Christ of Latter-Day Saints" thus defines the official
dogma:

> We believe in the literal gathering of Israel and in the restora-
> tion of the Ten Tribes; that Zion will be built upon this
> [North American] continent; that Christ will reign personally
> upon the earth; and that the earth will be renewed and receive
> its paradisaical glory.

The prophecy of Enoch, said to have been revealed to the
prophet Joseph Smith, is as follows:

> And the day shall come that the earth shall rest, but before that
> day the heavens shall be darkened, and a veil of darkness
> shall cover the earth; and the heavens shall shake, and also the
> earth; and great tribulations shall be among the children of men,
> but my people will I preserve; . . . and righteousness and
> truth will I cause to sweep the earth as with a flood, to gather
> out mine elect from the four quarters of the earth, unto a place
> which I shall prepare, an Holy City, that my people may
> gird up their loins, and be looking forth for the time of my
> coming; for there shall be my tabernacle, and it shall be called
> Zion, a New Jerusalem.
>
> [The Book of Moses, 7:16 ff.]

The companions of the prophet, however, explain that
"Zion" and the "New Jerusalem" are in fact separate places,
an ocean apart. Thus Orson Pratt says that the Jews, eventually to be converted, will reconstruct the Holy City just
before the second Advent. But, in the New World,

> a holy City called ZION or NEW JERUSALEM, is to be built
> upon this earth preparatory to Christ's second Advent; that it

is to be built by the elect of God under his direction; that righteousness is to be sent down from heaven, and truth sent forth out of the earth for the purpose of gathering the people of God from among all nations.[54]

He adds:

Both Zion and Jerusalem will remain on the earth during the Millennial reign of Christ; both will be preserved when the present heaven and earth pass away; both will come down out of heaven upon the new earth; and both will have place upon the new earth for ever and ever—the eternal abode of the righteous.

The books of Mormon relate how Christ preached the Gospel in the New World as well as the Old, and how the true believers (the "Former-Day Saints") were defeated and finally exterminated. Coincidentally, the Antichrist achieved dominion in the church of the Old World. So there ensued centuries of utter darkness, when the eternal priesthood of Melchisedec, established at the beginning of things, was in abeyance, and the true faith was held only secretly by a few. The pattern is essentially the same as that of the other Protestant interpreters of prophecy: in accordance with the predictions of John, Peter, and others, the long period of spiritual tyranny and perversion had to endure until the moment of liberation arrived with the Reformation. Parley P. Pratt, who in 1833 was commanded to found a school "in Zion," gives an account that has special authority, for Revelation 82 states that the Lord "will bless him with a multiplicity of blessings, in expounding all scriptures and mysteries to the edification of the school, and of the Church in Zion." (See *Doctrine and Covenants,* 1845 edition.) The "science of theology," Pratt says, had been lost to suffering mankind for many centuries, during which there was a terrible silence as the communion of God with man was broken.

For centuries, ages, there has been no voice from heaven among the Gentiles, any more than among the Jews. No Gentile

[54] Orson Pratt, *The New Jerusalem; or, The Fulfillment of Ancient Prophecy* (Liverpool, 1 October 1849), p. 4.

Prophet has arisen and uttered his voice. No kind angel has ministered unto them. No vision from the Lord. No answer. No inspired dream. No voice. No sound from the heavens. No revelation has burst upon the silence of midnight darkness which has brooded over the nations.[55]

The science of theology could not be restored "until the full time should arrive." Like the rest of the Protestant commentators, Pratt says that religious perversion has been the root, indeed the only cause of all the evils mankind has known in this long period.

All the darkness of the middle ages; all the priestcraft of every age, since the slaughter of the Apostles; all the oppressions, persecutions, or abuses of power; all the extravagances and idleness on the one hand, and all the sufferings and miseries of the toiling millions for want of the comforts of life, on the other; . . . have been the results of the decline, and loss of the keys and powers, of the science of theology, or for want of attention to them when existing on the earth.[56]

Consequently, all Christians must

welcome a messenger who comes in the name of the Lord, with a commission from heaven, and with keys committed by the Angels of God—a new Apostolic commission, a restoration of the Kingdom and Church, and power and gifts of God; a new dispensation, universally proclaimed in all the world, with power and signs following; and the whole consummated by the glorious restoration of Israel and Judah to their own land and nationality, and to the true fold of God; together with the second Advent of Messiah and all his Saints with him, to overthrow 'Mystery Babylon,' and reign on the earth.

Clearly, the prophecies are not to be interpreted allegorically only, as referring only to the triumph of Christian principles and spirit. Christ is to return, there is to be a first, physical resurrection, the earth is to be wonderfully and miraculously restored to its first glory. The function of the elect, in the short period to elapse before this consummation, is to prepare the way, by building Zion and evangelizing the world. More: there is to be, in effect, a preliminary

---

[55] Parley P. Pratt, *Key to the Science of Theology* . . . (Liverpool, 1855), pp. 16–17.
[56] *Ibid.*, p. 19.

reign of the saints, the first step in the organization of a
"theocratic government, that is, a government founded and
guided by Prophets, Priesthood, visions and revelations." [57]
When, as happened in the early centuries A.D., the commissioned priesthood has disappeared, it is necessary for the
last man or men having the keys to return to earth in angelic
form, and to restore the theocratic order. So Moroni, the
last survivor of the Mormons, has appeared as a spirit and
has called the messenger Joseph Smith as the first of the
new succession. This "Priesthood, including that of the
Aaronic, holds the keys of revelation of the oracles of God
to man upon earth; the power and right to give laws and
commandments to individuals, churches, rulers, nations, and
the world; to appoint, ordain, and establish constitutions and
kingdoms." [58]

The chosen people, then, are not identical with any one
nation or race. In some respects apparently like such ancient
sects as the Qumran, they are to be a separated, holy society,
a righteous community with some degree of communal
property, being "conscious of a vocation as heralds of the
approaching Messianic era." [59] But, unlike such sects, the
Saints claimed a special authority, and believed they had a
mission to all mankind.

Yet, if Enoch had prophesied "great tribulations" for the
latter days, it is plain, too, that the Saints were greatly
affected by the spirit of the age—by the sense that the
world was entering, physically as well as spiritually, into a
wonderful new time vastly better than the past. The restoration of spiritual and political liberty, the great flowering of
scientific experiment and invention, the fact that the "bright
constellation" had "displayed its glory in the West"—all
these phenomena were, Pratt says, harbingers of the millennial dawn.

Modern inventions and discoveries, for instance, the marine
compass,—the art of printing,—the discovery of America—steam

[57] *Ibid.*, p. 70.
[58] *Ibid.*, p. 66.
[59] Thus R. K. Harrison describes the Qumran community.
The Dead Sea Scrolls (London, 1961; New York: Harper &
Brothers, 1961), p. 102.

navigation and railway travelling, etc., are all so many preparatory steps to open the way for a short work on the earth, both
as it regards the spread of intelligence, the speed of news,
or the expeditious conveyance of those who are to be gathered
with their substance.[60]

The new Nephites, Parley Pratt writes in his poem "The
Millennium," a kind of epic of Mormon history, are rescued
by divine guidance when

> . . . the Gentiles break their foreign yoke,
> While tyrants tremble at the dreadful stroke,
> Assert their freedom, gain their liberty,
> And to the world proclaim Columbia free.[61]

Pratt's own verse demonstrates how completely the new
doctrine was in sympathy with optimism, for its images and
rhetoric at almost every line recall Pope, and particularly
"An Essay on Man." Pratt had been a follower of Campbell,
and it is obvious that the name of a journal he founded in
1840, *The Millennial Star*, was suggested by *The Millennial
Harbinger*. One paragraph in his "A Letter to the Queen,"
of 1841, could have come from Campbell's own pen:

> The discovery of America by Columbus 300 years since opened
> a new era upon the world, and poured a flood of light upon the
> startled nations. They awoke awake from the slumber of
> ages and gazed with astonishment and wonder. As the first
> transports of admiration subsided, a spirit of enterprise seized
> the people, and a new impulse was given to the minds of men,
> which has resulted in mighty changes in the scientific, commer-
> cial, and political departments, and which has mainly contrib-
> uted in forming all the great outlines of modern character.[62]

The ebullience of the times contributed, undoubtedly, to
the spiritual ferment of the Saints, to their conviction that
there had dawned a new age in which once again angels
would communicate directly with men, the Spirit would
enable the faithful to perform miracles, and a new and
perfect form of government would be instituted to end the

[60] *Writings of Parley P. Pratt*, ed. Parker Pratt (Salt Lake
City, 1952), p. 266.
[61] *Ibid.*, p. 319.
[62] *Ibid.*, p. 103.

tale of human woes. Columbus, Washington, and the inventors contributed to the certainty that now the realization of the visions of Isaiah and Micah was at hand.

Nor were the mystique of the westward movement and that of the continental heartland absent. We can gain an insight into the temper of the first generation of Latter-Day Saints from a kind of romance, called *The Angel of the Prairies: A Dream of the Future*, which Parley Pratt composed, during the terrible winter of 1843–44, and which he is said to have read in the presence of the prophet and the church council. It demonstrates how strong was the hold of the progressivist faith, even in the midst of the darkest period of the persecutions of the young, struggling church.[63]

The *Dream* begins with the appearance of a "messenger of a mild and intelligent countenance," who identifies himself as the Angel of the Prairies. This being says, "I hold the keys of the mysteries of this wonderful country, and to me is committed the fate of empires and the destiny of nations." In a "curious glass" the dreamer is able "to view the entire country," as it will be a century hence, "from a spot in the midst of the great American continent." The theme of *translatio imperii*, westward, appears, for the Angel informs the dreamer that

Here is the spot which is destined for the seat of empire, and here shall the ambassadors of all nations resort with a tribute of homage to a greater than Cyrus. . . . "The seat of empire," continued he, "began in the eastern Eden, but its progress has always been westward. It lighted on the plains of Euphrates, where, under Nimrod, Nebuchadnezzar, Cyrus, Alexander and others, it rested for a time. But, migrating still westward, it took its seat in Palestine, and finally on the banks of the Nile . . . and in course of time penetrated to the western islands of Europe, where it sojourned for a time as if to prepare for a

[63] *The Angel of the Prairies*, ed. Abinadi Pratt (Salt Lake City, 1880). The editor states that this "vision" is not to be taken as an authentic revelation, but that it has "inspired truth for its foundation." It was not printed until many years after the murder of its author, and, so far as I know, it has never been reprinted in Parley Pratt's later editions.

voyage. Holding still its sea-girt throne, it sent out a forlorn
hope, a kind of advance guard to prepare its way in the wilderness. These passed over the great waters and finally strengthened themselves until they founded a seat of government on
the eastern shore of this great continent."

Some "narrow minded mortals" have erroneously concluded
that the Atlantic shore was to be the permanent seat of
empire; but the capital, not alone of the United States but of
the world, will be in the middle of the North American
continent.

There are, here, some of the most extravagant demo-
graphic forecasts to be found in any American work—and
Americans have been given to extravagant forecasts of population. Iowa and Wisconsin, a century after the date of the
Dream, will have a hundred million inhabitants. The continental vision of Manifest Destiny is complete; Texas and
Mexico are included within the United States, and have no
fewer than two hundred million citizens living therein. This
land is no new Eden, but a great empire, the scene of intense
and vastly productive activity, and at its heart is the greatest
metropolis the world has known.

This metropolis, the seat of the last empire, appears in the
second vision the Angel of the Prairies presents. It is "an
immense city," composed of people from all nations. In its
midst is a "magnificent temple," seemingly the final form of
the one the Saints projected for Independence. This, the
Angel says, is the "sanctuary of freedom" and the seat of the
world government of the kingdom of the Saints. In the
throne room "an aged venerable man is seated," on a vast
"throne as white as ivory, and ascended by seventy steps."
On either side of the ruler a counselor is seated. The arrangement reflects the form of church government; the
three constitute the "First Presidency." Before them are
seated twelve—evidently the "Apostles," next in dignity and
power in the Latter-Day Saints. Below them are seated
thousands of Saints. This is "the grand Presiding Council
organized in wisdom and holding the keys of power to bear
rule over all the earth in righteousness and of the increase of
their Kingdoms there shall be no end." On the door of the
throne room is inscribed this verse:

Within is freedom's throne exalted high!
Where, crowned with light and truth and majesty,
A royal host in robes of bright array,
Their peaceful sceptre o'er the nations sway.

Here is the apotheosis of the ancient vision of the reign of the Saints, intertwined with expectations that America will be the millennial country. The Angel reveals that, after the destruction of the American union by its own internal corruptions and contentions, a remnant fled into the wilderness and established a noble, free form of government, to which the good, great, and patriotic from all nations repaired. To destroy the new state, the jealous and rapacious nations of the Old World eventually sent out an "Armada" (the word, of course, recalls the common Protestant belief that the fiasco of the Spanish Armada was a fulfillment of prophecy); but, like its predecessor, it was defeated by the patriots of "freedom." The example of the new country converts the world. "Thus, in one short century, the world is revolutionized; tyranny is dethroned; war has ceased forever; peace is triumphant, and truth and knowledge cover the earth."

Although this action clearly is inspired by the millennialist expectation of American destiny, there are significant differences from the usual conception. The perfect government, the Angel explains, is not a "human monarchy: not an aristocracy, not a democracy." All of these have been inclined to oppress minorities, and otherwise to demonstrate human weakness. "But it is a theocracy, where the great Elohim, Jehovah, holds the superior honor." Yet, as we have seen, this absolute reign of the Saints is described in the terminology and rhetoric of democratic liberty, as opposed to traditional tyranny. The council of the vision is revealed to be "the order of the Ancient of Days": it is "a government under the immediate, constant and direct superintendency of the Almighty." So ends the *Dream*.

This composition raises curious questions. The holy state certainly has the characteristics of the millennium. Yet it has come about without supernatural intervention, in the course of historical action. There has not, apparently, been a first resurrection, or a visible Advent. Is it, then, to be a kind of antemillennium? Is the return of Christ to set the seal only, so to speak, on the previously achieved victory of the Saints in this world? If so, the dire events predicted in Scripture and Enoch's prophecy of what was to occur just before the inauguration of the millennium—the "tribulations," earthquakes, and the like—must be allegories of great but historical disasters. In any case, Pratt's divine romance represents perhaps the most complete assimilation of the millenarian doctrine of the Latter-Day Saints with the American millennial dream.

The vicious persecutions of the church, combined with the murder of the prophet and his brother, necessitated a change in the immediate expectations of the organization. Although the church still regards the site of the temple as ultimately to be the one the prophet designated, in Independence, the location of Zion changed. Orson Pratt, like his brother an original member of the Council of Twelve, set forth the ideas of the church in 1849. In *The New Jerusalem; or, The Fulfillment of Ancient Prophecy*, a tract written for prospective English converts, he says that the ordained site of the new Zion in the wilderness of Utah was indicated in Isaiah 40:9—"O Zion, that bringest good tidings, get thee up into the high mountain." The Saints, fleeing from intolerable conditions in Nauvoo, have settled in "one of the most wild, romantic and retired countries on the great western hemisphere." The combination of the language of the Authorized Version with the typical adjectives of romantic aesthetics—"wild, romantic and retired"—shows how thoroughly the doctrine of the Latter-Day Saints combined fundamentalist interpretation of Scripture, traditions of the chosen people, revival of miracles, and the like, with current sensibilities and ideals of government.

The idea of "retirement"—that Zion must establish itself and prepare for its work in complete isolation—supersedes any hope that the Saints would decisively influence the course of political affairs in the great world, thus "overturning" the power of Satan. Yet, as late as February 1844, Joseph Smith had issued a manifesto announcing his candidacy for the presidency of the United States. It demonstrates that he was much under the influence of the most extreme progressivist, ardently reforming ideas of his time, and that he shared to the fullest the continental expectations for the nation. His political hero was Jackson, who, he says, was betrayed by Van Buren. If, according to the prophecies, terrible disasters and a time of sin were to be looked for just before the millennium, it is nevertheless clear that Smith had great confidence in the possibilities of sweeping betterment accomplished by the vote. Some of the planks in his platform, indeed, would be considered visionary in any age:

Abolish the cruel custom of prisons (except certain cases), penitentiaries, court-martials for desertion; and let reason and friendship reign over the ruins of ignorance and barbarity; yea, I would, as the universal friend of man, open the prisons, open the eyes, open the ears, and open the hearts of all people, to behold and enjoy freedom—unadulterated freedom.[64]

The conception that the American nation is called to manifest destiny appears in the statement that he would grant any petition to "possess the Territory of Oregon, or any other contiguous Territory . . . that they might extend the mighty efforts and enterprise of a free people from the east to the west sea, and make the wilderness blossom as the rose." It would seem that the wilderness may be made to blossom before the transformation of the earth to be achieved in the millennium; the American people need not wait for the Parousia. This conviction, we need not doubt, was strong in the Mormon pioneers who undertook the great migration to Utah.

Thus, if there was much that seemed strange in the new faith, it was, nevertheless, a product, also, of its nation and its time. Despite the theory of government by "theocracy" and the strong communal bonds of the new church, its central teaching in theology was, perhaps, the most characteristically "American" religious doctrine ever set forth. The prophet strongly emphasized that each individual has "free agency." It was his version of "free will." Impatiently

---

[64] *The Prophet Joseph Smith's Views on the Powers and Policy of the Government of the United States* (Salt Lake City, 1886), p. 22. (Originally published as *An Address to the American People*, February, 1844.)

casting aside all remnants of the dogma of original sin, he taught that by the redemption of Christ, each human being has been endowed with complete freedom, spiritual and psychological, to work out his own destiny, both here and hereafter. There are no limits on his power of decision and action. The choice of a word from business, rather than the usual theological term, is immensely indicative. Like Campbell, Smith believed that religion should adopt the forms and idiom of its time: hence, the church has a "president," and it is divided into "stakes." The church teaches that the American Constitution was inspired. Self-reliance has been canonized. For each person who makes the effort and accepts the truth, complete success is possible, now and throughout eternity. "Progress" unending, Smith further taught, is the divine law. Nor, in reality, was the apparent contradiction between "agency" and the duty of each individual to play his part in the ordained work of the organization atypical of the American spirit. For, as we have seen, the American nation, which stressed individualism to a degree previously unknown, also was a chosen people, whose collective identity claimed all its citizens. Zion could be built only in the United States.

VI

"The Ennobling War"

Confidence in the ideal of America as the new chosen people reached a peak of enthusiasm in the years immediately preceding 1860. A recent writer has remarked the mood of "cosmic optimism"; there was "a feeling that the millennium, if not at hand, was fast approaching"; there was "a . . . pervasive millennialism which looked hopefully on the American future as the fulfillment of divine promise." [1] All this is certainly true; but it would be a mistake to think that the Civil War came as a complete surprise, a great shock to an expectation of a smooth upward movement to the happy time. The mood of anticipation, for reasons I have set forth, was more complex than unalloyed optimism. In fact, there was a combination of great expectations, solemn apprehension, and wonder at it all. Whitman expressed much of the national mood in "Years of the Modern," which, under the more appropriate title "Years of the Unperformed," was first published in *Drum-Taps* (1865). There was a sense that the crisis of the apocalyptic drama was beginning, that the world shortly would go through experiences the like of which man had never known: so glorious and yet so awful.

I see not America only, not only Liberty's nation but other
    nations preparing,

[1] George M. Frederickson, *The Inner Civil War* (New York: Harper & Row, Publishers, 1965), p. 7.

I see tremendous entrances and exits, new combinations, the
    solidarity of races,
I see that force advancing with irresistible power on the world's
    stage,
(Have the old forces, the old wars, played their parts? are the
    acts suitable to them closed?)

The auguries of prophecy have come out of the books and
seem to be visible and audible.

What whispers are these O lands, running ahead of you, passing
    under the seas?
Are all nations communing? is there going to be but one heart
    to the globe?
Is humanity forming en-masse? for lo, tyrants tremble, crowns
    grow dim,
The earth, restive, confronts a new era, perhaps a general
    divine war,
No one knows what will happen next, such portents fill the
    days and nights;
Years prophetical! the space ahead as I walk, as I vainly try
    to pierce it is full of phantoms,
Unborn deeds, things soon to be, project their shapes around me,
This incredible rush and heat, this strange ecstatic fever of
    dreams
    O years!
Your dreams O years, how they penetrate through me! (I know
    not whether I sleep or wake;)

The "portents" were menacing as well as hopeful. For
some decades the abolitionists had been asking whether this
nation could possibly claim to be endowed with a world-
redemptive mission when it not only tolerated but supported by national law an institution as evil as any the
Enemy had ever invented. When the crisis of the Union
arrived, there was the further agonizing question whether a
nation, fragmented by internal discord, probably by divine
judgment, had lost the calling which it might once have
had: was it possible the United States had gone the way of
Judah? And if so, was there any millennial hope for the
world?

Although there was a great deal of complacency about
American superiority, the most responsible millennialists had
always warned that a chosen people would be subjected to

more severe tests than other peoples; for, as Strong said later, the "leverage" both of good and of evil must be greater in this country than anywhere else. A large part of Dwight's poetic-prophetic function, as we have seen, was to make clear this fact; in 1801, while assuring his countrymen that God has in all respects treated Americans as his chosen, he pointed out that we cannot take the future for granted: "We may be scourged, for we merit it, but I trust we shall not be forsaken; we may *be cast down*, but we shall not be destroyed." [2] The fear became greater, around the middle of the century, that a "scourging" might be at hand. For the power of Antichrist was still apparent in the slave market, even in the nation's capital itself, and the apocalyptic angel would surely have to pour out the vial of wrath to its fullest on this peculiar people if they failed to reform speedily. Urgent awareness of this possibility underlies *Uncle Tom's Cabin*. Harriet Beecher Stowe had lived in the atmosphere of millennialism; and, as she thought about the great question of the day, it was to be expected that she would see its prophetic aspect. As we have seen, it had long been assumed that Providence casts down evil, sometimes peacefully and sometimes violently. As we have seen, too, the will of Antichrist was still being done, and unless this "bad *system*" was ended by law, surely the apocalyptic angel would have to use the sword.

Mrs. Stowe was not wholly despondent. Like most people of her time, she had full confidence in the almost miraculous power of sentiment to arouse the "moral sense." Her father, moreover, in line with the "New Theology," had emphasized that the will is not absolutely free, as he says the Arminians teach, nor absolutely conditioned as the Antinomians (among whom he included rigid Calvinists) believe. Instead, the whole complex of "motives" in our minds directs the choice of action, for we have adequate natural powers to do good, but, after the Fall, lack inclination. God, through the Word, "both wounds and heals the soul, not as he would wound the body by a spear, and heal it by surgical

---

[2] Timothy Dwight, *A Discourse on Some Events of the Last Century* (New Haven, 1801), p. 43.

application; but he does it by an instrumentality which may be fitly represented by such metaphorical analogies."[3] Hence, the "occasions of volition" must be changed, by God's own shock treatment. But, he implies, the whole of one's experience determines motivation. "Edwards affirmed that there must be, and is, anterior to the exercise of free agency, some constitution of the agent and relevancy of motive, as the ground and reason of the certainty of choice, though not a coercive cause."[4] This "constitution" obviously would be much affected by means other than grace and the Word. Mrs. Stowe became more and more convinced that nature, poetry, and so forth, are means of improving the soul. I think it is not unjustified to say that *Uncle Tom's Cabin* was intended as a kind of shock treatment to the moral feelings; perhaps an aroused conscience in the nation, or at least in the North, would produce the purgation without the scourging. Her sense of something like divine inspiration in writing the book is understandable. Moral feeling, she says, is or can be a potent form of action; Motley was to call it the "electric chain," binding mankind.

But, what can any individual do? . . . There is one thing that every individual can do—they can see to it that *they feel right.* An atmosphere of sympathetic influence encircles every human being; and the man or woman who *feels* strongly, healthily and justly, on the great interests of humanity, is a constant benefactor to the human race. See, then, to your sympathies in this matter! Are they in harmony with the sympathies of Christ? or are they swayed and perverted by the sophistries of worldly policy? [Chap. 45.]

This last question was urgent for the whole nation.

This is an age of the world when nations are trembling and convulsed. A mighty influence is abroad, surging and heaving the world, as with an earthquake. And is America safe? Every nation that carries in its bosom great and unredressed injustice has in it the elements of this last convulsion.

[3] Lyman Beecher, *Views on Theology* (Cincinnati, 1836), p. 214.
[4] *Ibid.,* pp. 166–67.

Here is apocalyptic language. "Earthquake" always signifies the violent overthrow of evil, especially of the mystical Babylon in all its branches; the Reformation was the "earthquake" par excellence. In the death throes of Babylon, the nations are "trembling and convulsed"; every millennialist emphasized this point. And, of course, this is the *last* "convulsion": the great speed with which the world is moving to the conclusion makes the problem terribly urgent; a solution cannot be delayed, for, to recall Beecher again, "mighty causes, like floods from distant mountains, are rushing with accumulating power to their consummation of good and evil."

So, Mrs. Stowe addresses the churches in particular; they should understand the situation, they should be God's special agents.

O, Church of Christ, read the signs of the times! Is not this power the spirit of HIM whose kingdom is yet to come, and whose will is to be done on earth as it is in heaven? But who may abide the day of his appearing? 'For that day shall burn as an oven: and he shall appear as a swift witness against those that oppress the hireling in his wages, the widow and the fatherless, and that *turn aside the stranger in his right* and he shall break in pieces the oppressor.'

And she reminds the churches: "can you forget that prophecy associates, in dread fellowship, the *day of vengeance* with the year of his redeemed?" The guilt is national; it applies to free as well as to slave states. This is one nation, destined to play one part in the divine plan: it will not be permitted to ignore the evil still in its bosom.

Although her book failed to avert the judgment of blood, it may have helped prepare people to see the conflict, when it came, in terms that derived from the millennialist interpretation of the prophecies. A new rationale of national mission was constructed, and epitomized for all time in "The Battle Hymn of the Republic." Behind the surging optimism of the fifties, as we have seen, was the expectation of a "general divine war." The occurrence of the war did not, therefore, destroy confidence as we might expect. The struggle to eliminate slavery came to be explained as both a judgment on national wickedness and a way in which the chosen nation, by sacrificing its own sons, dealt a fatal blow at what Motley called "Privilege," not only here but throughout the world. And the outcome—the survival and strengthening of the Union—appeared as a decisive defeat of the powers of darkness; it seemed to validate the millennialist hopes. Perhaps, even, Armageddon had been fought.

The apocalyptic expectations in the first year of the Civil War were summarized by Hollis Read, a writer of popular works on history, in *The Coming Crisis of the World: or, The Great Battle and the Golden Age.* The "Introductory Note" is by S. H. Tyng, at that time the most renowned preacher of the Protestant Episcopal Church (a fact, incidentally, that demonstrates the denominational spread of millennialist doctrines; other writers I have cited were Presbyterian, Congregationalist, and Unitarian). Tyng strongly maintains the necessity, in Christian belief, of an earthly millennium: "Discard the idea of a yet to come golden age of the church, and how can we vindicate the ways of God in the dispensations of his grace among men?" [5] The age stands in breathless anticipation: "There is a feeling in the human breast that despotism, bloodshed, fraud, oppression and unbridled lust, have, in defiance of heaven, rioted long enough, and that a righteous God will soon rise in his wrath and make short work." For there are many signs that "great Babylon is toppling to her fall." The final battle is to be for "human freedom." And it is essential to remember that

The Enemy to be assailed and vanquished is generally *the same.* In India and China it finds its embodiment in a Pagan Priestcraft. In Europe it is the despotism of Rome. In America it is met in the system of African Slavery. Now in turn has this monster of sin come up in remembrance before Heaven and waits its final doom. [Italics added.]

In the last sentence is the essence of the rationale of the Civil War. Read's book expounds upon and gives details of

[5] Read, *The Coming Crisis of the World* . . . (Columbus, 1861), "Introductory Note." (The copy in the Library of the Berkeley Campus, University of California, has an inscription indicating it once was used by a Bible-study class.)

the proposition that, as we find from the chronology of Revelation, "God shall . . . in some remarkable manner avenge the cause of his elect" [6] within five or six years. By a remarkable coincidence, the Civil War came just before the time many commentators had predicted the millennium would begin. There was an old theory that Antichrist had gained supreme power about A.D. 606; this date, added to the 1,260 years (three and a half "prophetic years") of his permitted reign, adds up to 1866. How remarkable, therefore, that the "monster of sin" should be called up to remembrance just five years before this date!

The prophecies assure us that "Satan's empire is to be broken up." This, however, will be far more than a political or spiritual event alone, for it will involve the disintegration of ancient systems and of "manners, customs, maxims and practices interwoven with every fibre of life." [7] Tradition must not only be reexamined; it must in large part be swept away. Teaching and preaching have done much, but a change so radical will ultimately require violence; it can "only be broken to pieces by the sledge-hammer of WAR, or be starved out by gaunt *Famine*, or be burnt out by the devouring flame." For "the cause that has brought man into his present confused and suffering condition, is not as some suppose, simply that his civil and social relations are disordered and consequently all that is needed is a reorganization of society." This was the heart of the issue between Owen and Campbell; it is why, however much a millennialist might value orderly progress, he could never rely on it alone. The Golden Age must be won in a struggle supernatural in issue and direction, even if conducted on the natural plane.

The millennial state itself Read envisions in now orthodox terms. It is, essentially, the "triumph of Christianity" —which will rule the world like a conqueror. Sin and death will continue, and no bodies will emerge from the tomb. But it will be a time of universal peace, health and long life, and of "extraordinary knowledge" combined with

[6] *Ibid.*, p. 157.
[7] *Ibid.*, p. 26.

great cultural refinement. Isaiah's predictions will be fulfilled in that "The improved moral character of man—the
vastly increased industry, enterprise, and public spirit . . .
will do wonders to overcome the physical ruins of the fall,
and to renovate, beautify, and fertilize the whole face of the
earth." [8] The incessant busyness of the people in the millennium—engaged in "industry," in making inventions, in
public service, and the like—constitutes one of the greatest
contrasts between the holy utopia and the old idea of a
"world-sabbath" of rest and rich rewards. Carlyle's command "Work!" looms over the Happy Time. The stress on
these activities, moreover, helps explain the immense value
placed on them in the post-Civil War period: why, for
example, an Edison came to seem almost as much a religious
as a cultural hero. As we should expect, Read is ecstatic
about the laying of the transoceanic cable, whose completion Whitman was to celebrate with quasi-millennialist hy-
perbole, in "Passage to India." This achievement, Read
thinks, will be celebrated in more epics than "*our* 'ancients'
allotted to the labors of Hercules or the voyage of Argo";
but far more important is the fact that "It no doubt has a
most important part to play in the renovation of our world
and the establishment of Christ's kingdom on the earth." [9]
Yet we come back in the end to the fact that the door to the
Golden Age, like the gate of Eden, is guarded by a flaming
sword. The wonderful improvements are in their way also
dark portents, for they intimate that the winding-up of evil
is near, and in that time "men and angels are summoned to
survey the great battlefield and behold the dreadful displays
of incensed Omnipotence on his enemies." [10] To console us,
we have the probability that the conflict, though fierce, will
be short, and that once concluded, the matter will be settled.
Of course, prominent among the "civil commotions, wars
and revolutions," which are "sure precursors of that coming
kingdom for which we all look, and the efficient agents
which shall hasten it on," is the current crisis in the United

[8] *Ibid.*, p. 20.
[9] *Ibid.*, p. 218.
[10] *Ibid.*, p. 228.

States. "The great centre of conflict is for the present transferred to America."

Read now comes to grips with the supreme question: does this trial indicate that God in judgment is casting off the chosen people? The answer is unhesitating. God "hath made us his modern Israel—hath seemed to choose us as a peculiar people—hath made his goodness to pass before us as he did to his Israel of old; and yet in many respects, more abundantly." [11] Like Israel, we have sinned, "Especially in our failure to stand up before the nations of the earth as a model nation, to exhibit to them the beauty and glory of free institutions—of a self-governed people—a great moral fountain whose fertilizing streams should go out to bless a desert world." The present test is great indeed; but Read, like Dwight, concludes that the God who has promised the world salvation will not "give up the heritage, which he has cherished and watched over with such parental tenderness and care, to spoiling and final desolation." The whole national history, including the "great success and efficiency which has here been given to the Puritanical element and Anglo-Saxon type of our people" gives confidence in the triumph of the North, carrying the standard of Christ, against the South, ranged under that of the Beast. An implied distinction between the Israelites and the Americans as chosen peoples, moreover, is our possession, now, of the prophetic revelations. There was no such complete program revealed before the Advent; there was no indication that the end was approaching. All the prophecies of Isaiah and other Old Testament prophets now appear to refer not to the future of the Israelites only but to the world millennium. And we have the final comfort that the Reformation has occurred and is being completed.

The salient fact is that the apocalyptic vision of the Civil War was far more than a spontaneous response to a great crisis by a nation of Bible-readers, who naturally saw it as a moral conflict. It seemed to fit exactly into a pattern long established, and seemed to confirm the validity of that pattern. Thus it was more than just another war about a moral

[11] *Ibid.*, p. 241.

issue, even if a great one; it was *the* crisis of mankind, even if only one nation was involved. Read quotes the London *Standard*, which, although acknowledging that things so far have gone badly for the Union, asserted:

"Our sole remaining consolation arises from the fact that the Lord God omnipotent reigneth! In season due, He will avenge the oppressed and break in pieces the oppressor." Read proceeds to quote writers in various parts of the United States, on the "purging war." One, from Pennsylvania, says

This war is but the work of the Lord. He has this nation in the crucible of affliction, to burn up the dross. If I was ever thankful for anything, it is for this; and my prayer is, that the fires may not cease to burn until the gold of this nation shine in righteousness, clear and bright, reflecting the image of our Saviour.[12]

In conclusion to this part, Read expresses his confident hope, in a phrase that anticipates the Gettysburg Address:

Because we believe God is the friend and abettor of liberty, the friend and avenger of the oppressed; because we believe he will finish in this country the work he so nobly begun, and which, without let or hindrance, he has thus far so effectively carried on up to the present day, we believe the final victory shall be ours.[13]

There were many expressions of similar import. A representative one is an editorial article, "The War for the Union," in the *Presbyterian Quarterly Review*, January 1862. It takes, indeed, the extreme position that the war is solely about the abolition of slavery—not about the endurance of a republican form of government, or about secession.[14] The fixed "delusion" of the South can be destroyed by nothing "earthly." "It would seem, therefore, a case, especially, considering its importance as well as its inveteracy, in which we might expect a greater than man to intervene." Here is the intimation—a common one—that the

---

[12] *Ibid.*
[13] *Ibid.*, p. 233.
[14] *Presbyterian Quarterly Review*, 10 (1862):491.

conflict had its supernatural aspect, that angels and demons as well as human armies were in confrontation. There is the image of "breaking," which Mrs. Stowe had used. This metaphor seems to have replaced the earlier "overturn" in popularity. Its origin is significant: "The breaker is come up before them: they have broken up, and have passed through the gate, and are gone out by it: and their king shall pass before them, and the LORD on the head of them." (Micah 2:13.) Micah was especially appropriate, for he uttered the sternest predictions of judgments on the chosen people, immediately followed by one of the greatest visions of world redemption to be found in the Bible: "And many nations shall come, and say, Come, and let us go up to the mountain of the LORD, and to the house of the God of Jacob; and he will teach us of his ways, and we will walk in his paths; for the law shall go forth of Zion, and the word of the LORD from Jerusalem." (Micah 4:2.) Zion would be the historical type of the American people, but the prediction of final world salvation is more than type; it is the prophecy of *the* last epoch of world history, now upon us, and the judgment and purifying of new Zion is its prelude.

The apocalyptic trumpet sounded its clearest note in "The Battle Hymn of the Republic," first published in February, 1862.

(1) Mine eyes have seen the glory of the coming of the Lord:
     He is trampling out the vintage where the grapes of wrath
        are stored;
     He hath loosed the fateful lightning of his terrible swift
        sword:
                              His truth is marching on.
(2) I have seen Him in the watch-fires of a hundred circling
        camps;
     They have builded Him an altar in the evening dews and
        damps;
     I can read His righteous sentence by the dim and flaring
        lamps:
                              His day is marching on.
(3) I have read a fiery gospel writ in burnished rows of steel:
     As ye deal with my contemners, so with you my grace
        shall deal;

> Let the Hero, born of woman, crush the serpent with his heel,
>
>   Since God is marching on.
> (4) He has sounded forth the trumpet that shall never call retreat;
> He is sifting out the hearts of men before His judgment-seat:
> Oh, be swift, my soul, to answer him! be jubilant, my feet!
>   Our God is marching on.
> (5) In the beauty of the lilies Christ was born across the sea,
> With a glory in his bosom that transfigures you and me:
> As he died to make men holy, let us die to make men free,
>   While God is marching on.[15]

In this poem, which has become perhaps the most popular hymn of wars and moral crusades of the English-speaking peoples, were fused the images and interpretations that were associated with the great struggle. Even its authorship is revealing. Julia Ward Howe did not seem to be a person who would take seriously the fundamentalist millennialist notions, even in the desperate crisis. She and her husband were members of the Boston group of reformers and "advanced thinkers," parishioners of Theodore Parker, friends of Emerson and of Oliver Wendell Holmes (who called her "Madame Comment"). Needless to say, they had no faith in special revelation or mysteries in religion, and generally believed in the law of progress, and the perfectibility of human nature. The whole atmosphere was far removed from the old grim ideas of a cosmic war of good and evil. Thus the fact that she was the poet of the American apocalyptic faith is significant; it shows how deeply such ideas must have penetrated the national mind.

Although her own accounts of the origin of the poem vary, they agree in her impression that the one powerful work she wrote came to her mind as if it had shaped itself, after she had visited an encampment of the Army of the Potomac. What happened seems to have been that, as she brooded over this darkest moment of American history and whatever it might mean, childhood teachings rose out of

---

[15] The text of "The Battle Hymn," as first published in *The Atlantic Monthly*, 9 (1862): 145.

deep memory, and the images of the Apocalypse presented themselves—with their Protestant meanings. She says that her father was a strict Puritan, "not only a strenuous Protestant, but also an ardent 'Evangelical,' or Low Churchman, holding the Calvinistic views which then characterized that portion of the American Episcopal Church." [16] It seems likely that the Biblical training she received would have included the kind of interpretation of the prophecies I have described; and, of course, in her adult life she must have encountered many expressions of millennialist doctrines. Her experience, I suggest, is typical of what has happened to many other Americans. When urgent and baffling questions about the right course for the nation have arisen, the apocalyptic view of its history has come to the front: at such times as the expansionist eras, the Civil War, the First World War.

There has been a general impression that Mrs. Howe used the images from the Apocalypse only as fitting metaphors for a war between right and wrong; certainly most of those who have sung the hymn in recent years must have thought so. Analysis in the light of contemporaneous biblical theories, however, gives a very different impression. The images are not selected for poetic effect primarily; taken together, they are, as it were, a cipher which, decoded, conveys a message about the precise place and point of the war in the pattern of salvation.

The first line expresses the essential element of millennialism—that "the coming of the Lord" is an allegory of the victory of Christian principles. The "glory," however, is more specific; it is the wonder and the terror of the beginning of the transition to the millennium. The greatest event in the history of mankind is beginning; "mine eyes have seen. . . ." The second line sets that war in the sequence of predicted events. The image is that of the "reaping of the earth" (Rev. 14:19), which follows the proclamation, "Babylon is fallen, is fallen." An angel instructs the crowned figure "like the Son of man," who has in his hand a sickle: "Thrust in thy sharp sickle, and gather the clusters of the

---

[16] Howe, *Reminiscences, 1818–1899* (Boston, 1899), p. 49.

vine of the earth; for her grapes are fully ripe. And the angel thrust in his sickle into the earth, and gathered the vine of the earth, and cast it into the great winepress of the wrath of God." The MS version (reproduced in the *Reminiscences*) is even closer to this language than the published one: "He is trampling out the wine press. . . ." Mrs. Howe as a child must often have heard that the fall of mystical Babylon was the Reformation, the pivotal event of this history of Christendom; and so the grapes are "ripe" because the day of Antichrist is closing. Clearly, the Civil War is a major part of the "reaping" of the accumulated evils of the long reign of the Beast; Motley, it will be recalled, paralleled the "upward movement out of intellectual thraldom which we call the Reformation" and "the triumph of the Right in the recent four years' conflict in which all have been the conquerors." [17] The (subsequently added) refrain of the hymn, "Glory, Glory, Hallelujah," is derived from the shout of triumph that succeeds the pouring out of the seven vials and the fall of Babylon: "And after these things I heard a great voice of much people in heaven, saying, Aleluja; Salvation, and glory, and honour, and power, unto the Lord our God." Edwards had stated that there was a "coming" of the Lord in each of the four great judgments on the Enemy; the world is witnessing the last, and people now living are entitled to join the heavenly host in the great *Te Deum*.

The last stanza alludes to the event which made possible all the great triumphs over earthly evil—the Redemption. Only after divine grace had begun to transform human nature could the forces of right confront the power of darkness with hope of success. So Edwards sets forth the stages:

(1) Christ's earthly ministry and crucifixion, ending in the destruction of Jerusalem and 'bringing the church into the glorious state of the gospel'; (2) advancement of the church, in Constantine's time, to liberty from persecution; (3) the downfall of Antichrist, now being accomplished, accompanied by the advancement of the church to the 'glorious prevalence

[17] John L. Motley, *Historic Progress and American Democracy* (New York, 1869), p. 71.

and truth, liberty, peace, and joy which we so often read of in the prophetical parts of Scripture.' [18]

Political freedom, as we have seen, was considered to be the outgrowth and completion of spiritual liberty. Hence, the close association of Christ's dying to make men "holy," and the call to "make men free," in the hymn. It may be significant that the published version of the last stanza is more orthodox than the first draft, which reads "with a glory in his bosom shining out on you and me"; the implication in the first is that the example of Christ is a light only, whereas "transfigures you and me" suggests the operation of grace on the soul.

Each of the intermediate stanzas embodies in various images the point that the armies now fighting are powers symbolized in the Revelation. Thus "the trumpet that shall never call retreat" seems to epitomize the common belief that, once God has destroyed a form of evil, that particular menace is done for. "The terrible swift sword" obviously refers to the rider of the white horse in Revelation 19, "clothed with a vesture dipped in blood: and his name is called the Word of God. . . . And out of his mouth goeth a sharp sword, that with it he should smite the nations." Protestant commentators, especially those with Puritan sympathies, had from the early days of the Reformation stressed the mystical power of the Word in itself, when duly preached, to destroy evil; it generates, seemingly, its own power to overthrow the strongest forces of this world. Giovanni Diodati, for instance, had glossed the "sharp two-edged sword" (Rev. 1:16) as "a figure of the most effectual and penetrant power of God's word in the destroying of his enemies, and overcoming the world." [19] The Reformation having set free the Word, it has set in motion the irresistible march now visible in the Army of the Potomac.

The relation between symbol of prophecy and individual,

---

[18] Jonathan Edwards, *History of the Work of Redemption,* vol. 3 in *Works* (New York, 1830), p. 327.
[19] Diodati, *Pious Annotations upon the Holy Bible* (London, 1643).

in this view of history, is unique. The individual, as a component part of the group that the symbol designates, is both a spectator of and a participant in the sublime vision as it is realized. Symbols thus merge, in a unique manner, with actual persons and objects. The "terrible swift sword" is the armies, but is also each individual, each rifle. The soldiers in the Grand Army are actors in a drama, about which many of them had long been told. How great the destiny, to be the generation called upon to perform this crowning work! No army since Cromwell's ever had been endowed with such a sense of personal calling. And so the "fiery gospel" is both symbol and sacramental embodiment in action of the Word. In the revision, Mrs. Howe made another interesting change. The line originally ran, "burning Gospel writ in fiery rows of steel." By substituting "fiery gospel" and "burnished rows," she more effectively identified symbol and actual appearance; apocalyptic symbols were thought often to have some visual resemblance to the realities they foreshadowed. The "burnished" rows of guns and bayonets, shining in the sun, are symbol and fact merged; perhaps even the bayonets were foreshadowed by the "sickle." The bugles Mrs. Howe had heard in the camp *were* the trumpets of God.

Other images in the "Battle Hymn" are more obscurely related to those of the Revelation, and yet there are associations. The second stanza, for example, seems to be a description of the conditions in the camps, and of the dedication attributed to the soldiers. Yet even the "circling camps" may recall a verse descriptive of the final battle, against Gog and Magog: "And they went up on the breadth of the earth, and compassed the camp of the saints about." Since there was an increasing tendency to amalgamate Armageddon and the last battle, this image is not out of place. The second line of the third stanza condenses Revelation 13:10—"He that leadeth into captivity shall go into captivity: he that killeth with the sword must be killed with the sword." And God is "sifting out the hearts of men" as the judgment preparatory for the Great Day of the Lord, when the millennial state will be inaugurated; how important it is "to answer Him," to share in that supreme blessing!

2

As the likelihood of victory grew, attention shifted from "breaking" to the results of the purification by fire and blood: the residue of evil, which events had shown to be so much greater than most people had before realized, now at last had been decisively vanquished. What can we now expect from the chosen nation? An example of discussions of this question is the Thanksgiving sermon, "The Lord of War and of Righteousness," preached in 1864 by the Reverend Marvin R. Vincent in the First Presbyterian Church of Troy. The reelection of the President, just completed, he sees as proof that God is preparing the republic for a great future task: "God has been striking, and trying to make us strike at elements unfavorable to the growth of a pure democracy; and these and other facts point to the conclusion that he is at work, preparing in this broad land a fit stage for the last act of the mighty drama, the consummation of human civilization." [20] He employs a commonly used image: "Base alloy had wrought itself into the fabric; the lust of money and power, national idolatry and vanity, sensuality, brutality, and oppression of men for whom Christ died." Many discourses expounded this theme—that the Civil War had burned out not only the offense of slavery but the other vices that constituted part of the "base alloy." Earlier prophecies of a national role as political Messiah had been correct in essence, but had failed to take into account the dross from Babylon in the melting pot; now we may foresee "a national life crowned as with the glory of noonday; girt round with prayer, robed in purity, with love in its eyes and peace upon its lips, and in its hand the open charters of freedom." [21]

The sermon leaves no doubt that "the mighty drama" is not merely political and secular progress; the United States,

[20] Vincent, *The Lord of War and of Righteousness* (Troy, N.Y., 1864), p. 42.
[21] *Ibid.*, p. 40.

if she prove worthy, is to dominate the last act of the millennial "comedy":

Who shall say that she shall not only secure lasting peace to herself, but be, under God, the instrument of a millennial reign to all the nations? . . . In numerous respects democracy reveals itself as the natural ally and agent of Christianity. . . . God's purpose in the present state of affairs is a moral and not a political one.[22]

This country may perform that task by sending forth waves of influence; the dignity and power of the great democracy "will be felt as forces in the tremendous revolution which is gathering in its elements to remodel Europe; and the despot-ridden millions whose eyes have watched us through this shadow of death with straining eagerness, shall read in these manifestations new germs of hope for them and for the world." [23] The redemptive work has in fact begun in the nation itself. "Already the daughters and sons of the North have begun their mission, and sit enthroned in rude school-rooms, where the child of tender years and the child of gray hairs, bend together over the same page, and learn from their lips the rudiments of Christian education." [24] Perhaps this conviction of redemptive mission has found delayed expression in such projects as the Peace Corps; certainly no other nation has been moved to undertake, on such a scale, such a worldwide educational work.

The belief that the republic had been sanctified for an ordained and probably crucial service in world history was ubiquitous. A representative and important expression was Horace Bushnell's oration at the commemoration celebration held at Yale College, July 26, 1865. He repeats the common point of the millennialist commentators

. . . that, according to the true economy of the world, so many of its grandest and most noble benefits have and are to have a tragic origin, and to come as outgrowths only of blood. Whether it be that sin is in the world, and the whole creation groaneth in the necessary throes of its demonized life, we need

[22] *Ibid.*, pp. 36, 41.
[23] *Ibid.*, p. 23.
[24] *Ibid.*, p. 39.

not stay to inquire for sin would be in the world and the demonizing spell would be upon it.[25]

Mere "natural progress" could hardly break a "demonizing spell." It is indicative that Bushnell, a comparative liberal in theology and by no means a fundamentalist, expresses such an idea. We think of the nineteenth century as the period of the triumph of natural science; but it was also the last time in history when many responsible thinkers thought of human life and history as dominated or at least strongly affected by angels and demons. The spell must be annihilated by superior force; hence "Sentiments must be born that are children of thunder; there must be heroes and heroic nationalities, and martyr testimonies." [26] The destruction of evil by wrath, and the essential place of martyrdom, are two basic articles of the millennialist faith. Bushnell concludes that the great war has had something at least analogous to an apocalyptic consequence, and that at least the prototype of the millennial transformation of institutions has occurred: "Government is now become providential—no more a mere creature of our human will, but a grandly moral affair." We can understand why Motley, even in 1868, could observe the state of the Union with the eye of faith. It would seem that those who, having expected government to become providential, had got instead Congress and Andrew Johnson, would have been bitterly disillusioned. But the belief in national apotheosis had become fixed in the national mind, having entered the sacrosanct area of credal conviction; it has persisted despite many subsequent disappointments and disillusionments, and the halo of manifest millennial destiny around the head of Columbia is not wholly gone even yet.

If the United States is ultimately to be the "instrument of a millennial reign," it would seem inevitable that in her hour of trial, when the vial of judgment was poured out, she should have a leader of millennial stature. He was expected, indeed, before it was certain there would be a bloody purgation. Whitman's tract *The Eighteenth Presidency!* (written

[25] Bushnell, *Oration* (Yale, 1865), p. 14.
[26] *Ibid.*, p. 27.

in 1856) speaks of "the Redeemer President of These States." A redeeming nation, a Redeemer-President: the combination is appropriate. The fact that, in the crucial hour, there was elected a President who did indeed have qualities expected of such a figure was further proof that the millennial mission was no dream.

The utterances of Abraham Lincoln, as is well known, are permeated by the language of the King James Version. And the prophetic sections are not unrepresented. Consider the following paragraph, from the second inaugural address:

The Almighty has his own purposes. "Woe unto the world because of offenses! for it must needs be that offenses come; but woe to that man by whom the offense cometh." If we shall suppose that American slavery is one of those offenses which, in the providence of God, must needs come, but which, having continued through his appointed time, he now wills to remove, and that he gives to both North and South this terrible war, as the woe due to those by whom the offense came, shall we discern therein any departure from those divine attributes which the believers in a living God always ascribe to him? Fondly do we hope—fervently do we pray—that this mighty scourge of war may speedily pass away. Yet, if God wills that it continue until all the wealth piled by the bondman's two hundred and fifty years of unrequited toil shall be sunk, and until every drop drawn with the lash shall be paid by another drawn with the sword, as was said three thousand years ago, so still it must be said, "The judgments of the Lord are true and righteous altogether."

The quotation "Woe unto the world . . ." is, of course, slightly changed from Matthew 18:7, Jesus' sermon on the Kingdom of Heaven. It is not in itself dominantly apocalyptic (though not without eschatological implications), for it seems to state only that evil is in the nature of things as they now exist, that evil men must be expected until the end, but that they will inexorably receive their reward. Such a doctrine, taken by itself, would be a logical and appropriate justification for the war. But the preceding and succeeding sentences of the address alter the quotation to fit an idea of history as having an apocalyptic program. The first sentence suggests that the offenses are not only deeds of evil individuals, but integral parts of God's "own purposes." And why, as the third sentence states, is it that certain offenses "must needs come," being part of "the providence of God," and (most important of all) why must they last their appointed times? "Wills to remove" recalls Revelation 17:17—"For God hath put it in their hearts to fulfill his will, and to agree, and give their kingdom unto the beast, until the words of God shall be fulfilled." The "woe due to those by whom the offense came" in this context has taken on something like the meaning it has in the Revelation, where a series of three "woes," as parts of the progressive defeats of evil, are predicted (Rev. 9). The fact that the biblical quotation in the last sentence is said to have been uttered "three thousand years ago" would point to the Old Testament, probably Psalm 119:137—"Righteous art thou, O Lord, and upright are thy judgments"; but the actual wording is closer to the recollection of this verse in Revelation 16:7, where a voice from the altar exclaims, after the third angel has poured out his vial, "Even so, Lord God Almighty, true and righteous are thy judgments." And underlying the whole paragraph is what might be called the common doctrine of exact retribution: the judgment on an offense can be expected to be equal to the offense itself. Hence the terrible intensity of the "vials," for example: each must be awful enough to destroy a great evil.

This passage on sanguinary judgment seems curiously juxtaposed with the immediately succeeding call for reconciliation and mutual forgiveness—"With malice toward none. . . ." Perhaps Lincoln, familiar with the kind of thinking that must have influenced many minds, had a deliberate purpose in thus recalling the doctrine of judgments. As we have seen, it was assumed that a judgment, once completed, had finished the particular form of evil on which it was passed. Thus the destruction of slavery, although it had to be accomplished in its appointed time by a bloody war, is now almost finished, and the judgment on the slaveholding sections and on the nation as a whole is about to be terminated. This idea would be an argument against the kind of vindictiveness and fear of southern resurgence that Lincoln must have foreseen as the great imminent danger; even Horace Bushnell called for further retribution on the "rebels." But, if the divine wrath is ended, what right have men to continue theirs?

Disillusionment was inescapable for thinking people who lived through both the Civil War and the later decades of the century. There is a revealing passage in some notes Mark Twain made a few years before his death. He epitomizes in a memorable phrase the idealistic conception of what the war meant, and he sadly muses on the reasons for the failure of the great hopes its close had aroused:

Gould followed CIVIL WAR & California sudden-riches disease with a *worse* one, s. r. (secured riches?) by swindling and buying courts. Cal. & Gould were the beginners of the moral rot, they were the worst things that ever befel America; they created the hunger for wealth when the Gr. Civ. had just completed its youth, its ennobling WAR—strong, pure, clean, ambitious, impressionable—ready to make choice of a life-course & move with a rush; *they & circumstances* determined the choice. . . . Circumstance after Vand. wrought railways into systems; then Standard Oil; Steel Trust; & Carnegie. CALIF— causes Pac R. R. UNCLE TOM WAR TELEGRAPH. to *restrict* slavery —circum. *abolished* it.[27]

And the projected essay ends with a vision of a future in which Morgan takes over all power, actually meditating a monarchy; it is the final debacle of the whole democratic ideal.

The war, then, should have been "ennobling," the nation, to borrow Milton's words about England, "as an eagle mewing her mighty youth"; but, like the older Milton, Mark Twain was to be disillusioned. Why in fact had things turned out so badly? (The time when, presumably, he made this note was especially dark—the "Pacification" of the Philippines.) The traditional villains—Carnegie, the trusts, even the Gold Rush—are understandable; but the principal one, curiously, seems to be "circumstance," which here has something like the old meaning of "fortune." It seems to

[27] Untitled MS. DV127, in *Mark Twain Papers*, copyright 1964, Mark Twain Co. Quoted in *Mark Twain's Fable of Progress: Political and Economic Ideas in "A Connecticut Yankee,"* by Henry Nash Smith (New Brunswick: Rutgers University Press, 1964), p. 93.

have been Twain's greatest disappointment. The earlier
nineteenth century had been one of the few periods when a
large segment of the human race regarded fortune as
friendly, for there was the conviction that the whole complex of things was making for constant improvement. Mark
Twain had grown up in the era when voices on all sides,
both secular and religious, had incessantly proclaimed that
destiny was leading us to utopia, and that Americans especially are designed to be what the *Presbyterian Quarterly
Review* called "engineers of the mighty machinery."

But "circumstance" had turned out to be, not beneficent,
but capricious, and sometimes even carelessly malign. Circumstance had joined railways, made possible Standard
Oil—events that a Mark Hopkins would have expected to be
steps toward the millennium; but instead they only aided in
the old familiar enrichment of the few at the expense of the
many. And the final result had been Morgan and the prospect of restoration of the ancient root of all evil, monarchy.
Moreover, there was a suspicion that the "ennobling WAR"
had been in reality far less noble than it had seemed; that the
compromising goal of restricting slavery had been its real
purpose, and that circumstance, not national dedication, had
finished the work. The old abolitionists, even after the war,
had never admired Lincoln; his real purpose, they said, had
been to appease the slave-owning power. Twain seems to
have concluded that the nation only blundered along in the
old course of mankind.

Yet, despite post-Civil War disillusionment, the myth of
the Redeemer Nation kept a hold on the deepest feelings of
the country, and in critical moments asserted itself. A striking example of its latent strength is the series of addresses
President Wilson made on his 1919 tour in support of unre-
stricted American adherence to the League of Nations.
Frederick Lewis Allen says of them:

Again and again on that long trip of his, Woodrow Wilson
painted the picture of the Treaty and the League that lived in
his own mind, a picture which bore fainter and fainter resemblance to the reality. He spoke of the 'generous, high-minded,
statesman-like cooperation' which had been manifest at the
Paris Conference; he said that 'the hearts of men like Clemen-

ceau and Lloyd George and Orlando beat with the people of the world,' and that the heart of humanity beat in the document which they had produced. He represented America, and indeed every other country, as thrilling to a new ideal.[28]

The dream, I think we may now assume, was not only a "private" one; in the exaltation of his enthusiasm for the "Parliament of the World," the apocalyptic vision of America as "a spirit among the nations of the world" revived, and he saw the terrible events of the past four years as Armageddon. It had been won; the predicted consequences should follow. With the eye of the millennialist, he saw "this great nation marching at the fore of a great procession" to "those heights upon which there rests nothing but the pure light of the justice of God"; these words could have come from many a tract and sermon on God's prophesied plan. The picture of Clemenceau and Lloyd George illustrates the danger of fitting real, complex persons and events into a preconceived, simplified pattern of history. We have seen how commentators of high intellectual standing treated the French Revolution: this was in fact one of the most complicated events in all history, but it had to be fitted into a program, as an instrument wholly for good or wholly for evil, as if it were an actor in a morality play. So it was necessary for the Tiger, in Wilson's vision, to put on a mask, to act a preappointed part.

And in the process the American involvement was transformed. The United States, which, according to Wilson's messages of 1917, went to war to defend its rights under international law, now came to appear as the redemptive people of old. There is the familiar formula of world salvation, begun with Christ, and only partially achieved, apparently, with the Reformation:

When you look into the history not of our own free and fortunate continent, happily, but of the rest of the world, you will find that the hand of pitiless power has been upon the shoulders of the great mass of mankind since time began, and that only with that glimmer of light which came at Calvary

[28] Allen, *Only Yesterday* (1931; reprinted, New York: Harper and Row, Perennial Library, 1964), p. 28.

that first dawn which came with the Christian era, did men begin to wake to the dignity and right of the human soul, and that in spite of professions of Christianity, in spite of purposes of reform, in spite of theories of right and justice, the great body of our fellow beings have been kept under the will of men who exploited them and did not give them the full right to live and realize the purposes that God had meant them to realize.[29]

The oration at Salt Lake City magnificently sets forth the faith in American *destiny* (as opposed to potentiality alone); to this republic was given

. . . a liberating power, a power to show the world that when America was born it was indeed a finger pointed toward those lands into which men could deploy some of these days and live in happy freedom, look each other in the eyes as equals, see that no man was put upon, that no people were forced to accept authority which was not of their own choice, and that out of the general generous impulse of the human genius and the human spirit we were lifted along the levels of civilization to days when there should be wars no more, but men should govern themselves in peace and amity and quiet.[30]

It is Dwight's message, expressed far more eloquently than anything the poet created in laboriously elevated verse. No wonder, then, that in the last address, at Pueblo, Wilson saw the armies of the United States, in a vision rather resembling that of Julia Ward Howe, performing the bloody work of liberation:

I wish that they (opponents of ratification) could feel the moral obligation that rests upon us not to go back on those boys, but to see the thing through, to see it through to the end and make good their redemption of the world. For nothing less depends upon this decision, nothing less than the liberation and salvation of the world.[31]

[29] Wilson, at Oakland, September 18, 1919. In *Presidential Messages and Addresses, and Public Papers (1917–1924)*, ed. Ray S. Baker and William E. Dodd (New York and London, 1927), vol. 2, *War and Peace*, p. 268.
[30] *Ibid.*, p. 355.
[31] *Ibid.*, p. 414.

For, he said in the same speech, there is a "halo" around the "gun over the mantelpiece," and "the sword." The world accepted the American soldiers "as crusaders, and their transcendent achievement has made all the world believe in America as it believes in no other nation organized in the modern world." The sum of it all, as he said at Cheyenne, is that "America had the infinite privilege of fulfilling her destiny and saving the world." [32]

Of the sincerity and nobility of these statements, of the conviction that Isaiah's prophecy could be fulfilled with American leadership, there can be no question. Nor, I think, is there much question that the form of this vision was affected by the specific ideology I have been tracing. And, in general, to what extent was action affected or even initiated by these ideas of American destiny? No certain answer can be made, but perhaps the example of Wilson may be helpful. Most of the actual proposals of Wilson—the formation of the League, probably the Fourteen Points (although this latter might be debated)—I believe we may safely say, would have come about had Wilson and the American people had a very different background of expectations. The League, whatever its limitations, was in itself a necessary step if the world was to move out of the dreary cycle of power politics and wars. It certainly was true that the common man in the United States had reached a position hitherto unknown, and the freedom of the United States from feudal bonds and superstitions was a fact that would have exerted great influence in any case. That Wilson was no deluded idealist, wholly out of touch with realities, is shown by the very realistic predictions he made about the future of Europe, and there is no doubt that his desperate defense of the League was inspired in considerable measure by his awareness of the danger confronting the world. Yet his advocacy went far beyond practical political needs; his insistence on full acceptance of the Treaty provisions arose from faith. The "redemption of the world" is something far beyond any diplomatic device, which, in the last analysis, the League was. The general impression that it was the

[32] *Ibid.*, p. 367.

United States' "destiny" to save the world is the product, not of political idealism and observation, but of prophetic beliefs. America, he said several times, is inclined always "to go in only one direction." This is not the statement of a secular political philosopher. It implies that everything is moving to an ordained, climactic culmination.

We can say, I think, that millennialist ideas probably did not inspire the greatest decisions of our history simply by their own power. The expansion of the nation, the Civil War, the entry into the Second World War—all would have occurred in the course of things. But millennialist ideas did influence national expectations about their outcome and results.

Two extremes have alternated in our history. One is isolationist withdrawal—"innocent nation, wicked world." This, I suggest, has been what might be called the dominant motive in our history. It springs, as I have before indicated, from two sources, very different, but pointing to much the same outcome. The idea of world regeneration always was vague about means; presumably, they were to become evident as the time approached. But the general notion that the United States, as William Jennings Bryan said, would give "light and inspiration to those who sit in darkness" only by "silent . . . example," carried some weight.[33] To intervene actively would expose the chosen people to the temptations of Israel of old; the preaching of the prophets against any association with the gentiles carries a warning for us also. The other source of isolationism, the idea of America as a new Eden, to be preserved inviolate to make a new world of its own, is, on the other hand, largely rationalistic.

The generally less powerful idea, it would seem, was that of active messianism; yet, like a recessive gene, in the right situation it could become dominant. In the years immediately preceding American entry into each of the great wars, there was first a period of passionate non-involvement. This reaction no doubt was perfectly natural, but there was a special moral tone to the expressions of political leaders; the

[33] Quoted in *The Quest for Paradise*, by Charles L. Sanford (Urbana: University of Illinois Press, 1962), p. 230.

wars, it seemed, were designed to catch the righteous nation in the old web. Eventually, however, the trumpets of Zion began to be heard, and a millennialist kind of enthusiasm was generated. The great wars of our history have all to a considerable extent been regarded as Armageddon—which surely was near. After the war had been won, and evil conquered, a permanent era of peace and prosperity would begin.

It has often been remarked that Americans are inclined to expect each crisis to be final, to think each must be solved by a permanently decisive conflict. Nothing could be more characteristic of an apocalyptic attitude. The United States, Wilson told his people, *has* fulfilled its mission. In turn, after Armageddon turns out not to have been won after all, there has followed a reaction of disillusionment, accompanied by loud demands for complete withdrawal from the snares of the Old World. Perhaps some of the extreme reaction against "Bolshevism" may be traced to the fact that this antireligious movement, obviously a new and powerful strategy of Antichrist, came after centuries of predictions that his power was decaying and that his end was near. It looked as though he had more than seven lives; far from being in his last days, it seemed that he might be entering the most flourishing period of his empire.

Yet we should not ignore very real contributions of American millennialism. It certainly must have done much to make the Marshall Plan accepted with so little difficulty; in what other country would such a scheme, apparently so contrary to traditional ideas of national self-interest—and so expensive—have been undertaken? And the practical success of the Plan indicates, too, that millennialism was by no means wholly an idealistic dream: Christian principles, if really triumphant, would redeem the world.

APPENDIX

A Connecticut Yankee in the Mystical Babylon

It was to be expected that an ideology so widespread as American millennialism should in time be reflected in literature. In at least one major American work—Mark Twain's *A Connecticut Yankee in King Arthur's Court*—we see, I suggest, strong influences from millennialist beliefs about such questions as the nature and causes of the "Dark Ages," of the place of Americans in the great pattern of history, of the moral value of inventiveness, industry, individualism, and the rejection of the past. And it largely explains puzzles about the conclusion of the book—the failure of progress, which is foreshadowed in the fatalistic feeling throughout that Hank Morgan's model reforms are somehow doomed from the start. For reasons set forth below, I believe the millennialist faith must be added to the problems and themes that we can find in this complex novel.[1]

[1] *A Connecticut Yankee* has been extensively and intensively studied in recent years. I have found especially important the following studies: John C. Gerber, "The Relation between Point of View and Style in the Works of Mark Twain," in *English Institute Essays*, 1958; Roger Salomon, *Twain and the Image of History* (New Haven: Yale University Press, 1961); Henry Nash Smith, *Mark Twain, the Development of a Writer* (Cambridge: Harvard University Press, 1962); and Smith, *Mark Twain's Fable of Progress* (New Brunswick: Rutgers University Press, 1964). I need hardly add that the point I am making about this work is intended only as one more contribution and is not by any means intended to be an exclusive explanation.

Mark Twain's boyhood was passed in an area which was especially affected by the religious ferments of the 1840's and 1850's. The great, almost obsessive interest in religion that appears throughout his work perhaps reflects the interest, at times arising almost to hysteria, of the people of Hannibal in salvation. Despite the skepticism about church religiosity of his later years, it hardly seems wise to assume that religious attitudes ever were eradicated from his psyche. One biographer in fact has said that "he did not believe in Hell, but he was afraid of it." [2] Formally, he was brought up in the Presbyterian Church, and he described the terror inspired by sermons about predestination and the pains of hell. We may even suspect that the mature man reacted so strongly against the churches in part because these early teachings had made an ineradicable impression, and he resented their arrogated dominance over his heart and imagination. In *A Connecticut Yankee*, the author says:

Training—training is everything; training is all there is *to* a person. We speak of nature; it is folly; there is no such thing as nature; what we call by that misleading name is merely heredity and training. We have no thoughts of our own, no opinions of our own; they are transmitted to us, trained into us.[3]

Among the opinions transmitted to the young Sam Clemens, besides eternal damnation to the glory of God, must have been some form of the Protestant theory of history I have described. The Presbyterian Church itself was largely of these opinions; but there were other religious bodies of consequence in Hannibal. It was a center of Campbellites. The millennium, apparently, was one of the liveliest issues in the popular mind. Mark Twain, on his last visit to Hannibal, recalled how the Millerites donned their ascension robes and awaited the end, on October 22, 1844, and he pointed out the place where they gathered.

But for present purposes the Campbellites may have been

[2] Dixon Wector, *Sam Clemens of Hannibal* (Boston: Houghton Mifflin Co., 1952), p. 88.
[3] *A Connecticut Yankee in King Arthur's Court*, chap. 18. I have used the facsimile of the first edition (New York, 1889), edited by Hamlin Hill.

the most important. Young Sam's closest friend, Will Bowen, was the grandson of a notable Campbellite preacher, the Reverend Barton W. Stone. One may surmise that the boy saw issues of *The Millennial Harbinger*, and that millennialist doctrines were in the air. In his *Autobiography*, moreover, he recorded one personal encounter with Campbell himself, and we get an impression of the personal power of the celebrated revivalist. In Sam Clemens' early days on *The Courier*, "The farmers and their families drove or tramped into the village from miles around to get a sight of the illustrious Alexander Campbell and to have a chance to hear him preach." [4] The farmers raised the enormous sum of sixteen dollars to print the sermon of the illustrious preacher, and *The Courier* thus for the first time became a book publisher. It was Campbell who berated Wales McCormick for shortening "Jesus Christ" to "J. C." The great man dramatically irrupted into the newspaper office to direct that the blasphemy be corrected; unfortunately, he did not overawe McCormick, but something of the impression on Sam Clemens comes through. The sermon must have been almost engraved on the young man's mind; and, given Campbell's preoccupation with the millennium and with history as apocalyptic, we may speculate that the subject must have entered into that discourse.

Indeed, for all Mark Twain's distrust of doctrinalism and revivals, Campbell's conception of history had much that might well appeal to the grown man, Clemens. No other preacher more completely fused the religious and secular elements of the millennial utopia; none more strongly emphasized the need for social reform as preparation for the great age. One could say that for Campbell—who had come from Ireland at the age of twenty—"Americanizing" the world, in the right sense, is almost identical with millennializing it. As I have indicated before, he states in the Prospectus for the first issue of *The Millennial Harbinger* (January 4, 1830) that its purpose is to forward "the development and introduction of that political and religious order

[4] *Mark Twain's Autobiography*, ed. Albert Bigelow Paine (New York, Harper and Sons, 1925), 2:279.

of society called THE MILLENNIUM." The placing of "political" first is perhaps an unconscious revelation of his attitude. The wheel has come full circle from Augustine; Christianity to Campbell was of supreme importance because it and it alone would make possible the really good life and the good society.

Campbell's distrust of all sectarian dogmaticism matched even Mark Twain's; in the Prospectus he asserts "the incompatibility of any sectarian establishment, now known on earth, with the genius of the glorious age to come." Among the other principles of his faith are: "Inadequacy of all existing systems of education, literary and moral, to develop the powers of the human mind, and to prepare man for rational and social happiness. . . . Injustice now existing under the best governments, as contrasted with the justice of the millennium." The Campbellite theology might be called socioreligious; abstract issues of "justification," "calling," and the like yield to practical preparation "for rational and social happiness." In the Gospels, Jesus proclaimed a message of liberation and benevolence to all men. Promising remission of sins, Christianity "banishes all guilt and fear from the conscience"—thus dissipating the paralyzing fears inspired by sermons like those Mark Twain so vividly remembered.[5] The great purpose of the Gospel message is to free men from their own superstitions and selfishness and doubts, to create a new spirit in them, thus enabling them in turn to create the utopia in which they were made to live. God says, " 'I will revolutionize the world,' and how, my friends, but by introducing new principles of human actions?" [6]

Why, then, has not all this occurred? Why is faith in revelation necessary to solve the riddle of history? Here the prophecies furnished the answer. Campbell went so far as to say that he would share Owen's aversion to all religion, were it not for the prophecy of St. Paul that a great apostacy was

---

[5] *Debate on the Evidences of Christianity: Containing an Examination of the "Social System" and of All the Systems of Skepticism of Ancient and Modern Times* (Bethany, 1829), 2:106. (Stenographic report of impromptu speeches.)
[6] *Ibid.*, p. 111.

to occur. The explanation of the plan that makes sense of the chaos of human actions Campbell found in the great Protestant theory of history. All that has happened has been definitely predicted; so we may assume that Providence, in its beneficence, has foreseen and provided for everything; and, since the prophets have been vindicated thus far, we are justified in confidently expecting that the frequent predictions of a holy utopia to come will also be realized.

He makes a remark that might have come from Mark Twain himself: that only after the pagan emperors were replaced by a Christian one, did the popes usurp the honors of God.[7] This fact points up the absolute necessity of divorcing religion from the civil government, and of taking from the sects any power to coerce men's consciences. After the empire had nominally and forcibly been "Christianized"—and only then—could begin the great apostacy Paul had foretold (2 Thess. 2) and John had seen in vision.

Campbell's description of the dark era that followed is of special interest here, since it adumbrates the atmosphere of the world Hank Morgan is to find in sixth-century Britain.

The *mystery of iniquity* early began to work. She made mysteries of plain facts, that she might work out her own delusions. She it was that loved mysteries, that paralyzed the energies of the Christian spirit, and inundated the world with all the superstitions, fables, counterfeit gospels, and all the follies of Paganism in a new garb. . . . the lights of heaven were extinguished, or put under the bushel of these abominable, delusive mysteries, until a long, dark, and dreary night of superstition besotted the world. That man does not breathe whose mind is purified from all the influences of the night of superstition, which has so long obscured the light of the Sun of Righteousness.[8]

Artificial, metaphysical theology is being replaced, "and a religion, pure and social, springing from the meaning of gospel facts, will soon triumph over the speculations of the day." Campbell gives the impression of being a man who could easily have become a pessimist about the ingrained

[7] *Ibid.*, p. 84.
[8] *Ibid.*, p. 88.

folly and wickedness of human nature. His account of the human chronicle would accord with the spirit of *What Is Man?* His faith saved him from despair by assuring him that the erratic course of humanity carried out an infinitely benevolent plan, that men are capable of being redeemed. People ask, "How strange is it, . . . if Christianity orginated in divine benevolence, that there should be such a scene in the great drama as this long night of apostacy and darkness." Yet there it was; and the only explanation, apart from the fact that we cannot see all God's purposes, is that "it appears to be a law of human nature that man can only be developed and brought into proper circumstances to please himself, by what we call experience." [9] There is no short cut: first must be the germ, then the blade, then the stem, the blossoms, and last of all the fruit. "Therefore, as Paul said, the apostacy came first." Campbell, like all the other interpreters, believed that the light could break through only at the time fixed. The source of all evils was corrupted and perverted religion, and only when in the course of Providence religion was reformed—with much bloodshed—could progress occur. He goes back and forth over this question, but always comes to the same conclusion. To those who ask why all the agony of mankind intervening between the early church and the latter days was necessary, we can only say that "it is arrogance for us to arraign Omniscience at the tribunal of our reason, when we cannot tell the reason why the blossom precedes the fruit." [10] Perhaps we can afford to be more complacent because we know we are in the dawn, and know the full day is shortly to come.

If Campbell could have read *A Connecticut Yankee*, it is entirely possible that he would have welcomed it as one improving novel, even if in some details and in its breezy tone it might be somewhat objectionable. And, as must be evident by now, Campbell's views of history, though extreme, were in accord generally with those of a majority of American Protestants. Certainly, therefore, Mark Twain's readers were prepared for the picture of the Middle Ages

[9] *Ibid.*, p. 87.
[10] *Ibid.*, p. 101.

and of the American that his book presents; it appeared, we
may recall, about the time Strong's *Our Country* was a
best-seller. And, I suspect, some of the problems about the
book that now disturb us would not have occurred to most
readers.

Mark Twain unequivocally places the cause of the superstition that hung over Arthur's time in the perversion of the
true Christian church, and, like the Protestant commentators, sees in the feudal tyranny an offshoot and dependency
of the ecclesiastical:

There you see the hand of that awful power, the Roman
Catholic Church. In two or three little centuries it had converted a nation of men to a nation of worms. Before the day
of the Church's supremacy in the world, men were men, and
held their heads up, and had a man's pride and spirit and independence; and what of greatness and position a person got,
he got mainly by achievement, not by birth. But then the
Church came to the front, with an ax to grind; and she was
wise, subtle, and knew more than one way to skin a cat—or a
nation; she invented 'divine right of kings,' and propped it all
around, brick by brick, with the Beatitudes—wrenching them
from their good purpose to make them fortify an evil one."
[Chap. 8.]

History is patently falsified; to represent the Roman empire,
"two or three centuries" before, as a time when men got
ahead by "achievement" and "men were men" is so ludi-
crously distorted that it could come only from a preconceived idea of the historical pattern. Possibly, of course, he
is thinking of Britain alone; but the noble Anglo-Saxons had
not yet appeared. The statement could, in fact, almost be an
extension of Campbell's proposition that Antichrist came in
with the first Christian emperor; the "two or three centuries" would be about the length of time between Constantine and the date of the action in the novel. (Historical
periods, of course, are highly elastic, as they tend to be in
the commentaries; Twain treats the sixth century as if it
were the high Middle Ages.) And the thirteen centuries that
have elapsed since that date recall the 1,260 years Antichrist
was supposed to have been given power. (In fact, Hank
Morgan finds himself in King Arthur's court in 513; 1,260

plus 513 would come to 1773—just the time when the "hero of the West" appears.)

The whole novel is an extended illustration of something like Campbell's theory of progress as against those of Owen, Tom Paine, Godwin, and others. They, it will be recalled, maintained that, if institutions are reformed in a rational way and men are reached by enlightened education, social evils will necessarily disappear; the salvation of society is possible at any time. But Sir Boss has from the start a presentiment that some unconquerable power in the end will frustrate all his work. For some reason, "petrified training" cannot yet be broken up. The commentators, almost unanimously, had emphasized that "overturning" and "breaking" are necessary, along with education. So he meditates:

This was not the sort of experience for a statesman to encounter who was planning out a peaceful revolution in his mind. For it could not help bringing up the un-get-aroundable fact that, all gentle cant and philosophizing to the contrary notwithstanding, no people in the world ever did achieve their freedom by goody-goody talk and moral suasion: it being immutable law that all revolutions that will succeed must *begin* in blood, whatever may answer afterward. [Chap. 20.]

As we have seen, there was a school—of which Priestley and Price were notable exponents—which held the French Revolution, even with its Terror, to be a necessary step in the overthrow of the forces of the Enemy. Mark Twain's celebrated justification of the "ever memorable and blessed Revolution" in France, "which swept a thousand years of such villainy away in one swift tidal wave of blood—one" is entirely consonant with this view of history; the marvel is that, at the right time, only *one* upheaval could overturn such a mass of evil. Lincoln had expressed the doctrine of equivalent judgment: even if the destruction of the Civil War exactly matched in quantity the evil wrought by slavery, the Lord's judgments must be pronounced righteous. From this viewpoint, the wonder was not that the Terror came, but that it was relatively so short and mild. It was, by and large, the secular apologists of progress in the nineteenth century, not the eschatologists, who were given to "gentle cant and philosophizing."

And, as I have attempted to show, long before Mark Twain wrote, it had become a cardinal tenet of American Protestants in particular that the "liberty wherewith Christ hath made us free" is bound up with political freedom. The fact that political and religious reforms are a kind of Siamese twins underlies the Boss's strategy for overturning the medieval despotisms. The primary target is the established church, which by its very nature is "an established slave-pen." The Reformation could be completed, everyone agreed in principle at least, only when the last remnants of established religion had been abolished. And most American Protestants agreed in seeing a rear guard of the old Rome in the contemporary Church of England.

There is no suggestion that all religion is intrinsically an enemy to progress, that it is an "opiate of the people"; here again Mark Twain would be much closer to Campbell than to Owen.

I had started a teacher factory and a lot of Sunday schools the first thing; as a result, I now had an admirable system of graded schools in full blast in those places, and also a complete variety of Protestant congregations all in a prosperous and growing condition. Everybody could be any kind of Christian he wanted to: there was perfect freedom in that matter. But I confined public religious teachings to the churches and the Sunday schools, permitting nothing of it in my other educational buildings. [Chap. 10.]

Campbell himself would have approved; and he would have approved Hank Morgan's theory that "spiritual wants and instincts are as various in the human family as are physical appetites, complexions, and features."

The segregation of church from state is not merely a device to get the disturbing problems of religion out of the way so that political and social progress could go on; the "two schemes . . . which were the vastest of all my projects" were joined.

The one was to overthrow the Catholic Church and set up the Protestant faith on its ruins—not as an Established Church, but a go-as-you-please one; and the other project was to get a decree issued by and by, commanding that upon Arthur's death unlimited suffrage should be introduced. [Chap. 40.]

The Reformation is to be introduced, carried out, and completed with a rush. (But is "set up" a conscious or an unconscious irony?) Sir Boss's combination of advances in knowledge, democracy, and standard of living with advance of knowledge of the spiritual truths is entirely in consonance with the millennialists' frequent panegyrics of the telegraph, the printing press, improvements in agriculture, and the like as both means and results of spiritual improvement. His first official act, starting a patent office, is in keeping with the ideas of both Samuel and Mark Hopkins. The latter, as we have seen, found means of millennial grace in the mastery of nature, the assertion of the liberty and rights of the individual, and benevolence—all working together. Sir Boss's program could be an exemplification of Hopkins' opinion.

The problem of the new weapons Sir Boss introduces is more complex. They are undoubtedly products of the mastery of nature; are they instruments for attaining the millennium? There is curiously little interest in this question among religious writers. Julia Ward Howe has no difficulty in identifying the burnished rows of steel with the apocalyptic symbols; they are predestined, and necessarily right. I do not see much evidence that moral ambiguity is recognized consciously in Mark Twain's description of Sir Boss's electrical inventions. A millennial war is not only a just but, in Whitman's phrase, a "divine war." Means and ends are in predetermined harmony.

The dualistic nature of apocalyptic thought, of whatever type, leads inescapably to an emphasis on the destruction of evil, not to the working-out of problems. It is assumed that, once a specific work of the Enemy has been eliminated, the power of good, like a spring released, will at once assume its appointed shape. There is little recognition that new institutions, even though resulting from destruction of bad ones, may in their turn produce other evils. In Woodrow Wilson's glorification of the League, I think, something like this attitude is to be discerned. The "Parliament of the World," a cliché among millennialists, once established, will automatically take care of the old quarrels and selfish ambitions of nations; Wilson minimized the difficulties his opponents found in the proposal, even when there was some justification, and in effect presented the League as a kind of divine creation rather than as a great experiment that might or might not work. At Salt Lake City, he said, "The only force that outlasts all others and is finally triumphant is the moral judgment of mankind," seeming to assume that, Armageddon finally having been won, this force had been freed and so would infallibly succeed. In the same way Sir Boss was convinced that, once the vile oppressions of prelate and noble had been lifted, the judgment of the mass of the people—as soon as they were educated—would guarantee the establishment of a really good society.

Hank Morgan's conception of the role of the American in the movement of history is wholly predictable. If, as Strong asserted, the "world's scepter" is passing from Great Britain to "Greater Britain," the American is in his own manner the new lord of the creation—but not in the manner of the old lords. Hank Morgan exhibits a sublime assurance and jauntiness, what might be called democratic haughtiness, in keeping with this national belief. In the United States, the purgation of the old order has been carried much farther than even in the most advanced country of the Old World; and the new man has emerged. He has emerged only in very recent times. Hank agrees with Campbell, for example, that the old toxin still lingers, but has for the first time been virtually if not entirely expelled from some inhabitants of this earth.

Even down to my birth century that poison was still in the blood of Christendom, and the best of English commoners was still content to see his inferiors impudently continuing to hold a number of positions . . . to which the grotesque laws of his country did not allow him to aspire; . . . Of course that taint, that reverence for rank and title, had been in our American blood too—I know that; but when I left America it had disappeared—at least to all intents and purposes. The remnant of it was restricted to the dudes and dudesses. When a disease has worked its way down to that level, it may fairly be said to be out of the system.

As Milton's great pride in the leadership of England had been matched with anxiety lest the old corruptions should

return, so Mark Twain's seeming assurance that the healthy
state had been achieved in America for the first time was
accompanied by fear of relapse; and this fear, it may be, was
one motive for his writing this book. The power of superstition is infinite and tireless; victory over it is tenuous until
the entire world has been purged. Mark Twain's fear that
the American mind would be contaminated all over again
was lifelong; he was haunted by the prospect that the republic would sink to a monarchy.

And, in fact, we may suspect that *A Connecticut Yankee*
is a kind of counter-propaganda to reversionary tendencies
he feared were currently visible in the romanticization of
the Middle Ages. Dan Beard's illustrations for the first edition point to such a suspicion. There is, for example, the
curious fact that Merlin is represented with the features of
the seemingly innocuous Lord Tennyson (pp. 41 and 279).
If a joke, this was in bad taste, for Merlin is the epitome of
the malevolence as well as the fakery of the witch doctor.
But it may have seemed to Twain as well as to Beard that
this poet was indeed a kind of magician, who, in *The Idylls
of the King* and other works, had worked a kind of spell,
inducing people to regard the Dark Ages and chivalry as
noble and admirable. The fashion for medievalism would
certainly seem like a device of the Old One. And the adula-
tion of royalty, so marked in the later nineteenth century,
could well seem another peril. Beard's representations (p.
297) of aristocrats in *A Connecticut Yankee* show them with
the faces of contemporaneous rulers. For, as the text makes
clear, the latter are far worse than wastrels and parasites:
they constitute still vigorous parts of the continuing evil
conspiracy, just as the modern Catholic Church carries on
the work of the Beast.

Beard's illustrations are essential to a full understanding of
the novel. Mark Twain's approval of them was emphatic. He
told the artist, "What luck it was to find you! There are
hundreds of artists who could illustrate any other book of
mine, but there was only one who could illustrate this
one." [11] The first edition, in the popular manner of the time,

[11] Quoted on p. xxiv of Hamlin Hill's edition.

rather resembles an illuminated manuscript: the text often flows around an illustration, and, as Mark Twain intimates in this comment, the two form parts of an integral whole. The visual representations enhance the point that the perversion of Christianity is the root of all evils. Many of the drawings take the predictable form of Rabelaisian prelates or monks, drinking deep; some are carried by enslaved commoners. One cartoon (p. 218) reenforces the view that the master villain is the church; it represents a fat prelate, with miter and crosier, kicking a king, who is kicking a nobleman, who in his turn is kicking a long-suffering "freeman."

But in at least two of the illustrations there is a far more sinister note. One (page 93), exemplifying the statement (in Gothic lettering) "That was the church," is the portrait of a friar, drinking from a large bowl. Behind his cowled, almost obscured head arises a demonic spirit-face, vulpine, with two horns. The friar stands with one foot on "The Boss" and the other on a footstool; a capped serpent, with long protruding tongue, is reared up at the right; the cross hangs prominently from the friar's cincture. The theology is obvious. The fat friar, with belt and cross, is only the instrument of a dark spiritual master, and the serpent takes us back to the beginnings in Eden. The most horrendous of all (p. 283) depicts a wraith with a death's head, floating over a dark amorphous body, with a hand holding a censer. The death's head is crowned by miter and coronet, the first on top; the miter is labelled "Church," the crown, "State." It holds in one hand a bowl of blood, and in the other, a bloody dagger labelled "Policy." From the censer arise vapors, like the arms of an octopus, identified as "Slavery," "Superstition," "Ignorance." The inscription is Merlin's exorcism: "I command the fell spirit that possesses the Holy Fountain, to now disgorge into the Skies all the infernal fires that still remains [*sic*] in him!" The story of the Holy Fountain and its "spell" of course illustrates the workings of simple superstition. But the illustration suggests that there is indeed a spell on the land—not the one the ignorant nobles and populace imagine, but very real, very powerful. The question that gives suspense to the novel is whether reason and knowledge can exorcise it; can the American yet per-

form his mission? Such drawings would be good illustrations
for Defoe's account of the workings of Satan in the church,
or, for that matter, any Protestant commentary on the
prophecies. The corruptions in the church and their results
are far more than the work of ordinary human greed, cunning, and ignorance—as Chaucer represents them, for instance; they are, ultimately, the creations of a diabolism that
has gripped institutions and pejoratively changed human
nature itself. Commentators usually assume that there was a
real decline in the composition of most of humanity in this
Dark Age. Hank Morgan refers to the common people in this
time as "human muck," "sheep," etc. The word the commentators often used is "besotted"; it comes to much the
same thing. Adams, as we have seen, says there was an
improvement in human intelligence before the Reformation.
There had to be, Campbell said, "development"; but this is
not the linear growth the progressivists postulated. Ordinary reform, however energetic and sweeping, could not
redeem the world from such a curse. For the church-state,
in Beard's sketch, has the face of death: not only physical,
but spiritual as well.

An exception appears to be Arthur himself, who seems
well-intentioned if weak and understandably proud. This,
however, is in keeping with Protestant theories of history
from the beginning of the Reformation. It was held that the
force raised up by Providence to begin the undoing of
Antichrist included certain kings—that these were, so to
speak, preappointed enemies of the Papacy. Even Henry II
shared some of the glory of Wycliffe, as a pioneer of
Reformation. Patriotism and Protestantism were closely allied. Motley tells the story of a patriotic, righteous prince,
William of Orange, opposed to the tool of the Antichrist,
Philip II. The Protestant hero, William III, opposed James
II. True patriotism, even in monarchs, is the ally of true
religion.

The allegory of the monk foreshadows the inevitable
outcome of Sir Boss's efforts to redeem this forsaken age. He
is the very embodiment of redemptive Americanism. There
is the suggestion that he is really a forerunner of a kind of
superman—or true man—shortly to appear; and he is the

picture of Strong's "American Anglo-Saxon." "Here I was, a giant among pygmies, a man among children, a master intelligence among intellectual moles; by all rational measurement the one and only actually great man in that whole British world" (chap. 8). This is the naïve egotism of mission. In King Arthur's court, he says, he stood "at the very spring and source of the second great period of the world's history"; only by Protestant-apocalyptic interpretations could the Middle Ages be called the *second* great period. But the nineteenth century has the privilege of living in the rapidly moving third stage. What, he asks himself, "would I amount to in the twentieth century? . . . [I] could drag a seine downstreet any day and catch a hundred better men than myself."

The period is all. The great change from nineteenth to twentieth century man is no ordinary improvement, to be expected from the operation of progress; it will be as sudden as was the decline when the Roman Church gained its ascendancy. The course of history is indeed like the "wavering" of a battle—as one commentator on the Revelation put it.

The darkness of the medieval age cannot fully be lifted for thirteen centuries. Thus, although Sir Boss introduces schools on the best modern plan, technology, democracy, Protestant churches—reforming society and religion—all must finally come to naught. For the agents of darkness, even Merlin himself, are no more than agents. Antichrist himself is their chief; but the master of Antichrist is the Enemy, the sinister spirit who operates behind the monk's cowl. That master himself, the spider at the heart of the web, we never see, but we sense his malign power. In the final somber chapters we are told how (to use the language of prophecy) the Beast, feeling himself wounded in an extremity, bestirs himself to put an end to the danger; the interdict is invoked, and its effect is irresistible. Even so, the mechanical achievements of the nineteenth century for a moment seem on the point of annihilating the armed might of the great Beast; it seems as if the bloody battle Armageddon has been fought. But then occurs the most puzzling episode of the book. Sir Boss is wounded, but not seriously.

His followers carry him to a cave, with the assistance of an old woman, who turns out to be Merlin in disguise. The magician lays a spell on Sir Boss, and says, "with an accent of malicious satisfaction":

" 'Ye were conquerors; ye are conquered! These others are perishing—you also. Ye shall all die in this place—every one—except *him*. He sleepeth now—and shall sleep thirteen centuries." In the event, it seems that for the first and last time, the "parlor magic" of the old fraud has worked. Here, in a book dedicated to exposing the pretensions of dealers in the supernatural, the supernatural seems to triumph. But in reality it is not Merlin who has laid the spell on this missionary of progress from the New World; the enchantment is the work of destiny, which some call Providence, or God's plan of history. Morgan, a man from beyond the Reformation, is exempt from the curse on all men of the age. "For God hath put in their hearts to fulfill his will, and to agree, and give their kingdom unto the beast, until the words of God shall be fulfilled."

With the many complex problems about Mark Twain's own attitudes—how far we can identify Hank Morgan with the author—I do not attempt to deal in any depth. I might, however, suggest that Mark Twain seemed able to become imaginatively absorbed in an idea, embodying it in its fullness to the exclusion of everything else. He began, it seems, with a joke about the difficulties of wearing armor; in time, he became more and more taken with the idea of life in the medieval period. In the process, it would be natural that the conception of the Middle Ages he had been taught in his youth would strongly color the imaginative recreation of that time; and in Hank Morgan appears the idealized version of what the American would be to the world.

In the ending are frightening ambiguities, more evident, probably, to us than to the nineteenth-century audience. The display of the terrible destructiveness of electricity, the slaughter of the knights, reminds us that we have created, with our science and technology, a world that resembles the one John saw in his prophetic vision. The supernatural, cosmic battles and plagues would be matched, in terror and frightfulness, by our own weapons in an all-out war. Conversely, using this same technology, we can construct a world that matches the millennium. Certainly part of the message of the Revelation in our time would seem to be that we must make our choice between them. The old intermediate world of some good, much evil, but nothing totally catastrophic, is gone. And, as we have learned from totalitarian states, the Augustinian refuge of the City of God is becoming impossible. Too, the "leverage" of good and evil is increasing, at an incredible rate. Modern man is, it seems, faced by the final challenge of history: create the millennium, or go down into the lake of fire.

BIBLIOGRAPHICAL NOTE

It is unnecessary now to provide a detailed survey of books and articles on millennialism in general, since David E. Smith has recently published a review of what has been done in the field (*American Quarterly*, 17 [1965]:535–49). To this account, I should, however, make two reservations. Professor Smith, like many others, tends to include, at least partially, such movements as Fourierism and Owenism under the millennialist banner. In fact, although such groups had high hopes for the future, their basic ideologies were very different from those of millennial progressivists, and so their ultimate effects were different also.

Second, it is important to remember that—as I show in Chapter II—those who believed in a millennium were deeply divided. The Millerites, the Shakers, to a degree the Mormons, and others were not progressivists; they expected a divine intervention to establish a divinely ruled state, after evil had reached its fullest extent in the world at large. They, like Jehovah's Witnesses today, believed the faithful should separate from the world. Those whom I call "millennialists," on the other hand, thought that the kingdoms of this world are destined to become those of Christ: that is, that good is destined to triumph in the world at large. They therefore are progressivists and optimists. It is a common mistake to mix all kinds of believers in the millennium in one heterogeneous mass; in Chapter II, I remark that this is equivalent to putting Christian Scientists and Calvinists into one category. For this reason, we have failed to recognize that in the nineteenth century there were two "ideas of progress," not one.

There are many valuable studies that have furnished me background information. On the westward movement, for example, there are two basic works, Ray Billington's *Westward Expansion: A History of the American Frontier*, 2d ed. (New York: Macmillan Co., 1960), and Henry Nash Smith's *Virgin Land: The American West as Symbol and*

Myth (1950; reprinted, New York: Random House, 1957). In tracing one source for the anti-Catholic, nativist ideas in the first half of the nineteenth century, I have taken for granted the large body of information in such studies as Henry May's *Protestant Churches and Industrial America* (1949; reprinted, New York: Harper and Brothers, 1964), and Ray Billington's *The Protestant Crusade, 1800–1860: A Study of the Origins of American Nativism* (1938; reprinted Chicago: Quadrangle Books, 1964). One book not in Professor Smith's bibliography deserves special mention: H. Richard Niebuhr's *The Kingdom of God in America* (1937; reprinted New York: Harper and Brothers). This pioneering work in some respects can never be replaced; its consideration of the problems for Christian faith which the idea of a literal "holy utopia" raises, and of the relations of millennialism to the social gospel movement, is unique. But Niebuhr was not very much interested in the relations of the millennialist idea to American history and the American mind in general, and he wrote before much was known about the beginnings in Protestantism of historical interpretations of the prophecies. As a consequence, Niebuhr's book is in need of supplementation.

As Professor Smith's bibliography shows, interest in the millennial theme in American thought is steadily increasing. Three recent works have taken notice of the millennial expectations as an important fact in American history. Sacvan Bercovitch's article "Typology in Puritan New England: The Williams-Cotton Controversy Reassessed" (*American Quarterly*, 19 [1967]: 166–91) brings forth striking evidence that the Puritans of the early churches were motivated by their interpretation of the prophecy; this article supplements what I say above on the subject. Alan Heimert's *Religion and the American Mind, from the Great Awakening to the Revolution* (Cambridge: Harvard University Press, 1966) cites many examples of millennialist expressions. Perry Miller's *The Life of the Mind in America from the Revolution to the Civil War* (New York: Harcourt, Brace & World, 1965) shows the continuity of thinking and writing about the millennial theme. None of these works, however, traces the origin and sets forth the rationale of the conception of what I have called "American millennial mission"; consequently, the nature of its potent influence on American national thought and history necessarily remains undetermined.

INDEX